Frances Willey

The Model Cook Book

Containing Over 1000 Thoroughy Tested Recipes

Frances Willey

The Model Cook Book
Containing Over 1000 Thoroughy Tested Recipes

ISBN/EAN: 9783744786522

Printed in Europe, USA, Canada, Australia, Japan

Cover: Foto ©Lupo / pixelio.de

More available books at **www.hansebooks.com**

CONTAINING OVER

1000 THOROUGHLY TESTED RECIPES

FOUNDED UPON THE PRINCIPLES OF ECONOMY, AND
ADAPTED TO THE USE OF PRIVATE FAMILIES,

BY

MRS. FRANCES WILLEY.

TROY, N. Y.:
E. H. LISK, PUBLISHER AND PRINTER, 312 RIVER STREET.
1884.

PREFACE.

There is scarcely a woman who does not feel, at times, the need of advice as to the best manner of performing the various duties of housekeeping. Young wives, when first entering upon their duties, are frequently made to keenly feel their ignorance of the many customs to which all are expected to conform, and allowance is scarcely ever made for inexperience. Perhaps in no other branch of housekeeping is criticism oftener heard than that of cookery and table etiquette, and to those who are "in the dark," so to speak, this book—containing, as it does, over eleven hundred well-tried recipes, bills of fare, etc.—will prove very acceptable.

The universal cry has been, "We can do nothing with cook books; the receipts are so expensive." To this stereotyped phrase, our reply is, that it has been the endeavor of the author to combine, in this work, economy with excellence; and with this end in view that the book might be prepared in the best manner and free from the impress of one woman's ideas, the recipes have been selected with great care from English, French, German and American authors whose opportunities have rendered them well-fitted to treat the subjects on which they have written. In this way we are enabled to furnish the ladies of America with the most complete work on home and foreign cookery ever yet produced.

It has been the earnest aim of the compiler to give such a variety of recipes that the housewife of limited means, as well as she of greater financial resources, may be able to select a suitable repast and to properly serve it. Believing there is a genuine need of such a book, we offer it to the public, trusting it may meet with cordial approbation.

INDEX TO SUBJECTS.

Bread and Biscuits........................... 163
Breakfast and Tea Cakes...................... 171
Bills of Fare................................ 381
Cake... 190
Confectionery................................ 326
Canned Fruits................................ 298
Dishes for Dessert........................... 267
Drinks....................................... 313
Eggs... 115
Fish... 29
Jellies...................................... 298
Meats.. 49
Miscellaneous 353
Miscellaneous Observations to Housekeepers...   7
Pickles...................................... 145
Pies, Pastry and Meat........................ 220
Plants, Pertaining to........................ 340
Poultry and Game............................. 79
Puddings..................................... 240
Rare bits, Cheese, Cakes, Etc................ 123
Sauces and Dressings for Meats and Fish...... 95
Sauces for Puddings.......................... 263
Salads....................................... 107
Shell-fish................................... 41
Sick Room, for the........................... 333
Soups 15
Table Etiquette.............................. 11
Vegetable.................................... 125
Yeast.. 161

MISCELLANEOUS OBSERVATIONS TO HOUSEKEEPERS.

In every rank, they deserve the most praise who best acquit themselves of the duties which their station requires of them. Indeed if we would maintain our characters as rational beings, this line of conduct is not a matter of choice, but of necessity.

In the variety of female accomplishments, domestic arts do not stand so high in esteem as they formerly did; yet when neglected they produce much human misery. There was a time when ladies knew little beyond their own family ideas of cookery, but in this age of advancement progress should be made, and a universal knowledge obtained of the proper conduct of the household. The experience of others should be brought into requisition, and to this end this volume will prove invaluable.

Instances may be found of women in the highest walks of life, who examine the accounts of their house stewards, and, by overlooking and wisely directing the expenditures of their husband's income, save much financial embarrassment. How necessary, then, is domestic knowledge to those whose limited incomes compel them to consider even the slightest expense. The management of the table is no inconsiderable part of a woman's education; it involves judgment in outlay, respectability of appearance, the comfort of her family and those who partake of her hospitality. There are few incidents in which the honest pride of a man is more immediately felt than in the style of the dinner to which he may bring a friend. If but two or three dishes are well served with the usual sauces, the table linen clean, the table neatly laid, and all that is necessary at hand, the husband and friend are gratified because no irregularity of domestic arrangement will disturb the social intercourse. The same observations hold good on a larger scale. In all situations of life the entertainment should be no less suited to the station than to the fortunes of the entertainer. The mistress of a family should always remember that the welfare and good management of the house depend upon the eye of the superior. If a woman has not been accustomed, while single, to the management of a family, let her not, on that account, fear she cannot attain to it; she may study a good book on cookery, and consult with others who are more experienced than herself. Many families owe their prosperity full as much to the expediency of female management as to the knowledge and activity of the head of the family.

Ready money (cash) should be paid for all things, if possible; the best places should be selected for purchasing, that is, reliable dealers upon whose word you can depend; a common-place book should be kept at hand in which to enter such hints as sensible, experienced women give of useful knowledge. Want of attention to what is advised, or supposing things to be too minute to be worth remembering, is the main cause why so much ignorance prevails on such important subjects.

If economy of time was duly considered, early breakfasts had and regular hours kept, there would be more time to execute the duties of the day, and far more pleasure in their performance. "A place for everything and everything in its place," is a rule that must be observed in every well-regulated household.

A part of every person's fortune should be devoted to charity, by which a pious woman builds up her house before God, while she that lends nothing to the Lord destroys it with her own hands. There are many ways by which the poor may be relieved and comforted, the expense of which would not be felt. To give promiscuous relief cannot be attempted. A person's conduct should harmonize with his circumstances. To do the best we can, and be of the greatest good possible to God and our fellow-men, is all that is required of us. Let us endeavor to excel.

TABLE ETIQUETTE.

Manners are made for the convenience of man. All social observances are founded upon good reason and common sense. It may seem to us that society has adopted a great many useless customs, but, generally speaking, it is not so. The distinction between the gentleman and the boor is more clearly noted at the table than anywhere else. Nothing reflects more upon home training than bad manners here. If, then, we would merit the title of lady or gentleman, it is necessary that we be able, naturally and easily, to show our good breeding by gentility at the table. Here, especially, it may be said, good manners cannot be assumed for an occasion. Children must be taught by parents, both by precept and example, to be attentive and polite to each other at every meal—to observe proper rules of etiquette regularly. If they are so taught, there is no danger that they will appear rude, awkward or unmannerly when they are entertaining, or are entertained as guests. This every day encouragement of the observances of simple and sensible table manners promotes the comfort and cultivation of the family, and takes the embarrassment out of important occasions. The hour of dining should be made an hour of solid pleasure and comfort; the dining room, the table, and all the appurtenances belonging thereto, should be as cheerful as possible. The room should be comfortable, bright and cosy, and at the table the mistress should wear her brightest smile. If you have trials do not bring them to the table; brooding over them impairs digestion and sends husband and children to business and to school gloomy and morose instead of strengthened and refreshed. Taste will add beauty to the plainest room; neatness and skill will give a relish to the plainest fare—little attentions to the decorations or pretty arrangement of the table will tempt the appetite, charm the eye and make the home table powerfully attractive. It is not our purpose here to write special rules of etiquette to be observed at great dinners and receptions, but rather to speak of common rules of table manners which are to be observed constantly in the family, both at home and abroad.

GENERAL RULES ON TABLE ETIQUETTE.

When you are at the table do not show restlessness; do not play with the table utensils or crumble your bread; do not put your elbows on the table, nor sit too far back in your chair, nor lounge; do not talk loud or boisterously; be cheerful in conduct and conversation; never, if possible, cough or sneeze while at the table; do not bend the head down to the plate, as the food should go to the mouth and not the mouth to the food; never tilt back your chair at the table or elsewhere; do not talk when the mouth is full; never make a noise while eating; keep the lips closed, as it is not necessary to show persons how you masticate your food; never indicate that you notice anything unpleasant in the fare; chew your victuals well, but quietly, and slowly. Break your bread when not buttered; do not bite it. Never leave the table in advance of the rest of the family or guests without asking to be excused. Eat soup from the side of the spoon, and without noise. The fork is used to convey food to the mouth, except when a spoon is necessary, as is the case with sauces, puddings and liquids. Raw oysters are eaten with a fork. If you wish to be served with tea or coffee a second time place your spoon in your saucer. Tea or coffee should not be poured into the saucer, but sipped from the cup. If a dish is passed to you, help yourself and then pass it on. Avoid all gross heaping up of plates. At a large dinner party it is better to confine your conversation to your immediate neighbor. There is one good rule which, if followed, will make you acceptable everywhere. "Be not obtrusive; do everything smoothly and quietly; talk in a low tone of voice; handle your knife, fork and dishes without clatter, and eat without smacking of the lips."

Observe the following rules regarding the dressing of the table: It is a good plan to cover the table with baize or cotton flannel to prevent noise. Place the knife on the right hand, the fork on the left and a napkin on each plate; water glasses to the right; finger glasses should be half full—a slice of lemon or a geranium leaf is pretty in them. The soup, salad and dessert should be placed before the hostess, and all other dishes before the host. Soup should be put on the table first; if wine is served it should follow the soup. For ordinary dinners the following bill of fare is sufficient: One kind of soup, one kind of fish, two entrees, a roast, a boil, game, cheese, desserts, ices, coffee. The hostess is the first to rise from the table.

We cannot do better, in closing this chapter, than

to quote from an eminent authority in housekeeping etiquette: " Let no one suppose that, because she lives in a small house, and dines on plain fare, the general principles here laid down do not apply to her. Taste may be quite as well displayed on a pine table as in the grouping of silver and china on the table of the rich. The charm of housekeeping lies in the nice attention of little things, not in a superabundance."

SOUPS.

We would here give the housewife an idea in regard to spices and herbs for soups. In the early fall buy all the herbs you think sufficient for the coming year; dry, pound, and sift them and keep in well corked bottles. Sage, thyme, bay leaves, marjoram, rosemary, sweet basil, parsley, and, when you are using lemons, where the rind is not required, as in lemonade, grate, dry, and bottle it in the same way. You will find all of the above very desirable in soups. Use very little of each, as the flavor should be quite delicate. The excellence of French cooking is the combination of flavors, all so delicate that none predominates. All kinds of spices should be kept on hand, though not in large quantities— say one-quarter of a pound each, and kept in tightly covered tin boxes.

Coloring for Soups and Gravies.

Put four ounces of lump sugar, a gill of water, and half an ounce of the finest butter into a small tosser, and set it over a gentle fire. Stir it with a wooden spoon until it becomes a bright brown. Then add half a pint of water; boil, skim, and, when cold, bottle and cork it tight. Add to soup or gravy as much of this as will give a proper color.

A CLEAR BROWN STOCK FOR GRAVY-SOUP OR GRAVY.

Put a knuckle of veal, a pound of lean beef, and a pound of the lean of a gammon of bacon, all sliced, into a stew-pan with two or three scraped carrots, two onions, two turnips, two heads of celery sliced, and two quarts of water. Stew the meat quite tender, but do not let it brown. When thus prepared it will serve either for soup, or brown or white gravy. If for brown gravy put in some of the above coloring, and boil a few minutes.

TOMATO SOUP.

Put on a piece of beef, mutton or lamb, to boil; skim off all the fat before seasoning, then add two sliced onions, a little pepper and salt, two cloves, and about a dozen tomatoes; boil three hours, then add a little thickening of flour. If the tomatoes are very sour, add a tablespoonful of sugar.

PORTABLE SOUP.

Boil one or two knuckles of veal, one or two shins of beef, and three-pounds of beef in as much water as will cover them. Take the marrow out of the bones; put in any kind of spice you like and three large onions. When the meat has cooked to pieces strain it off, and put it in a very cold place. When cold take off the cake of fat, put the soup in a double bottomed tin sauce pan, and set it on a pretty quick fire, but do not let it burn. It must boil fast and uncovered, and be stirred constantly for eight hours. Put it into a pan, and let it stand in a cold place a day; then pour it into a round soup china-dish, and set the dish into a stew-pan of boiling water on a stove, and let it boil, and be now and then stirred, till the soup is thick and ropy, then it is done enough. Pour it into the little round part at the bottom of cups or basins turned upside down, to form cakes; and when cold turn them out on flannel to dry. Keep them in tin canisters. When they are to be used, melt them in boiling water; and if you wish the flavor of herbs, or any thing else, boil it first, strain off the water, and melt the soup in it. This is very convenient in the country where fresh meat is not always at hand; as by this means a basin of soup may be made in fifteen minutes.

Noodles Soup—German.

Make a good beef soup. When almost done take two eggs and beat well; when light, work in as much flour as they will absorb, and then roll out as thin as a wafer; dust over with flour; make in a roll, cut in thin strips and shape out. A teaspoonful of salt should be put into the flour. Boil in the soup ten minutes.

English Mock Turtle Soup.

Take a calf's head, cut it in half, clean it well and then boil it until half done; cut all the meat off in small square pieces, break the bones of the head and put back in the kettle. Fry some shallot in butter, and dredge in flour; when it is nicely browned put it into the kettle and let it boil gently for one hour; skim well. About ten minutes before serving, season with basil, tarragon, parsley, cayenne pepper, and salt to your taste; also two tablespoonfuls of mushroom catsup and one pint of Madeira wine. This will make four quarts of splendid soup.

English White Soup.

Three pounds of knuckle of veal, two slices of salt pork; cover with cold water and boil gently until it falls off the bones. Take out the bones and pork; blanch a quarter of a pound of almonds in a mortar with a tablespoonful of water to prevent oiling; add to this a pint of cream and stir into the soup; add one cupful of vermicelli that has been soaked in milk one hour Season with white pepper, salt and a little grated lemon peel. This will make five quarts of excellent soup.

A Plain White Soup.

One pound of knuckle of veal, covered with cold water and boiled gently until the meat falls from the bones; take out the bones, season with white pepper and salt to taste; add one quart of sweet milk, a little butter, and some cooked rice. This will make four quarts of good soup.

Partridge Soup.

Skin two old birds and cut them into pieces, with three or four slices of ham, a stick of celery, and three large onions sliced. Fry them all in butter till brown, and take care not to burn them. Then put them into a stew-pan with five pints of boiling water, a few pepper-corns, a shank or two of mutton, and a little salt. Stew it gently two hours; then strain it through a sieve, and put it again into a stew-pan with some stewed celery and fried bread; when it is near boiling, skim it, pour it into a tureen and serve it up hot.

Grouse Soup

Is made the same as Partridge soup, only using one onion, and adding Jamaica pepper and half a dozen cloves, but no celery.

Macaroni Soup.

Boil a pound of the best macaroni in a quart of good stock till quite tender; then take out half, and put it into another stew-pot. To the remainder add some more stock, and boil it till you can pulp all the macaroni through a fine sieve. Then add together that, the two liquors, a pint or more of cream boiling-hot, the macaroni that was first taken out, and half a pound of grated Parmesan cheese; make it hot, but do not let it boil. Serve it with the crust of a French roll cut into pieces the size of a shilling.

English Gravy Soup.

Take four pounds of shin of beef, break the bones, cover with cold water; add a bunch of sweet herbs, two onions fried a fine brown, two blades of mace, three cloves, ten allspice berries, and forty black peppers; stew until very rich; take two carrots, two turnips, one head of celery and simmer them together until tender, then add to the soup also one tablespoonful mushroom catsup. Strain and send to the table clear. Salt to taste. This will make six quarts of strong, clear soup.

Tomato Soup.

Boil one quart of ripe tomatoes in one quart of water ten minutes; then add one teaspoonful of salt, one teaspoonful of pepper, one teaspoonful of white sugar and a piece of butter the size of an egg; lastly add one quart of milk and let all simmer.

Scotch Barley Broth.

Set on the fire two ounces of pearl barley, with three pints of salt water; when it boils, skim it, and add what quantity of salt beef, or fresh brisket, you choose, and a marrow-bone, with a good quantity of leeks, cabbages, or savoys, and let it simmer four or five hours. Or you may use turnips, onions, and grated carrots.

Scotch Mutton Broth.

Soak a neck of mutton in water for an hour; cut off the scragg, and put it into a stew-pan with two quarts of water. As soon as it boils, skim it well, and then simmer it an hour and a half; then take the best end of the mutton, cut it into pieces (two bones in each), take some of the fat off, and put in as many as you think proper; skim the moment the fresh meat boils up, and every quarter of an hour afterwards. Have ready four or five carrots, the same number of turnips, and three onions, all cut, but not small; and put them in soon enough to get quite tender; add four large spoonfuls of Scotch barley, first wet with cold water. The meat should stew three hours. Salt to taste, and serve all together. Twenty minutes before serving, put in some chopped parsley and some salt. It is an excellent winter dish.

Ox Tail Soup.

Make the same as gravy soup taking two ox tails; they should be soaked over night in cold water with salt in it. It is a very nourishing dish.

Dried Pea Soup with Salt Pork.

Soak a quart of split peas over night in soft water, next morning wash them, put them in four quarts of water, with a teaspoonful of sugar, two carrots, two small onions, one stalk of celery—all cut in small pieces; let them boil three hours; boil a pound of salt pork in another pot for an hour, take off the skin, and put the pork in the soup, and then boil one hour longer.

French Vegetable Soup.

Take a leg of lamb of moderate size, and four quarts of water; of potatoes, carrots, cabbage, tomatoes and turnips·take a teacupful of each, chopped fine; salt and black pepper at the rate of one small teaspoonful of salt to each quart of water and one-sixth as much pepper; wash the lamb and put it into the four quarts of cold water; when the scum rises, take it off carefully with a skimmer; after having pared and chopped the vegetables, put them into the soup. Carrots require the most boiling and should be put in first. The soup requires about three hours to boil.

Green-Pea Soup.

Wash a small quarter of lamb in cold water, and put it into a soup-pot with six quarts of cold water; add to it two tablespoonfuls of salt, and set it over a moderate fire; let it boil gently for two hours, then skim it clear; add a quart of shelled peas, and a teaspoonful of pepper; cover it, and let it boil for half an hour; then, having scraped the skins from a quart of small young potatoes, add them to the soup, cover the pot, and let it boil for half an hour longer ; work a quarter of a pound of butter and a dessert-spoonful of flour together, and add them to the soup ten or twelve minutes before taking it off the fire. Serve the meat on a dish with parsley, sauce· over, and the soup in a tureen.

Ham or Pea Soup.

The bone of the ham may be used when the meat has been removed from it before cooking, or it will do equally well if it has been already boiled in the ham (if in the former case, cleanse it thoroughly from all particles of mould). Put it over the fire in three quarts of cold water, with one pint of split peas which have been previously soaked in cold water for three hours. Cook very slowly for seven hours, and then strain the broth, rubbing the peas through the colander. Season to taste, and pour over small squares of dry toast.

Split-Pea Soup.

Put a quart of split peas in water to cover them at night, with half a teaspoonful of saleratus; next day take them from the water in which they were soaked, and put to them two quarts of water and a pound of salt pork, with a bone of beef; let it boil gently until the peas are tender, then add five or six potatoes, and pepper to taste; cover it for fifteen minutes, then add a tablespoonful of butter and flour each, worked together; cover it until the potatoes are done, which will be about fifteen minutes. Serve in a tureen.

Common Soup.

Take shank or neck of beef or meat of fowls; cut fine; crack the bones; put in a pot and stew slowly several hours, until all the meats are cooked to shreds. Pour on a little boiling water and keep boiling till nearly ready to serve. Skim off all grease. Add vegetables, potatoes, carrots, barley or rice as you may prefer—the vegetables having been previously cooked by themselves—and then add a little butter to give it richness.

Beef Soup.

One pound of lean beef, cut very fine, and one pint of cold water. Heat slightly for two or three hours, till it comes to boiling point. Then boil briskly two or three minutes, and strain through a coarse bit of cloth. Season with salt and pepper. Add roast onions or burnt sugar to color brown if desired.

Chicken Broth.

Cut the chicken into very small pieces and put in a jar filled with water, adding a little salt. Cover tight and let it simmer all day on stove or range. Strain and season to taste.

Mock Stewed Oysters.

One bunch oyster plant, eight teaspoonfuls butter, a little flour or corn starch, vinegar and water for boiling, pepper and salt, one-half cup of milk. Wash and scrape the oyster plant very carefully; drop into weak vinegar and water, bring quickly to a boil, and cook ten minutes; turn off the vinegar water, and rinse the salsify in boiling water; throw this out, and cover with more from the tea kettle; stew gently ten minutes longer; add pepper and salt and two tablespoonfuls of butter; stew in this until tender. Meanwhile beat, in a farina kettle, the milk; thicken, add the remaining butter, and keep dry until the salsify is done, then transfer it to this sauce; pepper and salt; let all lie together in the inner kettle, the water in the outer at a slow boil, for five minutes; pour into a covered dish.

Bean Soup.

Wash and boil your beans with a piece of salt pork. When the beans are soft take them out, and press through a colander; then put them back in the water they were boiled in, together with four hard boiled eggs quartered, and a half a lemon sliced, a little pepper if you like it. Boil up and serve.

Soup, a la Sap.

Boil half a pound of grated raw potatoes, a pound of beef sliced thin, a pint of gray peas, an onion, and three ounces of rice, in six pints of water; strain it through a colander; then pulp the peas to it, and turn it into a sauce-pan again with two heads of celery, sliced. Stew it tender, and add pepper and salt; when you serve add fried bread.

Eel Soup.

Take three pounds of small eels; put to them two quarts of water, a crust of bread, three blades of mace, some whole pepper, an onion, and a bunch of sweet herbs; cover them close, and stew until the fish is quite broken; then strain it off. Toast some bread, cut it into dice, and pour the soup on it boiling. A piece of carrot may be put in at first. This soup will be as rich as if made of meat.

American Lobster Soup.

After having boiled a lobster, take it from the shell; roll two or three crackers, and put them to the meat, which must be cut small; put of milk and water each a quart into a stewpan, with a tablespoonful of salt and a teaspoonful of pepper; when it is boiling hot, add the lobster, cut small, and the green inside if liked, and a quarter of a pound of sweet butter; let it boil closely covered for half an hour; break a dozen butter-crackers, or six or seven soda-biscuits, into a tureen, pour the soup over, and serve.

English Lobster Soup.

Take the meat from six small lobsters; do not use the brown nor the green; chop the fins and the claws fine, and boil all gently in two quarts of water; add butter, nutmeg and a teaspoonful of flour mixed into a quart of cream. Force-meat balls may be served in the soup if desired.

CLAM SOUP.

Put two quarts of water into your kettle with one quart of potatoes sliced very thin; put in pepper, salt and butter; set it over the fire to cook. Take a slice of salt pork and cut it into diamonds; take one onion, cut very fine, and fry with the pork until brown, then put it in the kettle; now add one quart of clams; lastly add one teacup of milk with a teaspoonful of flour stirred in it. Let it boil ten minutes.

FRENCH STEWED OYSTERS.

Wash fifty large oysters in their own liquor, strain the liquor into a stew pan, putting the oysters into a pan of cold water, season the liquor with a half pint of sherry or madeira, the juice of two lemons, and a little mace. Boil this liquor, and skim and stir it well; when it comes to a boil, put in the oysters well drained; let them get heated through, but do not boil them. Many people consider this the nicest way of stewing oysters.

OYSTER STEW—No. 1.

Make a paste of one tablespoonful of butter and two of flour, a teaspoonful of salt and a pinch of pepper; put in a stew-pan on the fire one pint of milk and one of water; when this comes to a boil, put in two quarts of oysters and stir in the paste, a small lump at a time; stir frequently, so as to melt the paste. As soon as it comes to a boil remove it from the fire, pour into a tureen and serve at once with crackers.

OYSTER STEW—No. 2.

Open and separate the liquor from them and strain; wash the oysters till free from grit and put with them a bit of mace and lemon-peel and a few white peppers. Simmer them very gently, and put in some cream and a little flour and butter. Serve with bread broken in. The beards of the oysters should be removed. But few minutes are required to prepare the stew.

Soup Powder.

Two ounces each of parsley, summer savory, sweet marjoram, and thyme, one ounce each of lemon peel and sweet basil. Dry, pound, sift and keep in a tightly corked bottle.

FISH.

TO SELECT FISH.

In every sort, stiffness and redness of the gills, and brightness of the eyes, are invariable signs of freshness; thickness of flesh generally marks the good condition of all fish.

OBSERVATIONS ON DRESSING FISH.

If the fishmonger does not clean it, fish is seldom very nicely cleaned. Common cooks are not apt to slit the fish low enough, by which, and not thoroughly washing blood, etc., from the bone, a very disgusting mass is left within, and mistaken for liver; but fishmongers in great towns wash it beyond what is necessary for cleaning, and by perpetual watering diminish the flavor. Salt should be put into the water in which all fish is boiled; and cod is rendered firmer by the addition of two or three spoonfuls of vinegar. Cod, haddock and whiting eat firmer if a little salt be put into their gills, and they be hung up a few hours before dressing.

Care must be taken to preserve the roe, melt and liver whole to let them be sufficiently dressed; and to place them conspicuously when served. The sound adhering to the bone must be left there, but very carefully cleaned.

Fish that is to be boiled must be put on the fire in cold hard water; when it boils, skim with the greatest care; throw in a little cup of cold water to check the extreme heat, then keep it *simmering only*, lest the outside break before the thick and inner be done. Crimped fish should be put into boiling water, and simmered a few minutes.

To judge if a large fish be sufficiently boiled, draw up the fish-plate, and with a thin knife try if the fish easily divides from the bone in the thick parts, which it will when done enough. Keep it hot, not by letting it sodden in the water, but by laying the fish-plate crosswise on the kettle, and covering it with a thick cloth. If left in the water after it is done, fish loses its firmness, and becomes woolly. Serve fish on a napkin. The fish looks more complete if fried fish be served round the boiled, alternately placed with the roe or melt, and handsomely garnished.

Great care is necessary to drain the water from the boiled fish, that the dryness and color of the fried around it may not be lessened.

TO FRY FISH.

Having nicely cleaned and washed it, dry it completely; dip it in yolks of eggs beaten, and then in a dish of bread-crumbs or cracker-dust; if you wish it to look extra nice, repeat the egg and crumbs, and instantly plunge it into a thick-bottomed frying-pan, in which have ready a sufficient quantity of drippings or lard, *boiling hot*, to cover the fish. Let it gently fry until it becomes a beautiful yellow brown, and is done enough; if the latter, before the color be obtained, the pan must be drawn to a cooler part of the fire to finish. The frying liquor must not be suffered to become black, as it will answer again with a little fresh ; but it gives a bad color. Oil is the best thing to fry in, if the expense be no objection.

Frying-pans suited to the sizes of fish, and oblong instead of round, will be found particularly useful, as much waste of lard will be prevented.

Turbot.

If necessary turbot will keep a couple of days or more in perfection if a little salt be sprinkled over it, and it be hung in a very cool place.

Boiled Turbot.

The turbot-kettle must be of a proper size and in the nicest order. Set the fish in cold water sufficient to cover it completely ; throw a handful of salt and a glass of vinegar into it, and let it gradually boil. When thick, the fish is apt to be unequally done ; to prevent which, cut a slit down the back of two inches, close to the bone, and the same on the belly side, with a small, sharp knife. Be very careful that there fall no blacks ; but skim it well, and preserve the beauty of the color. Serve it garnished with a complete fringe of curled parsley, lemon and horse-radish. The sauce must be the finest lobster, anchovy butter and plain butter, served plentifully in separate tureens.

Baked Turbot.

Boil five or six pounds of haddock or cod. Take out the bones and shred fish very fine. Let a quart of milk, one-quarter of an onion, and a piece of parsley come to a boil. Stir in one-half cup flour, which has been smoothed with one cup of milk and the yolks of two eggs (a little more flour may be needed). Season with one-half teaspoonful white pepper, same quantity of thyme, one-half cup butter and plenty of salt. Butter a stone pan, put in first a layer of sauce, then one of fish and so on, finishing with sauce on top; sprinkle over it cracker-crumbs and a light grating of cheese. Bake for an hour in a moderate oven.

To Dress Fresh Sturgeon.

Cut slices an inch thick, rub egg over them, then sprinkle with crumbs of bread or cracker dust, parsley, pepper and salt; fold them in paper, and broil gently. Sauce: Butter, anchovy and soy.

Another.

Put a piece of butter rolled in flour in a stew-pan, with four cloves, a bunch of sweet herbs, two onions, some pepper and salt, half a pint of water, and a glass of vinegar. Stir it over the fire till it boils; then let it become lukewarm, and steep the fish in it an hour or two. Butter a paper well, tie it around, and roast it without letting the spit run through. Serve with sorrel and anchovy sauce. Three or four pounds of sturgeon will make a handsome dish.

To Boil Salmon.

Let it be put on in cold water, unless the fish be split; then in warm. If underdone, it is very unwholesome. Shrimp or anchovy sauce.

To Broil Salmon.

Cut slices an inch thick, and season with pepper and salt; lay each slice in white paper well buttered; twist the ends of the paper, and broil the slices over a slow fire six or eight minutes. Serve in the paper with anchovy sauce.

To Pot Salmon.

Take a large piece, scale and wipe, but do not wash it; salt very well; let it lie till the salt is melted and drained from it, then season with mace, cloves and whole pepper; lay in a few bay leaves, put it into a pan, cover it over with butter, and bake it; when well done, drain it from the gravy, put it into the pots to keep, and, when cold, cover it with clarified butter. In this manner any firm fish may be done.

Collared Salmon.

Split such a part of the fish as may be sufficient to make a handsome roll, wash and wipe it, and having mixed salt, white pepper, mace and Jamaica pepper, in quantities to season it very high, rub it inside and out well. Then roll it tight and bandage it; put as much water and one-third vinegar as will cover it with bay leaves, salt, and both sorts of pepper. Cover close, and simmer till done. Drain and boil quick the liquor, and put on when cold. Serve with fennel. It is an elegant dish.

An Excellent Dish of Dried Salmon.

Pull some into flakes; have some eggs boiled hard and chopped; put both into half a pint of thin cream, and two or three ounces of butter rubbed with a teaspoonful of flour; skim it and stir till boiling hot; make a wall of mashed potatoes round the inner edges of a dish, and pour the above into it.

Pickled Salmon.

Boil a salmon, and, when done, take it out Take a sufficient quantity of vinegar to cover your fish and heat it hot; while hot add a few bay leaves and a few pepper-corns. Pour over the fish when cold.

To Dress Salt Cod or Ling.

Soak and clean the piece you mean to dress, then let it lay all night in water, with a glass of vinegar. Boil it enough, then break it into flakes on the dish; pour over it parsnips boiled and mashed, and then boil up with cream and a large piece of butter rubbed with a bit of flour. It may be served as above, with egg-sauce instead of parsnip, and the root served whole; or the fish may be boiled and served without flaking, and sauces as above.

To Dress Salt Fish that has been Boiled.

Break it into flakes, and put it into a pan with sauce thus made; mash some boiled parsnips, then add to it a cup of cream, and a good piece of butter rolled in flour, a little white pepper, and a half teaspoonful of mustard, all boiled together; keep the fish no longer on the fire than to become hot, but not boil. This is an excellent dish.

Soles.

If boiled, they must be served with great care, to look perfectly white, and should be covered with parsley. The roe or melt of soles must not be taken out.

Soles that have been fried are nice eaten cold with oil, vinegar, salt and mustard; or, cut into large dice, in a bowl with salad.

Soles, a la Portuguese.

Take one large, or two small; if large, cut the fish in two; if small, they need only be split. The bones being taken out, put the fish into a pan with a bit of butter and some lemon juice; fry, then lay the fish on a dish, and spread a force-meat over each piece, and roll it round, fastening the roll with a few small skewers. Lay the rolls into a small earthen pan, beat an egg and wet them, then strew crumbs over, and put the remainder of the egg, with a little meat gravy, a spoonful of caper sauce, an anchovy chopped fine, and some parsley chopped, into the bottom of the pan ; cover it close, and bake in a slow oven till the fish are done. Then place the rolls in the dish for serving, and cover it to keep them hot till the baked gravy is skimmed ; if not enough, a little fresh, flavored as above, must be prepared and added to it. The heads of the fish are to be left on one side of the split part, and kept on the outer side of the roll ; and when served, the heads are to be turned towards each other in the dish. Garnish with fried or dried parsley.

Stuffing for the Above.

Chop cold beef, mutton or veal, a little ; then add some fat pork that has been lightly fried, cut small, and some onions, a little garlic or shallot, some parsley, anchovy, pepper, salt and nutmeg ; chop all fine with a few crumbs, and bind it with two or three yolks of eggs.

Red Mullet.

It is called the sea woodcock. Clean, but do not open or wash the inside, fold in oiled paper, and gently bake in a small dish. Make a sauce of the liquor that comes from the fish, with a piece of butter, a little flour, a little essence of anchovy, and a glass of sherry. Let it boil, and serve in a boat, and the fish in the paper case it was dressed in.

Flounders.

Let them be rubbed with salt inside and out, and lie two hours to give them some firmness. Boil, if so chosen ; but they are better fried ; for which observe the usual directions. Serve garnished with fried parsley. Sauce: Anchovy and butter.

An Excellent Way of Dressing a Large Plaice, Especially if there be a Roe.

Sprinkle with salt, and keep twenty-four hours; then wash and wipe it dry, wet over with egg, cover with crumbs of bread; heat some lard or fine dripping and two large spoonfuls of vinegar, boiling hot; lay the fish in, and fry it a fine color, drain it from the fat, and serve it with fried parsley and anchovy sauce. You may dip the fish in vinegar, and not put it into the pan.

Fried Herrings.

Serve them of a light brown, with onions sliced and fried round them; or without onions.

Broiled Herrings.

Flour them first, and boil to a good color; plain butter for sauce.

To Dress Pike.

Scale it, and open as near the throat as you can, and, after cleaning well, stuff it with the following: Grated bread, anchovies, oysters, suet, salt, pepper, mace, half a pint of cream, four yolks of eggs; mix all over the fire till it thickens, then put it into the fish, and sew it up. Boil or bake; if the latter, bits of butter should be put over it, and half a pint of rich broth in the dish; and, when the fish is ready, take the gravy out of the dish, add a dessert-spoonful of essence of anchovy, the same of soy, and a squeeze of lemon, to some butter rolled in flour, and boiling it up, pour it into the dish. *Note:* If, in helping a pike, the back and belly are slit up, and each slice gently drawn downwards, there will be fewer bones given.

To Fry Smelts.

They should not be washed more than is necessary to clean them. Dry them in a cloth, then lightly flour them, but shake it off. Dip them into plenty of egg, then into bread or cracker crumbs, and put them into a pan of hot lard; let them fry a few minutes a bright yellow-brown. Take care not to take off the light roughness of the crumbs, or their beauty will be lost.

Scrambled Codfish.

Beat two eggs into one cup of milk, stir in half a cup of codfish properly freshened, put into a buttered pan, and stir briskly while cooking; cook to the consistency of scrambled eggs.

Codfish Cakes—A Yankee Dish.

Take salt codfish that has been cooked slowly, *simmered*, not boiled, the day before. Remove the bones and mince it. Mix it with warm potatoes, mashed with butter and milk, in the proportion of one-third codfish, and two-thirds mashed potatoes; add sufficient beaten egg to make the whole into a smooth paste. If it seems dry, add a little butter, Make into cakes an inch thick, and as large round as a teacup.

Fried Eels.

If small, they should be curled round and fried, being first dipped into egg and crumbs of bread or crackers.

Collared Eel.

Bone a large eel, but do not skin it; mix pepper, salt, mace and allspice, add a clove or two, in the finest powder, and rub over the whole inside; roll it tight, and bind with a coarse tape. Boil in salt and water and two bay leaves, till done, then add vinegar, and when cold keep the collar in pickle. Serve it whole or in slices. Chopped sage, parsley and a little thyme, knotted marjoram and savory, mixed with the spices, greatly improve the taste.

Excellent Fish Cake.

Take any sort of dressed fish (the remains of a turbot do well), cut the meat from the bones, put them, the head and fins, over the fire, with a pint of water, an onion, herbs, pepper and salt to stew for gravy. Mince the meat, put to it a third part of crumbs of bread or cracker dust, a little minced onion, parsley, pepper and salt, and the least bit of mace; mix well, and make it into a cake with white of an egg and a little melted butter; cover it with raspings, and fry it a pale brown, keeping a plate on the top while doing. Then lay it in a stew-pan with the fish gravy, and stew it gently a quarter of an hour; turn it twice, but with great care not to break it; cover it closely while stewing.

Cake of dressed meat, done in the same way, is remarkably good.

Fish Chowder.

Five pounds of any kind of fish (the light salt-water fish is the best), half a pound of pork, two large onions, one quart sliced patatoes, one quart water, one pint of milk, two tablespoonfuls of flour, six crackers, salt, pepper. Skin the fish, and cut all the flesh from the bones. Put the bones on to cook in the quart of water, and simmer gently ten minutes. Fry the pork, then add the onions, cut into slices. Cover and cook five minutes, then add the flour and cook eight minutes longer, stirring often. Strain on this the water in which the fish bones were cooked and boil gently for five minutes, then strain all on the potatoes and fish. Season with salt and pepper, and simmer fifteen minutes. Add the milk and crackers, which were first soaked for three minutes in the milk. Let it boil up once, and serve. The milk may be omitted and a pint of tomatoes used, if you like.

Broiled Fresh Fish.

Split open on the back; broil first on one side, then on the other; it should not be broiled rapidly, but should be thoroughly cooked, three-quarters of an hour being about the time required for broiling an ordinary fish; spread with butter as soon as taken from the gridiron, and serve hot.

Fried Brook Trout.

This is an important recipe, and they are delicious when well cooked. The best method is to cut thin slices of salt pork and place them in a frying-pan until the fat has cooked out; then, after cleaning the trout nicely and washing them well, rub them thoroughly with salt and allow them to stand for a little time; then dry and roll each one in cracker dust, and place them in the fat smoking hot, watch them, constantly turning first one and then another to avoid burning, frying until thoroughly cooked through. If they are not cooked enough they will not be good and will also be spoiled by allowing them to burn, which they do very easily.

Cream Baked Trout.

Clean the trout, put in pepper and salt, and close them. Place the fish in the pan, with just cream enough to cover the fins, and bake fifteen minutes.

SHELL-FISH.

CLAM CHOWDER—NO. 1.

The materials needed are fifty quahogs or round clams, a large bowl of salt pork cut into fine pieces, the same quantity of onions chopped fine, the same quantity of potatoes (or more, if you choose) cut in eighths or sixteenths. Wash the clams very thoroughly, put them in a pot with a half pint of water. When the shells open they are done. Take them from the shells and chop them fine, saving all the clam water for the chowder. Fry out the pork very gently, and when the scraps are a good brown take them out and put the chopped onions into the fat to fry. The chief secret in chowder making is to fry the onions so delicately that they will be missing in the chowder. They should be fried in a frying-pan, and the chowder-kettle be made very clean before they are transferred to it, or the chowder will burn. Add a quart of hot water to the onions, and put in the clams, clam water and pork scraps. After it boils add the potatoes, and when the potatoes are cooked the chowder is finished. Just before it is taken up thicken it with a cup of powdered crackers and add a quart of fresh milk. If too rich add more water. No seasoning is needed but good black pepper.

Clam Chowder—No. 2.

Take three slices fat pork ; cut small and fry crisp six potatoes and six onions ; then put into a kettle some of the pork and fat ; then alternate a layer of potatoes with a layer of onions ; then add pepper, salt and rolled cracker ; then repeat, and put in enough hot water to cook. Cook slowly, and, when nicely done, add half a pound of butter, one quart of milk and one quart of clams. Before serving, add a few large crackers.

To Pickle Oysters.

Wash four dozen of the largest oysters you can get in their own liquor, wipe them dry, strain the liquor off, adding to it a dessert-spoonful of pepper, two blades of mace, a tablespoonful of salt if the liquor be not very salt, seven of vinegar. Simmer the oysters a few minutes in the liquor ; then put them in small jars and boil the pickle up ; skim it, and when cold pour over the oysters ; cover close.

Fried Oysters—No. 1.

Make a batter of flour, milk and eggs ; season it a very little, dip the oysters into it, and fry them a fine yellow-brown. Take off the beards previously. A little nutmeg should be put into the seasoning, and a few crumbs of bread into the flour.

Fried Oysters—No. 2.

Take fine, large oysters, put them in a colander and drain off the liquor. Have a beaten egg on one plate and cracker dust on another. Lift the oysters, one at a time, with a fork; dip first in the egg, then in the cracker dust ; lay them two together, making them look like one, place them in the palm of your hand

and pat them together, so that they will not come apart; lay them on a dish until you have them all ready to fry; place on the fire a frying-pan, with one tablespoonful of lard and one of butter in it; as soon as it is boiling hot lay in the oysters; sprinkle a little salt on them and fry them a nice brown; when done lift them out and put them in a colander and set them in the oven until wanted; serve on a warm dish.

Oyster Patties.

Put one quart of oysters into a saucepan, with liquor enough to cover them; set it on the stove and let it come to a boil; skim well and stir in two tablespoonfuls of butter, a little pepper and salt. Line some patty-pans with puff-paste, fill with oysters, cover with paste, and bake twenty minutes in a hot oven. The upper crust may be omitted, if desired.

Oyster Pie.

Line a deep dish with pastry and bake it; then fill with oysters, seasoned with salt, pepper, a teaspoonful of butter and two of cream; cover with pastry and set it in the oven and bake for twenty minutes. Serve at once.

Steamed Oysters.

Leave a covered dish where it will heat; wash and drain the oysters, then put them in a shallow tin and place it in the steamer; cover and leave it over boiling water until the oysters are puffed and curled. Then they may be dressed at table when eaten, or butter, salt and pepper may be added in the kitchen, when served in the heated dish.

Roasted Oysters.

Wash the shells perfectly clean, wipe them dry and lay them on a gridiron, the largest side to the fire ; set it over a bright bed of coals. When the shells open wide and the oysters look white, they are done. Fold a napkin on a large dish or tray ; lay the oysters on the shells, care being taken not to lose the juice ; serve hot. When oysters are served roasted, there should be a small tub between each two chairs to receive the shells.

Scalloped Oysters.

Line the bottom of a pudding dish with cracker or stale bread crumbs; then put in a layer of oysters seasoned with salt, pepper and butter, and so on until the dish is full, having the top layer of crumbs. Lay small lumps of butter over the top, pour over half a pint of cream; set it in the oven and bake half an hour. Serve at once.

Oyster Loaf.

Cut a piece, five inches across, from the top of a round loaf of bread; remove the crumbs, leaving the crust half an inch thick; make a nice oyster stew, and put in the loaf in layers, sprinkled with bread crumbs; place the cover over the top, and cover the loaf with the beaten yolk of an egg, and put it in the oven to glaze. Make a wreath of curled parsley on a platter, with the stems turned in, and place the loaf on them, concealing all but the leaves.

Oyster Toast.

Scald a quart of oysters in their own liquor; take them out and pound them in a mortar; when they form a paste, add a little cream, and season with pepper. Get ready some nice pieces of toast, spread the oyster paste upon them, and place them for a few minutes in an oven to heat. A little finely-chopped pickle may be strewn on the top before serving.

OYSTER MACARONI.

Boil macaroni in a cloth to keep it straight. Put a layer in a dish seasoned with pepper, salt and butter, then a layer of oysters, until the dish is full. Mix some grated bread with a beaten egg, spread over the top, and bake.

OYSTERS—FANCY ROAST.

Toast a few slices of bread and butter them; lay them in a shallow dish; put on the liquor of the oysters to heat, add salt and pepper, and just before it boils add the oysters; let them boil up once, and pour over the bread.

OYSTERS BAKED IN THE SHELL.

Open the oysters, place them in a dripping pan in the shell, season with salt and pepper and bake half an hour. Just before taking them out, put a piece of butter into each shell. Serve in the shells.

OYSTER FRITTERS.

Beat four eggs until very light, and add to them one pint of milk; stir in flour enough to make a stiff batter; add a little salt; scald one quart of oysters in their own liquor, then drain and dry them. Season with pepper and salt, and put into the batter and fry.

LOBSTER PUDDING.

Divide the body in two, and having cleared the back shell and dressed the meat of the whole as for patties, lay it in the shell hot; cover with crumbs of bread, and brown with a salamander. If the lobsters are small, use two.

RISSOLES OF LOBSTERS.

Chop the flesh of a large lobster, or two small ones, and mix with it a very little lemon peel, pepper, salt, nutmeg or mace, a small piece of butter, cream and a little cracker dust. Roll the mass and cover it in small quantities, the size of sausages, with a light puff paste. Rub over them the yolks of eggs; and dip them in fine cracker dust. Fry to a yellow brown, and serve them with crisped parsley.

BUTTERED LOBSTER.

Pick the meat out, cut it, and warm with a little weak brown gravy, nutmeg, salt, pepper, butter and a little flour. If done white, serve with a little white gravy and cream.

TO POT LOBSTERS.

Half boil them, pick out the meat, cut it into small pieces, season with mace, white pepper, nutmeg and salt; press close into a pot, and cover with butter; bake half an hour; put the spawn in. When cold take the lobster out and put it into pots, with a little of the butter. Beat the other butter with some of the spawn; then mix that colored butter with as much as will be sufficient to cover the pots, and strain it. Cayenne may be added, if approved.

LOBSTER PATTIES.

For lobster patties use the meat of a cold boiled lobster, and follow the directions given for oyster patties.

ADDITIONAL RECIPES.

Aitch Bone of Beef.

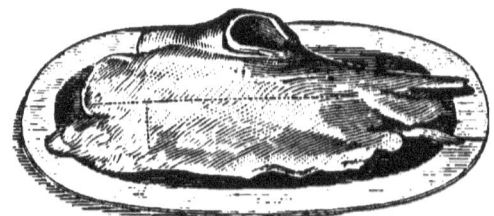

Half a Calf's Head.

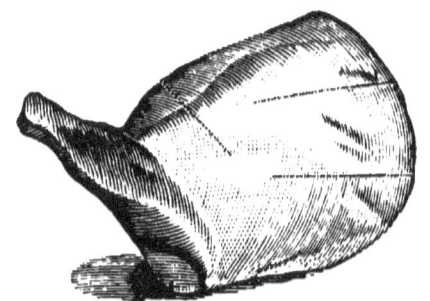

Shoulder of Mutton.

Leg of Mutton.

Quarter of Lamb.

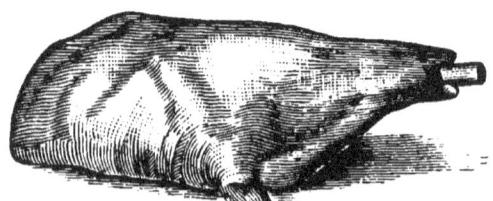

Haunch of Venison.

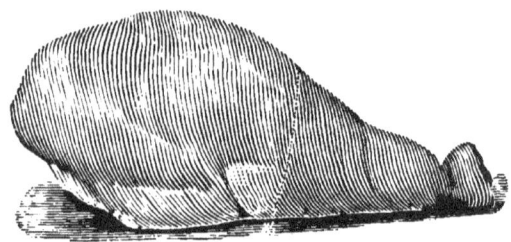

Ham.

MEATS.

To Select Beef.

Nice beef may be known by its color. The fat will be of an oily smoothness, and white, rather than yellow. The lean will be of an open grain and bright red. Yellow fat is a sure sign of an inferior quality of meats.

A Few Practical Hints.

Particular care should be taken to well skim all boiled meats and to well baste all roast meats.

The more soups and broths are skimmed, the clearer and better they will be.

Meats boiled quick will be hard.

A ham weighing ten pounds will take four hours' gentle boiling.

A leg of pork to boil will take twenty minutes to the pound.

Beef or mutton fifteen minutes to the pound, either to boil or bake.

A tongue takes four hours' boiling. A pickled tongue two hours and a half.

Drippings, if sweet, will baste everything as well as butter, except game.

Meat and vegetables that have been touched with the frost should be soaked in cold water for two hours before using.

Roast Venison.

Lay three long slices of salt pork on a haunch of venison; place in a dripping pan, and add salt and pepper and hot water; baste very often. It will take about four hours to bake well. Serve with jelly sauce. To make a gravy, take up the venison and pour one quart of boiling water in the dripping pan; work flour smoothly into a piece of butter the size of an egg and turn into the pan; let it boil and then strain. Serve in a gravy boat.

Spiced Beef.

Cover a 'round of beef, weighing about sixteen pounds, with a pound of salt, and turn it every day for a week. At the end of that time, wash it in cold water, rub it well with two ounces of black pepper and a quarter of an ounce of mace. Fry three or four onions sliced, add a few cloves, then put in the meat, cover it with water, and bake in a stone-covered stewing-pan for five hours. To be eaten cold, for breakfast or supper.

Stewed Shoulder of Venison.

Take the bone out of a shoulder of venison, and beat the meat with a rolling-pin or hammer; lay among it some slices of mutton fat that have been soaked and stewed tender in port wine; sprinkle a little pepper and allspice over it, and then roll it up tight and tie it; set in a stew-pan that will only just hold it, and add some mutton or beef gravy, half a pint of port wine and some pepper and allspice. Simmer it as slow as you can, closely covered, for three or four hours, or until tender. Take off the string, set the meat on a dish and strain the gravy over it. Serve with currant jelly sauce.

Breast of Venison.

Follow the directions for stewing the shoulder, or make into a small pastry In the latter case, bake it with good mutton gravy in a pan the day before, and season with pepper, salt and some Jamaica pepper when you put the crust on.

Italian Beefsteaks.

Cut a fine, large steak from a rump that has been well hung (or it will do from any *tender* part); beat it, and season with pepper, salt and onion; lay it in an iron stew-pan with a close-fitting cover, and set it by the side of the fire without water. Take care it does not burn, as it must have a strong heat; in two or three hours it will be quite tender, and then serve with its own gravy.

Beefsteak.

Good beefsteak should be cut three-quarters of an inch thick, and broiled over or before a clear, bright fire. Serve on a hot dish with butter, pepper and salt, or if desired, mushroom or tomato sauce. Pounding steak is a bad but prevalent habit, and should be avoided, as much of the juice (the most nutritious part) of the meat is wasted. When broiling turn frequently, as the juice should not be drawn out on either side.

Beefsteaks and Oyster Sauce.

Strain off the liquor from the oysters, and throw them into cold water to take off the grit, while you simmer the liquor with a bit of mace and lemon-peel; then put the oysters in and stew for a few minutes; add a little cream if you have it, and some butter rubbed in a little flour; let them boil up once; have your steak well seasoned and broiled, ready for the oyster sauce, the moment you are to serve.

Staffordshire Beefsteaks.

Flour and season your steak, and fry with sliced onions; then lay into a stew-pan, after frying, and pour as much boiling water over it as will serve for sauce; stew very gently for half an hour, and add a teaspoonful of catsup or walnut liquor before you serve.

Beef, a la Mode.

Make a stuffing of rich herbs, spices and suet, and stuff the beef with it; one and one-half bottles of port or claret wine, according to the size of the beef, and five quarts of water. Do not let it boil, but simmer until it is done.

Beef Heart.

Wash it carefully and stuff it nicely; roast or bake it, and serve with the gravy, which should be thickened with some of the stuffing. It is very nice hashed, with a little port wine added.

Beef Palates.

Simmer them in water several hours until they will peel; then cut the palates into slices, or leave them whole, as you choose; stew them in a rich gravy until as tender as possible. Before serving, season them with pepper, salt and catsup. If the gravy was drawn clear, boil it with some butter and flour. If to be served white, boil them in milk, and stew them in fricassee sauce, adding cream, butter, flour, mushroom powder and a little mace.

To Pickle Beef Palates.

Clean four fine palates, simmer them in a quart of water, skim them well, and then put as much mace, cloves, pepper and sweet herbs as will flavor them highly, in which boil them until perfectly tender, which will take about five hours; take the skin off, cut them into small pieces and let them cool, being covered. Make a pickle sufficient to cover them with equal parts of white wine and vinegar, the spices before used, and some salt; strain when cold, and pour the liquor on the palates, with a little fresh spice and four or five bay-leaves. Cover very close.

To Pot Beef.

Take two pounds of lean beef, rub it with saltpetre, and let it lie one night; then salt and cover it with water four days in a pan. Dry it with a cloth, and season with black pepper; lay it into as small a pan as will hold it; cover it with coarse paste, and bake it five hours in a very cool oven. Put no liquor in. When cold, pick out the strings and fat; chop the meat fine with a quarter of a pound of butter, just warmed, but not oily, and as much of the gravy as will make it into a paste; put it into very small pots, and cover it with melted butter.

Another.

Rub three pounds of beef with two ounces of dark brown sugar, and a quarter of an ounce of saltpetre let it lie forty-eight hours; wash it clean, and dry it; season with pepper, salt, mace and twelve cloves; lay it in an earthern pot, with four ounces of butter put over it in pieces. Bake it three hours; then cut off the hard outside and chop it fine. Melt four ounces of fine butter in this and the gravy which comes from the beef, and chop with the beef as fine as possible. Add seasoning to your taste. Put it into pots; cover deep with clarified butter, and keep in a cool, dry place.

Minced Beef.

Mince your beef with onions, pepper, and salt; add a little gravy, and put it into scollop shells or saucers, making them three parts full; then fill them up with potato, mashed with a little cream; put a small piece of butter on the top of each, and brown them in an oven, or with a salamander

To Dress the Inside of a Cold Sirloin of Beef.

Cut out all the meat, and a little fat, into pieces as thick as your finger and two inches long; dredge them with flour, and fry in butter; drain the butter from the meat, from which make a rich gravy, seasoned with pepper, salt, anchovy, and shallot. Do not let it boil on any account. Before you serve add two spoonfuls of vinegar. Garnish with crimped parsley.

To Dress an Ox Cheek.

Soak half a head three hours, and clean it with plenty of water. Take the meat off the bones, and put it into a pan with a large onion, a bunch of sweet herbs, some ground allspice, pepper, and salt. Lay the bones on the top; pour on three pints of water, and cover the pan close with brown paper, or a dish that will fit tightly. Let it stand eight or ten hours in a slow oven. When done tender, put the meat into a clean pan, and let it get cold. Take the cake of fat off, and warm the head in pieces in the soup, adding truffles, morels, and force-meat balls. Put in what vegetables you choose.

Tripe.

May be served in a tureen, stewed tender with milk and onions, or fried in bits dipped in batter. In both the above ways, serve melted butter for sauce. Or, if preferred, cut the thin parts in oblong bits, and stew in gravy; thicken with butter rolled in a very little flour, and add a spoonful of mushroom catsup.

Soused Tripe.

Boil the tripe, but not quite tender; then put it into salt and water, which must be changed every day till it is all used. When you dress the tripe, dip it into a batter of flour and eggs, and fry it to a good brown.

Savory Beef.

Take a shin of beef from the hind quarter, saw it into four pieces and put it in a pot; boil it until the meat and gristle drop from the bones; chop the meat very fine and put it in a dish; season it with a little salt, pepper, cloves and sage, to your taste; pour in the liquor, in which the meat was boiled, and place it away to harden. Cut in slices and eat cold.

To Curry Meat.

Take slices from cold beef or mutton, and from your jar of ready-made gravy take enough to cover your meat; let it cook slowly for twenty minutes; then rub some butter and flour together to thicken it; add curry powder to taste; one teaspoonful will be enough.

Tongues to be Eaten Cold.

Season with salt, saltpetre, brown sugar, pepper, cloves, mace and allspice for a fortnight; then take away the pickle and put the tongue into a small pan; lay some butter on it and cover with brown crust; bake slowly till so tender that a straw would go through it.

To Select Veal.

When the kidney is well surrounded with fat, you may be sure the meat is of good quality. Always choose that which is whitest and fattest. If the vein in the shoulder, which is very perceptible, is a bright red or blue, it is a sure sign that the meat is fresh.

Shoulder of Veal.

Cut off the knuckle for a stew or gravy. Roast the other part with a stuffing; you may lard it. Serve with melted butter. The blade-bone, with a good deal of meat left on, is extremely palatable with mushrooms or oyster-sauce, or mushroom catsup in butter.

Roast Fillet of Veal.

Make a stuffing of a little beef suet, chopped fine, the same quantity of bread crumbs, a little sweet marjoram, the rind of two lemons, grated, a tablespoonful of grated horse-radish, a little pepper and salt; if you choose add the yolks of two hard boiled eggs, cut up fine. Introduce the stuffing through the fillet and secure it with skewers and twine; baste it well while it is roasting, and make a gravy of the drippings, thickened with flour.

Veal Sweet-breads.

Take two or three fresh sweet-breads, parboil them for a few minutes, then take them from the hot water, and put them into cold. Take some bread crumbs or cracker dust and add the yolks of two eggs, well beaten, to the crumbs. When the sweet-breads are perfectly cold, place them on a skewer, and roll them in the prepared crumbs, lay them in a stew-pan with a small bit of butter and a little veal gravy, and cook them a nice brown. Take the gravy in which they are cooked, add the juice of a lemon, a little salt and pepper; toast some slices of bread, dip them into the gravy, and lay the sweet-breads on.

To Dress Calf's Head like Turtle.

Let them boil an hour and a half, with salt in the water; tie the brains in a cloth bag, and boil half an hour; when all is done, take out the bones and cut up in pieces. Add to your liquor a little sweet marjoram, a nutmeg, grated, clove, mace, and pepper to taste, half a pint of catsup, half a pound of butter, and a pint of claret, or port wine; then put in the meat, and boil a few minutes, and it is done.

Breast of Veal.

Before roasted, if large, the two ends may be taken off and fried or stewed, or the whole may be roasted. Butter should be poured over it. If any is left, cut the pieces into handsome sizes, put them into a stew-pan, and pour some broth over them; or if you have no broth, a little water will do; add a bunch of herbs, a blade or two of mace, some pepper and an anchovy; stew till the meat is tender; thicken with butter and flour, and add a little catsup; or the whole breast may be stewed, after cutting off the two ends. Serve the sweet-bread whole upon it, which may either be stewed or parboiled, and then covered with crumbs, herbs, pepper and salt, and browned in an oven.

To Collar a Breast of Veal.

Bone it, take off the thick skin and gristle, and beat the meat with a rolling-pin. Season it with herbs chopped very fine, mixed with salt, pepper and mace. Lay on it some thick slices of fine ham, or roll into it two or three calves' tongues of a fine red, boiled first an hour or two and skinned. Bind it up tight in a cloth and tie it. Set it over a slow fire to simmer in a small quantity of water, till it is quite tender; this will take some hours. Lay it on the dresser, with a board and weight on it till cold. Pigs' and calves' feet boiled, and taken from the bones, may be put in or around it. The different colors laid in layers look well when cut; you may also put in yolks of eggs boiled, beet-root, grated ham and chopped parsley, in different parts. When it is cold, take off the string, and pour over it the liquor, which must be boiled up twice a week, or it will not keep.

A Ragout of Cold Veal.

Cut the veal into slices; put a large piece of butter into a frying-pan, and as soon as it is hot, dredge the meat well with flour, and fry a nice brown. Remove the meat, and put into the pan as much of your cold gravy as you think proper; season with pepper and salt, and a wine glass of tomato catsup; then cut a few slices of cold ham, lay into the gravy, and add your slices of veal. It must be sent to the table hot.

Chump of Veal, a la Daube.

Cut off the chump end of the loin; take out the edgebone; stuff the hollow with good force-meat, tie it up tight and lay it in a stew-pan with the bone you took out, a small bunch of herbs and anchovy, two blades of mace, a few white peppers, and a pint of good veal broth. Cover the veal with slices of fat pork, and lay a sheet of white paper over it. Cover the pan close; simmer it two hours, and then take out the pork and glaze the veal. Serve it on mushrooms, or sorrel sauce, or what else you please.

Hashed Veal.

A most excellent recipe for hashed veal is to cook it fine, put in just enough water to moisten it, butter, salt, pepper and a little juice of a lemon (some like a little lemon rind grated in), heat it through but do not let it fry, as it injures cooked meats to cook them again. Put it on buttered toast and garnish with lemon.

Fricandeau of Veal.

What is called a fricandeau of veal is simply a cushion of veal trimmed into shape, larded and braised. Cut three or four pounds from a fillet of veal, form it into an oval-shaped loaf, and lard it on top. Put some pieces of pork into a sauce-pan with two slices of carrot, an onion with cloves stuck in, a stick of celery and some parsley. Place the veal on this, larded side up. Sprinkle over pepper, salt and a little flour, and cover it with well-buttered paper. Now fill the pan with boiling stock, or water enough to just cover the meat. Cover with a tight lid and put it into a hot oven. It will take about two or two and a half hours to cook. It may be garnished with green peas, spinach or sorrel. It is often served on a bed of mashed potatoes, or garnished with potato balls. The best sauce for a fricandeau is a tomato sauce.

Cutlets Maintenon.

Cut slices about three-quarters of an inch thick, beat them with a rolling-pin, and wet them on both sides with egg; dip them into a seasoning of cracker crumbs, parsley, thyme, knotted marjoram, pepper, salt, and a little nutmeg, grated; then put them into papers folded over, and broil them. Have in a boat melted butter with a little mushroom catsup.

Cutlets, Another Way.

Prepare as above, and fry them, lay them into a dish, and keep them hot; dredge in a little flour, and put a little butter into the pan; brown it; then pour a little boiling water into it and boil quick; season with pepper, salt and catsup, and pour over them. Or pepper, salt, and broil them, especially neck steaks. They are excellent with herbs.

Veal Collops.

Cut long, thin collops, pound them well, and lay on them a piece of thin pork of the same size, and spread force-meat on that, seasoned high, and also a little garlic and cayenne pepper. Roll them up tight, about the size of two fingers, but no more than two or three inches long; put a very small skewer to fasten each firmly; rub egg over; fry them to a fine brown, and pour a rich brown gravy over.

To Dress Collops Quick.

Cut them thin, with a very sharp knife, and in small pieces. Throw the skin, and any odd pieces of the veal, into a little water, with a little pepper and salt; set them on the fire while you beat the collops; then dip them into a seasoning of herbs, bread, pepper, salt and a scrape of nutmeg, but first wet them in egg. Then put a piece of butter into a frying-pan, and give the collops a very quick fry; for as they are so thin, two minutes will do them on both sides; put them into a hot dish before the fire, then strain and thicken the gravy.

Veal Olives.

Cut long, thin slices, beat well and lay on them thin slices of fat pork, and over these a layer or force-meat, seasoned high with some shred shallot and cayenne pepper. Roll them tight, about the size of two fingers, but not more than two or three inches long; fasten them round with a small skewer, rub egg over them and fry them to a light brown. Serve with brown gravy, in which boil some mushrooms, pickled or fresh. Garnish with balls fried.

Excellent Dish made from Roasted Veal.

From a joint, not overdone, cut thin slices and remove the skin and gristle; put some sliced onion and a shallot over the fire with a piece of butter and some flour, fry and shake them. Put in some veal gravy and a bunch of sweet herbs; simmer ten minutes; strain off the gravy, and put it to the veal, with some parsley, chopped fine, and a little grated lemon peel and nutmeg; let it simmer one minute; then add the yolks of two eggs, beaten up with two spoonfuls of cream and a very little pepper; stir over the fire one way, until the same be thick and smooth; squeeze a little lemon juice in and serve.

To Collar Calf's Head.

Scald the skin of a fine head, clean it nicely, and take out the brains. Boil it tender enough to remove the bones; then have ready a good quantity of chopped parsley, mace, nutmeg, salt, and white pepper, mixed well; season it high with these; lay the parsley in a thick layer, then a quantity of thick slices of fine ham, or a beautifully-colored tongue skinned, and then the yolks of six nice yellow eggs stuck here and there about. Roll the head quite close, and tie it up as tight as you can. Boil it till the tape slackens, and then lay a weight on it (without removing the bandage) till quite cold.. Keep it in a pickle of the liquor, vinegar and salt. A cloth must be put under the tape, as for other collars.

CALF'S LIVER.

Slice it, season it with pepper and salt, and broil nicely; rub a bit of cold butter on it, and serve hot, with small slices of fat pork, or on fried herbs.

SWEET-BREADS, A LA DAUBE.

Blanch two or three of the largest sweet-breads and lard them with small pieces of pork. Put them into a stew-pan with some good veal gravy, a little browning, and the juice of half a lemon; stew them till quite tender, and just before serving thicken with flour and butter. Serve with their gravy, around which place bunches of boiled celery.

Sweet-breads for every mode of dressing, should be prepared by half-boiling, and then putting them in cold water. This, called blanching, makes them whiter and thicker, as well as firmer.

HASHED MUTTON WITH HERBS.

Put into a sauce-pan a good piece of butter, some finely minced shallot, parsley, and half a pint of mushrooms; boil them gently in the butter; then, by degrees, mix in a large spoonful of flour, half a pint of broth, and stew till the flavor of all is obtained; let it become a little cool and then mince some under-done mutton in it, without boiling.

MUTTON KIDNEYS.

With a very sharp knife cut mutton kidneys in the thinnest possible slices; flour, and fry quickly till they are quite crisp. While frying, add pepper and salt. Serve them in a good gravy, to which a little garlic has given a very slight flavor.

Mutton Steaks with Beans.

Wash the beans and drain the water from them; then simmer them with pepper and salt in a good piece of butter, a few minutes before serving. Add the beaten yolk of an egg, and shake the pan over the fire, but they must not boil. In the meantime have three mutton steaks ready, neatly trimmed and seasoned with pepper, salt and a few crumbs, and nicely broiled or fried. Serve them on the beans.

Mutton, a la Venison.

Take a fat loin, remove the kidney, and let it hang a week, if the weather permits. Two days before dressing it for cooking, take ground allspice, cloves and pepper, mix them, and rub into the meat a tablespoonful of each twice a day for two days. Before cooking, wash it off, and roast as a leg. To preserve the fat and keep it in, make a paste of flour and water, and spread thickly over the meat. Over this tie a double sheet of coarse paper, well buttered. About a quarter of an hour before it is done, remove the paper and paste, return to the oven and baste, and dredge with flour. It is equal to venison.

Mutton Kidneys.

Take half a dozen fine mutton kidneys, clear them of fat and skin, and cut them into thin slices; powder them immediately with sweet herbs in fine powder, a little cayenne pepper and salt. Put into a stew-pan two ounces of fine butter or fresh lard; put in the slices of kidney, and fry them nicely; dredge a little flour over them, and moisten with lemon juice, and in five minutes they will be done; lay them on a hot dish, around which place slices of fried bread. Pour into the gravy two glasses of white wine; boil it, pour over the kidneys, and serve hot.

HARRICO.

Take off some of the fat, and cut the middle or best end of the neck into rather thin steaks, flour, and fry them in their fat a fine light brown, but not enough for eating. Then put them into a dish while you fry the carrots, turnips and onions—the carrots and turnips in dice—the onions sliced; but they must only be warmed, not browned, or you need not fry them. Then lay the steaks at the bottom of a stew-pan, the vegetables over them, and pour as much boiling water as will just cover them; give one boil, skim well, and then set the pan on the side of the fire to simmer gently till the meat is tender. In three or four hours skim them, and add pepper, salt, and a spoonful of catsup.

FILLET OF MUTTON GLAZED.

Take off the chump end of the loin, butter some paper, and put over it, and then paste as for venison; roast it two hours. Do not let it be the least brown. Have ready some boiled beans, drained on a sieve; while the mutton is being glazed, heat them up once in the gravy, and lay them on the dish with the meat over them.

ROAST SADDLE OF MUTTON.

Let it be well kept first. Raise the skin, and then skewer it on again; take it off a quarter of an hour before serving, sprinkle it with some salt, baste it and dredge it well with flour. The rump should be split, and skewered back on each side. The joint may be large or small, according to the company; it is the most elegant if the latter. Being broad, it requires a high and strong fire.

BREAST OF MUTTON.

Cut off the superfluous fat, and roast; serve the

meat with stewed cucumbers; or if to eat cold, covered with chopped parsley. Or, half-boil, and broil it over the fire, in which case cover it with crumbs and herbs, and serve with caper-sauce. Or, if boned, take off a good deal of the fat, and cover it with bread, herbs and seasoning; then roll and boil till tender; pour over it chopped walnuts in butter. Or, make it into a pie.

To Collar a Breast of Mutton.

Bone it, and rub it with the yolk of an egg; strew over it a little grated lemon-peel, pepper and salt; then mix a teacup of capers, two anchovies, a handful of parsley, a few sweet herbs, all minced fine, with bread crumbs or cracker dust, which spread over the mutton; roll it very tight, boil it two hours, and when cold, unbind the tape, and put it into a pickle of strong salt and water one pint; and vinegar half a pint.

Mutton Chops.

They should be cut from a loin or neck; if from a neck, the bone should be long. They should be broiled on a clear fire, seasoned when half done, and often turned; take them up into a very hot dish, rub a bit of butter on each, and serve hot the moment they are done.

Mutton Cutlets in the Portuguese Way.

Cut chops, and half-fry them with sliced shallot or onion, chopped parsley and two bay-leaves; season with pepper and salt; then lay a force-meat on a piece of white paper, put the chop on it, and twist the paper up, leaving a hole for the end of the bones to go through. Broil on a gentle fire. Serve with a little gravy

Steaks of Mutton or Lamb, and Cucumbers.

Quarter cucumbers, and lay them into a deep dish, sprinkle them with salt, and pour vinegar over them. Fry the chops to a fine brown, and put them into a stew-pan; drain the cucumbers and put over the steaks; add some sliced onions, pepper and salt; pour hot water or weak broth on them; stew and skim well. If the gravy is not thick enough, put in a piece of butter rolled in a little flour.

Leg of Lamb.

Boil the leg in a cloth, as the meat will look much whiter. Fry the loin in steaks and serve, garnished with dried or fried parsley, or dressed separately, or roasted. A hind-quarter is seldom roasted, but if fat and young it is far more juicy and well-flavored than the fore-quarter, or either joint dressed separately.

Fore-Quarter of Lamb.

Roast it, either whole or in separate parts. If left to be cold, chopped parsley should be sprinkled over it. The neck and breast together are called a scoven.

China Chilo.

Mince a pint basin of undressed neck of mutton, or leg, and some of the fat; put two onions, a head of lettuce, a pint of green peas, a teaspoonful of salt, a teaspoonful of pepper, four spoonfuls of water, and two or three ounces of butter, into a stew-pan closely covered; simmer two hours, and serve in the middle of a dish of boiled rice. If cayenne pepper is approved, add a little. This cannot be done too slowly.

Lamb Cutlets with Spinach.

Cut the steaks from the loin, and fry them; the spinach is to be stewed and put into the dish first, and then the cutlets around it.

Lamb's Head and Hinge.

Soak in cold water; boil the head separately till very tender; have ready the liver and lights, three parts boiled, and cut small; stew them in a little of the water in which they were boiled, season and thicken with flour and butter, and serve the mince around the head.

Lamb's Sweet-breads.

Blanch them, and place in cold water a short time. Then put them into a stew-pan, with a ladleful of broth, some pepper and salt, a small bunch of small onions, and a blade of mace; stir in a piece of butter and some flour, and stew half an hour. Have ready the yolks of two or three eggs, well beaten in cream, with a little minced parsley and a few grates of nutmeg. Put in some boiled asparagus tops with the other things. Do not let it boil after the cream is in; but make it hot, and stir it well continually. Take great care it does not curdle. Young beans or peas may be added, first boiled, of a beautiful green.

To Select Pork.

In fresh pork the flesh is firm, smooth, a clear color, and the fat set. Dairy fed pork bears the palm over all others. In young pork, the lean, when pinched, will break. Excellent bacon may be known by the lean being tender and of a bright color, the fat firm and white.

Roast Leg of Pork.

Choose a small leg of fine young pork; cut a slit in the knuckle with a sharp-knife and fill the space with sage and onion chopped, and a little pepper and salt. When half done, score the skin in slices, but do not cut deeper than the outer rind.

Boiled Leg of Pork.

Salt it eight or ten days, turning it daily, but do not rub it after the first. When to be dressed, weigh it; let it lie half an hour in cold water to make it white; allow a quarter of an hour for every pound, and half an hour over from the time it boils up; skim it as soon as it boils, and frequently after, but do not boil it fast, or it will be hard. Allow water enough. Save some of it to make pea-soup. Some boil it in a very nice cloth, floured, which gives a very delicate look.

Pork Steaks.

Cut them from a loin or neck, and of middling thickness; beat the lean part with a broad knife; pepper and broil them, turning them often; when nearly done, put on salt, rub a piece of butter over, and serve the moment they are taken off the fire, a few at a time.

Spare-Ribs.

They should be basted with very little butter and a little flour, and then sprinkled with dried sage crumbled. Apple-sauce and potatoes for roasted pork.

Pettitoes.

Boil them, the liver and the heart, in a small quantity of water, very gently; then cut the meat fine, and simmer it with a little of the water, and the feet split, till the feet are quite tender; thicken with a piece of butter a little flour, a spoonful of cream, and a little salt and pepper; give it a boil, pour over it a few sippets of bread, and put the feet on the mince.

To Roast a Sucking Pig.

If you can get one when just killed, it is of great advantage. Let it be scalded, which the dealers usually do; then put some sage, a large piece of old white bread, salt and pepper, into the belly, and sew it up. Observe to skewer the legs back, or the under part will not crisp. Lay it by a brisk fire till thoroughly dry; then have ready some butter in a dry cloth, and rub the pig with it in every part. Dredge as much flour over as will possibly lie, and do not touch it again till ready to serve; then scrape off the flour very carefully with a blunt knife, rub the pig well with the buttered cloth, and take off the head while at the fire. Take out the brains and mix them with the gravy that comes from the pig. Cut it down the back and belly, lay it into the dish, and chop the sage and bread quickly and as fine as you can; mix them with a large quantity of fine melted butter that has very little flour. Put the sauce into the dish after the pig has been split down the back, and garnished with the ears and the two jaws; take off the upper part of the head down to the snout. It will require from an hour to an hour and a half to roast.

Pigs' Feet and Ears Soused.

Clean carefully, soak them some hours and then boil them tender; after having prepared a pickle of some of the liquor that they were boiled in, and a quarter part of vinegar and salt, boiled, pour over them cold. When to be dressed, dry them, cut the feet in two, slice the ears and fry them. Serve with butter, mustard, and vinegar, in a boat. They may be dipped in batter, or only floured.

To Cure Hams.

Hang them a day or two; then sprinkle them with a little salt, and drain them another day; pound an ounce and a half of saltpetre, the same quantity of salt, half an ounce of sal-prunella, and a pound of the coarsest sugar. Mix these well, and rub them into each ham every day for four days, and turn. If a small one, turn it every day for three weeks; if a large one, a week longer; but do not rub after four days. Before you dry it, drain and cover with bran. Smoke it ten days.

Pork and Beans.

One pound of pork to one quart of beans. Wash the beans at night and pour over one quart. of tepid water; in the morning add two quarts of water, after pouring off the water that has stood over night. Drain and put them in a pot, cut the pork rind into small squares and put it in the centre of the beans; sink to the rind; then pour a quantity of hot water over them, cover the pot and bake slowly for three hours.

Head Cheese.

Boil the head and feet very tender; remove all the bones; put the meat into a strainer and press out all the grease possible; when cool, chop fine, season with pepper and salt and pack the same as sausage meat.

How to Choose a Ham, and Other Useful Information.

First, Never buy a ham because it is offered at a low price. Cheapness counts one against its being choice.

Second, Do not select too lean a joint. The fat of a ham is often considered so much waste meat; so it may be in many families. But one would not select a very lean piece of beef for roasting; it would surely be dry and tough when cooked. Now, a well-fed and quickly fatted pig will furnish tender, juicy and fine-flavored meat. Bear this in mind, and you will be willing to lose a little extra fat for your gain in the superior qualities of every other ounce of the flesh. Let the joint be well-rounded and plump rather than thin and flat, and see that the skin is thin and pliable.

Third, Choose freshly-cured hams. Formerly the year's supply was packed in the winter, and, after smoking, must needs be canvassed to preserve it against the ravages of flies, and in this shape be carried to meet the demands through the summer and fall. This necessarily resulted in a considerable loss of the juices of the meat by evaporation; while the surface of the flesh gradually became densely covered with mildew, which often gave a mouldy flavor to the entire ham. This has now been entirely obviated by such improvements in curing by ice, that hams of the very finest quality are now prepared even in the hottest weather; and so the market affords, to all buyers who will insist upon having them, new-cured hams for every day in the year. Wines improve by age; but not so meats. The more recently the joint has come from the curing-cask (other things being equal), the better it will please you when cooked.

Fourth, The size of a ham has much to do with the way in which it should be served. A whole ham will boil more satisfactorily than a part of it. For broiling or frying never use a ham of less than twelve pounds, and one weighing fifteen or sixteen is better still for this purpose. Only the centre of such a ham, however, should be sliced. Take off at least two inches from the large end of the ham in one cut. Then slice up the remainder as it is needed, until the upper joint in the bone is reached.

Fried Ham and Eggs.

Cut the ham in rather thin slices, take off the rind

and pour cold water on them; then wipe dry. Put your lard into the spider which should be hot, and fry quickly. If fried this way the ham will be red and tender. Break the eggs in a cup; the lard should not be too hot. Do not put too many in the pan together, and dip the hot lard over them; do not turn them as they should be kept whole. Lay the ham in the centre of the platter and garnish with the eggs.

Roast Ham.

The most delicious way to cook ham is to boil a small pig ham in the ordinary way until the skin will peel off, then stick in cloves over the surface of the ham; cover with bread crumbs or cracker dust, place in a dripping-pan, raising it a little from the pan by sticks and bake three or four hours.

Another.

A roasted ham is simply a boiled ham nicely browned in a hot oven; therefore thoroughly cook, and remove the skin. Have ready some oven-dried bread or crackers, of which roll fine, and sift a teacupful. Break in two eggs, and stir well with two tablespoonfuls of sugar. Use a little water if the eggs do not sufficiently moisten it. Spread this evenly over the fat, and dress with pepper and spices.

Ham Croquets.

Chop the ham fine, and season with pepper or mustard. With a little flour in hand make up small balls, and dip in beaten egg; roll in crumbs of bread or cracker, and fry to a light brown in hot lard.

Ham Toast.

Melt in a stew-pan a small piece of butter till it is browned a little; put in as much finely minced ham as will cover a large round of buttered toast, and add gravy enough to make it moist. When quite hot stir in quickly with a fork one egg. Place the mixture over the toast which may be cut in pieces of any shape you may fancy.

Rice Hash.

Chop remnants of fresh meats with salt pork or cold ham; season with salt, pepper, and a little sugar; add two eggs and a little butter. Then make alternate layers with this and slices of cold boiled rice, and bake it half an hour.

Veal Sausage.

Chop equal quantities of lean veal and fat bacon, a handful of sage, a little salt and pepper, and a few anchovies. Chop all in a bowl; and when used, roll and fry it, and serve it with fried sippets, or on stewed vegetables, or on white collops.

Mutton Sausage.

Take a pound of rawest part of the leg of mutton that has been either roasted or boiled; chop it very fine, and season it with pepper, salt, mace, and nutmeg; add to it six ounces of beef-suet, some sweet herbs, two anchovies, and a pint of oysters, all chopped very fine; a quarter of a pound of grated bread, some of the anchovy-liquor, and the yolks and whites of two eggs well beaten. Put it all, when well mixed, into a little pot, and use it by rolling it into balls.

Pork Sausage.

Chop fat and lean pork together; season it, for one hundred pounds, with one and three-quarter pounds of salt, six ounces of pepper and four ounces of sage, and you may add two or three berries of allspice;

half fill hog casings that have been soaked and made extremely clean; or the meat may be kept in a very small pan closely covered; and rolled and dusted with a very little flour before it is fried. Serve on stewed red cabbage; or mashed potatoes put in a form, browned with a salamander, and garnished with the above. They must be pricked with a fork before they are dressed, or they will burst.

An Excellent Sausage to Eat Cold.

Season fat and lean pork with some salt, saltpetre, black pepper and allspice, and rub into the meat; the sixth day cut it small, and mix with it some shred shallot or garlic, as fine as possible. Have ready an ox-casing that has been scoured, salted, and soaked well, and fill it with the above stuffing; tie up the ends, and hang it to smoke as you would hams, but first wrap it in a fold or two of old muslin. It must be well-dried. Some eat it without boiling, but others like it boiled first. The skin should be tied in different places, so as to make each link about eight or nine inches long.

Salting Beef.

To one hundred pounds beef put eight pounds fine salt, three pounds brown sugar, one-quarter pound salt petre. Scald and skim. Keep under cover from the air.

Sausage.

To one hundred pounds of meat put in one and three-quarter pounds salt, six ounces pepper and four ounces sage.

MEATS.

FORCE-MEAT INGREDIENTS.

Cold fowl, veal or mutton.	Cold sole.
Scraped ham or gammon.	Oysters.
Fat bacon or the fat of ham.	Anchovy.
	Lobster.
Beef-suet.	Tarragon.
Veal-suet.	Savory.
Butter.	Pennyroyal.
Marrow.	Knotted marjoram.
Crumbs of bread.	Thyme and lemon thyme
Parsley.	Basil.
White pepper.	Sage.
Salt.	Lemon peel.
Nutmeg.	Yolks of hard eggs.
Yolk and white of eggs, well beaten to bind the mixture.	Mace and cloves.
	Cayenne.
	Garlic.
	Shallot.
	Onion.
	Chives.
	Chervil.
	Jamaica pepper in fine powder, or two or three cloves.

The first column contains the articles of which the forcemeat may be made, without any striking flavor; and to those may be added some of the different ingredients of the second column, to vary the taste.

ADDITIONAL RECIPES.

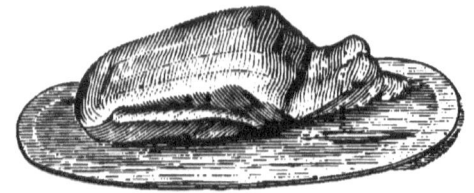

Goose.

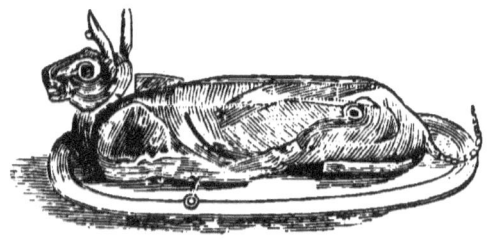

Hare.

A Roast Fowl.

Partridge.

Pigeon.

POULTRY AND GAME.

To Blanch.

Put the article to be blanched in cold water over the fire, and when it boils up, take it out and plunge it into cold water, and there let it remain until thoroughly cold. This gives plumpness and whiteness. Tongues, palates, etc., are said to be blanched when, after long boiling, the skin can be peeled off; and the latter will become thicker by being put into cold water as above.

To Braise.

Put the meat you would braise into a bright stew-pan, and cover it with thick slices of fat pork; then lay round it six or eight onions, a bunch of sweet herbs, some celery, and if to be brown, some thick slices of carrots, and trimmings, or fresh meat bones, if you have them, and a pint and a half of water, or the same quantity of stock. Over the meat lay a sheet of white paper. According to what the meat is, add seasoning. Cover the pan close, and set over a slow fire; it will require two or three hours. as its size and quality may direct. Then put the meat and gravy into a colander to drain, and keep it quite hot; skim the gravy carefully, and boil it as quick as you can till it thickens; then baste, and if that has been larded, put it into the oven for a few minutes. This is called glazing, and is much in use for made dishes. The glaze should be a clear yellow brown. A glass of sherry may be put to it before it is set to thicken over the fire. If properly braised and cooked slowly and thoroughly, tough meat will become tender and juicy, but if the cooking is hurried the dish will be spoiled.

To Glaze, Without Braising.

Fowls or meat may be dressed in any way chosen, without pork, and a gravy, boiled to a glaze, basted over, as above. Hams, tongues and stewed beef, to serve cold, are thus prepared.

To Force Fowls, Etc.,

Is to stuff any part with force-meat, and is usually put between the skin and the flesh.

To Lard Meat, Fowls, Sweet-breads, Etc.

Have ready larding pans of the right sizes, and, according to the article to be larded, cut slices of pork of the proper length, which put in a dish of broken ice to harden. Put a strip of the pork in a needle, with which pierce the skin and a very little of the meat, and draw underneath the skin. Lard in rows. For chicken, turkey, veal or beef, the strips should be about as large as a lead pencil, and about three or four inches long. For birds, sweet-breads and chops, they should be not much larger around than a match.

Dressing for Turkey or Chicken.

Grate stale white bread fine or use powdered crackers, and mix with it butter, pepper, salt, thyme, summer savory and sweet marjoram; wet with cold milk; add the beaten yolks of two eggs. If preferred, one dozen finely-chopped oysters may be added. Stuff the craw of the fowl, tie a string tightly around its neck to prevent the escape of the stuffing; then fill the body and sew it up with strong thread. The stitches should be cut and the neck untied before serving.

Dressing for Duck, Goose and Sucking Pig.

Follow closely the above directions, and substitute onions and sage for thyme and marjoram.

Boiled Turkey—No. 1.

Prepare your turkey as for roasting; put it in a cloth, and boil it slowly; if from eight to nine pounds, an hour and a half. Throw into the water a few cloves, a little black pepper, sweet marjoram and salt. It is to be served with oysters. Skim the turkey well while boiling, or it will not be white.

Boiled Turkey—No. 2.

If a boiled turkey is not well managed it will be quite tasteless. Choose a hen turkey. It must be well trussed and tied. Cut the legs at the first joint and draw them into the body. Fasten the small ends of the wings under the back, and tie them securely with strong twine. Sprinkle over plenty of salt and pepper and lemon-juice, and put it into boiling water. Boil it slowly two hours, or until quite tender. It is often served in a bed of rice with oysters; sometimes with caper-sauce, celery sauce and Hollandain sauce. Pour part of the sauce over the turkey. Reserve the giblets for giblet soup. It can be stuffed or not, the same as for roasting.

Baltimore Turkey.

Take out the breast bone and cut off the legs—not the thigh part—of a small, fat turkey. Clean it thoroughly and fill the inside with oysters; sew it up and lay in a floured cloth; place it in cold water, and boil one hour and a half, very slowly; take it out, lay on a dish, and draw out the thread with which the turkey was sewed. Make a jelly of calf's feet, without sugar, but flavored with lemon and wine; when cool, but not cold, pour over the turkey and set it aside to jelly. Serve with celery.

Deviled Turkey.

On the rump, gizzard and one leg put salt and cayenne pepper. Let them be broiled and brought to the table as hot as possible. Cut them in small pieces and pour over a ladle of mustard, a ladle of melted butter, a spoonful of soy, a spoonful of lemon-juice and some of the gravy out of the dish; mix quickly and serve.

To Boil Fowls.

Flour them and rub in salt, and put into boiling water. Simmer gently until tender. Choose those that are not black-legged for boiling. Serve with parsley and butter, oyster, lemon, liver or celery sauce. If for dinner, ham, tongue or bacon is usually served with them; as likewise greens or young cabbages.

To Stew a Fowl with Rice.

Stew the fowl very slowly in some clear mutton broth, well skimmed, and seasoned with onion, mace, pepper and salt. About half an hour before it is ready put in a quarter of a pint of rice, well washed and soaked. Simmer till tender; then strain it from the broth, and put the rice on a sieve before the fire. Keep the fowl hot and lay it in the middle of the dish, with the rice round it, without the broth. The broth will be very nice to eat as such; but the less liquor used in cooking the better. Gravy or parsley and butter for sauce.

Broiled Spring Chicken.

Pick and wash the fowl and split it down the back; crack the breast bone and flatten the chicken; make a small incision in each side and insert the legs; season with salt and pepper; lay it in a broiler and put it over bright coals; or put it in a pan and set it in front of the grate with a bright fire; broil a half or three-quarters of an hour, turning it frequently; when done, baste with butter and serve on buttered toast.

Chicken and Cream.

One pair of chickens; joint them; wash the pieces in cold water; dry them in a cloth; roll them or pat them in fine bread crumbs. Take a pint of cream or milk, chop a quantity of parsley very fine; add it to the cream, with a little salt and pepper. Fry the chicken in butter; when done, lay the pieces on a hot dish; then pour the prepared cream slowly into the frying-pan, stirring quickly; when all in, and well done, turn the cream over the chicken.

Baked Spring Chicken.

Cut them open at the back and spread them out in a baking pan; sprinkle on plenty of pepper, salt and a little flour. Baste them well with hot water, which should be in the bottom of the pan: also at different times with a little butter. When done, rub butter over them, as you would beefsteak, and set them in the oven for a moment before serving.

CHICKEN, A LA MODE.

Pick and draw a fine young chicken; wash and wipe dry and season with salt and pepper. Make a nice pastry and roll out an inch thick; wrap the chicken in it; tie in a cloth, and boil an hour or two, according to the tenderness of the fowl. Make a dressing of one tablespoonful of flour, one of butter, and sufficient boiling water to make a smooth paste. Place the chicken on a dish, and pour the dressing over it; garnish with parsley or celery leaves and a hard boiled egg cut in slices.

CHICKEN CROQUETTES.

One pound of finely-chopped cooked chicken; season with one-half teaspoonful of pepper, one-half tablespoonful of salt, one-half tablespoonful of butter, mix with this one egg and nearly half a pint of cream, a little lemon juice and one-half a teaspoonful of onion juice; have the board lightly sprinkled with fine cracker crumbs and roll the croquettes until they are shaped in the form of little cylinders; when they are so shaped, beat the eggs light and cover the croquettes with it; now have the board thickly covered with cracker crumbs and roll the egg-covered croquettes in these; fry in a croquette basket in boiling fat until a light brown. Instead of cream, chicken stock may be used. Veal, mutton, lamb and turkey croquettes may be thus prepared.

TO ROAST A FOWL OR CHICKEN.

Have a bright, clear and steady fire for roasting poultry; split it, put a pint of hot water in the dripping-pan, add to it a small tablespoonful of salt, and a small teaspoonful of pepper; baste frequently, and let it roast quickly, without scorching; when nearly done, put a piece of butter the size of a large egg to the water in the pan; when it melts, baste with it, dredge a little flour over, baste again, and let it finish; half an hour will roast a full-grown chicken. if the fire is right. When done, take it up, let the giblets (heart, liver and gizzard) boil tender, and chop them very fine, and put them in the gravy, add a tablespoonful of browned flour and a bit of butter; stir it over the fire for a few minutes, then serve in a gravy-tureen; or put the giblets in a pan and let them roast.

Roast Poultry.

When thoroughly picked and cleaned rub the inside of the fowl with salt; then make a dressing with bread or crackers; season to the taste with butter, pepper and salt, to which a little salt pork may be added, chopped fine, and wet up until quite moist with one egg and milk; fill the fowl with this dressing and sew up; tie down the legs and wings; place in a dripping-pan with a teacupful of salted water, having previously rubbed the outside of the fowl with salt and dredged it with flour; lumps of butter should be placed on the fowl and thin slices of salt pork tucked under the wings; bake from three to five hours in a moderate oven, basting often; when done, remove the fowl; thicken the gravy with brown flour and strain. Some prefer the giblets chopped fine and added to the gravy. Parsley or thyme may be used for garnishing roast meats.

Chicken Pot-pie.

Take a full-grown chicken or fowl; cut it as for stewing or pie; rinse it in cold water, and put it in a stew-pan with hot water to cover it; add half a pound of salt pork, cut in thin slices if liked, or a large teaspoonful of salt; let it boil gently for half an hour, unless it be a young chicken, when it need not be parboiled; take off the scum; make a pie or pot-pie crust; make it rather more than half an inch thick; line the sides only of a dinner-pot (if it extends too low down, it will burn); put the meat in the bottom; take a piece of butter the size of a large egg and cut it in small bits; put it over the meat; not half as much butter will be required if pork is used; dredge it white with flour; put in the water from the stew-pan, and, if it does not reach nearly to the top of the crust, add more hot water; lay skewers across the top; roll out the paste; reserve enough to cover the pie; cut the remainder in small squares, and drop them in the pie; then put on the top crust; cut a slit in the centre and cover the pot. Set it over a moderate fire, to boil gently for three-quarters of an hour; then take a fork and try the top-crust; if it is done, take the pie up. The side-crust should be four or five inches wider, and, if a large pie, reach nearly to the top of the pot, that there may be plenty of gravy.

Chicken Short Cakes.

Cut the chicken up, put it in a pan; and cover it over with water; let it stew as usual, and when done make a thickening of cream and flour, adding a piece of butter, and pepper and salt; have made and baked a pair of short-cakes, made as for pie-crust, but roll thin and cut in small squares. This is much better than chicken pie, and more simple to make. The crusts should be laid on a dish, and the chicken gravy put over it while both are hot.

Fricassee of Chickens.

Rather more than half boil in a small quantity of water; let cool, and then cut up and put to simmer in a little gravy made of the liquor in which they are boiled, and a bit of veal or mutton, onion, mace and lemon peel, some white pepper and a bunch of sweet herbs. When tender, keep hot while you thicken the sauce, as follows: Strain it off and put it into the sauce-pan with a little salt, nutmeg and a little flour and butter. Give it one boil, and when you are going to serve, beat up the yolk of an egg, add half a pint of cream, and stir over the fire, but do not boil. The gravy may be made of the necks, feet, small wing bones, gizzards and livers.

To Braise Chickens.

Bone and fill them with force-meat. Lay the bones and other poultry trimmings into a stew-pan; on them put the chickens; add a few onions, a bunch of herbs, three blades of mace, a pint of stock and a glass of sherry. Cover the chickens with slices of pork, and then white paper. Then cover the whole close, and put over a slow fire for two hours. Take up, strain and braise, and skim off the fat carefully. Set it on to boil very quick, to a glaze, and baste. Serve with a brown fricassee of mushrooms. Before glazing put the chickens into an oven a few minutes to give a good color.

To Roast Wild Fowls.

The flavor is best preserved without stuffing. Put pepper, salt and a piece of butter into each. Wild fowls require much less dressing than tame, and should be served in a fine color A rich brown gravy should be sent in the dish, and when the breast is cut into slices, before taking off the bone, a little lemon with pepper and salt added, is a great improvement to the flavor. To take off the fishy taste, which wild fowls usually have, put an onion, salt, and hot water in the dripping-pan, with this baste them for the first ten minutes; then take away the pan and baste constantly with butter.

WILD DUCKS, TEAL, WIDGEONS, DUN-BIRDS, ETC.,

Should be taken up with the gravy in. Baste them with butter, and sprinkle on a little salt before they are taken up; put a good gravy upon them, and serve with shallot sauce in a boat.

TO PULL CHICKENS.

Take off the skin, and pull the flesh off the bone of a cold fowl, in as large pieces as you can; dredge it with flour, and fry it a nice brown in good butter. Drain the butter from it, and then simmer the flesh in a good gravy, well-seasoned, and thickened with a little flour and butter. Add the juice of half a lemon.

BROILED QUAILS.

Clean, wash and split down the back. Lay in cold water half an hour. Wipe carefully, season with salt and pepper, and broil on a gridiron over a bright fire. When done, lay in a hot dish, butter on both sides well, and serve at once.

Pigeons, woodcock and small birds may be broiled in the same manner and are delicious and nourishing fare for invalids.

QUAIL PIE.

Clean, truss and stuff the birds. Loosen the joints with a penknife, but do not separate them. Parboil them for ten minutes. Line a deep dish with puff-paste, put in the bottom some shreds of salt pork; next, a layer of hard-boiled eggs, buttered and peppered; then the birds, sprinkled with pepper and minced parsley. Squeeze some lemon juice upon them, and lay upon the breasts pieces of butter rolled in flour. Cover with slices of egg, then with shreds of pork; pour in some of the gravy in which the quails were parboiled, and put on the upper crust, leaving a hole in the middle. Bake over an hour.

STEWED PIGEONS.

Clean the pigeons and cut them in quarters; put them with their giblets into a stew-pan, with a little water salted; season well with salpicant and butter; cover the pan closely, and stew until tender. Thicken the gravy with the yolk of an egg beaten with three tablespoonfuls of milk, and a little butter rolled in flour.

PIGEON PIE

May be made the same as quail pie, except that the pigeons are cut into four pieces each, and not stuffed. Parboil and lay in the dish in alternate layers with the pork and boiled eggs. Make the gravy richer than for quails.

ROAST PIGEONS

Should be stuffed with parsley, either cut or whole, and seasoned within; serve with parsley and butter. Peas or asparagus should be dressed to serve with them.

Pigeons left from dinner may be either stewed ten minutes in a good gravy with force-meat balls ready fried, or made into a pie. If the latter, let a beef-steak be stewed tender in a little water, and put both at the bottom of the dish, the pigeons next, and cover them with a piece of fat pork to keep them moist; season as usual, and add the yolks of eggs boiled hard. The crust in this case must be thin, that it may not require long baking.

BROILED PIGEONS.

After cleaning, split down the backs, pepper and salt them and broil very nicely; pour over them either stewed or pickled mushrooms in melted butter, and serve as hot as possible.

ROASTED DUCKS.

Stuff one with sage and onion, a dessert-spoonful of crumbs, a bit of butter, and pepper and salt; let the other be unseasoned. They should be well done and served with a rich gravy in the dish.

BOILED DUCKS.

Choose a fine, fat duck; salt it two days; then boil it slowly in a cloth. Serve it with onion sauce, but melt the butter with milk, instead of water.

ROAST SNIPE.

Clean and truss, but do not stuff. Lay in rows in the dripping-pan; sprinkle with salt, and baste well with butter, then with butter and water. When they begin to brown, cut as many slices of bread as there are birds. Toast quickly, butter, and lay in the dripping-pan, a bird upon each. When the birds are done, serve upon the toast, with the gravy poured over it. The toast should lie under them while cooking at least five minutes, during which time the birds should be basted with melted butter seasoned with pepper. The largest snipe will not require above twenty minutes to roast. Another way is to dip an oyster in melted butter, then in bread crumbs, seasoned with pepper and salt, and put in each bird before roasting. Small birds are very nice cooked in this way

GROUSE.

Roast them like fowls, with the head twisted under the wing. They must not be overdone. Serve with a rich gravy in a dish, and bread sauce. Garnish with parsley.

BAKED RABBIT.

Skin the rabbit and let it be extremely well washed; then soak it an hour or two in water, and, if old, lard it, which will make it tender. Give it a large, relishing stuffing and then sew it up. Baste it well with milk till half done, and afterwards with butter. If the blood has settled in the neck, soak the part in warm water and prick the skin here and there with a knife, which will remove it. Serve with a rich gravy, melted butter and currant jelly sauce. For the stuffing use the liver, an anchovy, some fat pork, a little suet, herbs, pepper, salt, nutmeg, a small onion, crumbs of bread or cracker dust, and an egg to bind it all. The ears must be nicely cleaned and singed and made crisp. They are a dainty.

FRICASSEED RABBIT.

After skinning and cleaning, cut up the rabbit, and season it with pepper, salt, allspice, mace and a little nutmeg; put it into a jar with an onion, a clove or two, a bunch of sweet herbs, a piece of coarse beef and the carcass bones over all. Put the jar into a saucepan of water up to the neck, but no higher; tie it down. Keep the water boiling five hours. When it is to be served, boil the gravy up with a piece of butter and flour, and if the meat gets cold, warm it in this, but not to a boil. Force-meat balls may be served, if desired, but are not necessary.

To Pot Rabbits.

Cut up two or three young, but full-grown rabbits; take the leg-bones off at the thigh, and pack them as closely as possible in a small pan, after seasoning them with mace, cayenne pepper, salt and allspice. Make the top as smooth as you can. Keep out the heads and the carcasses, but take off the meat about the neck. Use a good supply of butter, and bake the whole gently. Keep it two days in the pan; then put it into small pots, adding butter. The livers should also be added.

ADDITIONAL RECIPES.

Sauces and Dressings for Meats and Fish.

Gravies.

Gravy may be made quite as good of the skirts of beef and the kidneys as of any other part of the meat. Ox kidney or milt makes a good gravy, which should be finely cut and prepared as other meat gravies. Shank bones of mutton add greatly to the richness of the gravy, but must be first soaked well and scoured clean. Tarragon gives the flavor of French cookery, and in high gravies is a great improvement; but it should be added only a short time before serving.

To Dress Gravy that will Keep a Week.

Cut lean beef thin, put it into a frying-pan without any butter, and set it on the fire covered, but take care it does not burn; let it stay till all the gravy that comes out of the meat is dried up into it again; put as much water as will cover the meat, and let that stew away. Then put to the meat a small quantity of water, herbs, onions, spice, and a bit of lean ham; simmer till it is rich, and keep it in a cool place. Do not take off the fat till it is to be used.

Clear Gravy.

Slice beef thin; broil a part of it over a very clear, quick fire, just enough to give color to the gravy, but not to dress it; put that and the raw into a stew-pan, with two onions, a clove or two, whole black peppers, berries of allspice and a bunch of sweet herbs; cover it with hot water, give it one boil, and skim it well two or three times; then cover it and simmer till quite strong.

DRAWN BUTTER SAUCE.

Take six tablespoonfuls of butter, half a teaspoonful of salt, two teaspoonfuls of flour or fine bread crumbs worked into the butter, and one teacupful of hot water; heat very hot, but do not let it boil. Two hard boiled and chopped eggs improve it much. For fish, add a tablespoonful of vinegar and chopped capers or green nasturtium seeds.

WORCESTERSHIRE SAUCE.

Ten peppers, one large onion, twenty-four ripe tomatoes, two tablespoonfuls salt, one teaspoonful each of allspice, nutmeg, ginger and cloves, one quart vinegar; chop peppers, onions and tomatoes fine, and let all simmer two hours.

ANCHOVY SAUCE—No. 1.

To half a pint of drawn butter add three tablespoonfuls of essence of anchovy, a teaspoonful of lemon extract; salt and pepper; boil up at once, and serve with baked or boiled fish.

ANCHOVY SAUCE—No. 2.

Soak some anchovies in a basin of cold water for two or three hours; then put them in a stew-pan with cold water, and set them on coals to simmer until the anchovies are dissolved; then strain the water, add to it a wineglass of red wine and half a pint of melted butter; let it simmer for quarter of an hour; then serve with boiled fish or meat.

Shallot Sauce.

Take half a pint of water in which meat has been boiled, add a wineglass of vinegar and two or three shallots, cut fine, and half a teaspoonful of salt; put these into a saucepan over the fire; work a teaspoonful of flour into a piece of butter the size of an egg, and stir them into the hot water, and let them simmer for fifteen minutes. Serve with boiled meat.

Chutney Sauce.

Four dozen large ripe tomatoes, six green peppers, eight onions, four tablespoonfuls each of sugar, salt and mustard, three tablespoonfuls each of cloves and black pepper, one quart vinegar; chop the onions and peppers and cut the tomatoes; then boil all together for two hours; strain through a sieve. Add, lastly, just before bottling, one bottle of Worcestershire sauce.

Celery Sauce.

Make a drawn butter of the broth from the meat of fowls, and season with celery salt. Serve with boiled meats or fowls.

Onion Sauce.

Peel six or seven good-sized onions and boil tender; drain and chop fine; heat one pint of milk in a saucepan, and add one tablespoonful of flour and two of butter; stir in the onions and season with salt and pepper; boil a few minutes and serve with roast pork.

An Excellent Currie Powder.

Reduce to the finest powder six ounces and a half of coriander seeds, one ounce and a half of cumin seeds, a quarter of an ounce of cardamom seeds, three ounces of turmeric, and half an ounce of ginger, after being cleared of the outsides. Put each before the fire to dry; then mix thoroughly. When quite cold, put together twenty drops of oil of cinnamon, ten drops of oil of cloves, and ten drops of oil of nutmeg; and, mixing them well, rub by degrees the whole of the powder in a mortar. Keep it in tightly corked bottles, each containing enough for twice using.

LOBSTER SAUCE.

Pound the spawn and two anchovies; pour on them two spoonfuls of gravy; strain all into some melted butter; then put in the meat of the lobster; give it all one boil, and add a squeeze of lemon.

A VERY GOOD SAUCE FOR BOILED CHICKENS.

Take the heads and necks, with a small bit of the scrag of veal or mutton; put them into a saucepan with two blades of mace, a few white peppercorns, an anchovy, a head of celery sliced, a bunch of sweet herbs and a small piece of lemon peel. Boil these in a quart of water to half a pint. Strain, and thicken it with a quarter of a pound of butter and some flour; boil it five minutes; and then put in two teaspoonfuls of mushrooms; having beaten up the yolks of two eggs with a teacup of cream, put it into your sauce and keep shaking it one way over the fire till it is near boiling; then put it into a sauce-tureen.

BREAD SAUCE FOR FOWL OR FISH.

Boil a large onion, cut into quarters, with some black peppers and milk, till the onion is quite soft; pour the milk, strained, on grated white stale bread, and cover it. In an hour put it into a saucepan with a piece of butter mixed with a little flour; boil the whole up together and serve.

Caper-sauce for Mutton.

Work two tablespoonfuls of flour into a piece of butter the size of an egg; into this stir one pint of boiling milk; add your capers, cut once in two; let it boil up and then serve in a tureen.

Mint Sauce for Lamb.

Take fresh mint, wash and chop very fine, and put into your gravy boat; over this pour good cider vinegar, and sweeten to taste with white sugar.

Tomato Sauce.

Gather your tomatoes when fully ripe, and, after washing them, mash them in some suitable vessel; then place them in a kettle over a moderate fire, and when just warmed through, press a colander down upon them; then dip from the colander all the watery juice possible. After boiling a short time, strain the mass through a wire sieve just fine enough to retain the rind of the fruit; then return it to the kettle, and boil it down to the desired consistency (some prefer it thin, as it retains more of the flavor), taking care that it does not become scorched in the process. Heat the bottles you intend to use, in a steamer, to boiling heat, and while they retain this heat fill them with sauce in a boiling state; then cork them immediately with good corks, and place them where they will cool slowly. Tomatoes thus prepared will keep good, and retain all their original freshness and flavor throughout the entire season.

Horseradish Sauce.

Two tablespoonfuls of mustard, the same of vinegar, three tablespoonfuls of cream or milk, and one of pounded white sugar, well beaten up together with a small quantity of grated horseradish. This is, of course, to be served cold.

Oyster Sauce for Turkeys, Etc.

Strain fifty oysters; put the juice into a saucepan and add one pint of new milk; let it simmer, and skim off any froth which may arise; then rub a large spoonful of flour and two of butter together; stir this into the liquor; add a little salt and pepper. Let it simmer five minutes, but do not add your oysters till just as they are to be sent to the table, as, if they are cooked too much, they are hard.

Oyster Sauce.

Save the liquor in opening the oysters, and boil it with the beards, a bit of mace and lemon peel. In the meantime throw the oysters into cold water, and drain it off. Strain the liquor, and put it into a saucepan with them, and as much butter, mixed with a little milk, as will make sauce enough; but first rub a little flour with it. Set them over the fire and stir constantly, and when the butter has boiled once or twice, take them off, and keep the saucepan near the fire, but not on it; for if done too much the oysters will be hard. Add a little lemon juice and serve.

Trout in White Sauce.

Boil the fish gently in as much water and light white wine, in equal quantities, as will only cover them; keep them hot, when done, while you boil the liquor with a bit of butter and a little flour. Meantime have ready beaten two eggs, with a spoonful of cold water, and pour them and the sauce to and fro at a little distance above the stove, till they are of due thickness; serve the fish in it, adding a little salt.

Trout in Green Sauce.

Chop quite fine half an anchovy, a tablespoonful of capers, one each of chives and parsley, previously minced, a good lump of butter and a dessert-spoonful of flour. When the trout is ready, keep it hot while this mixture is boiled with the liquor, in which serve it.

Mushroom Sauce for Fowls or Rabbits.

Wash and pick a pint of young mushrooms and rub them with salt to take off the tender skin. Put them in a saucepan with a little sauce, some nutmeg, a blade of mace, a pint of cream, and a good piece of butter rubbed in flour. Boil them up, and stir them till done; then pour it around the chickens, etc.; garnish with lemon. If you cannot get fresh mushrooms, use white pickled ones, with a mushroom powder without cream.

Giblet Gravy.

Take the livers, gizzards and hearts from fowls; boil very tender and chop fine; make a nice thin, drawn butter sauce of the water in which they were boiled and stir in; season with pepper and salt.

Lemon White Sauce for Boiled Fowls.

Put the peel of a small lemon, cut very thin, into a pint of sweet, rich cream, with a sprig of lemon thyme and ten white peppercorns. Simmer gently till it tastes well of the lemon and strain it; thicken it with a quarter of a pound of butter, and a dessert-spoonful of flour rubbed in it. Boil it up; then pour the juice of the strained lemon into it, stirring it well.

Sauce for Wild Fowls.

Simmer a teacupful of port wine, the same quantity of good meat gravy, a little shallot, a little pepper, salt, a grate of nutmeg, and a bit of mace, for ten minutes; put in a bit of butter and flour, give it all one boil, and pour it through the birds. In general, they are not stuffed, but may be done so if liked.

Another for the Same, or for Ducks.

Serve a rich gravy in the dish; cut the breast into slices, but do not take them off; cut a lemon, and put pepper and salt on it; then squeeze it on the breast, and pour a spoonful of gravy over it before you serve.

Veal Gravy.

When all the meat has been taken from a knuckle of veal, divide the bones, and lay them, and a pound of the scrag of a neck, in a stew-pot; and, if you like it, an ounce of lean bacon, a bunch of parsley, a little thyme, a bit of lemon peel and a dessert-spoonful of pepper; add as much water as will cover them. Boil and skim it nicely; cover the pot down close, and let it simmer as slowly as possible three hours. Strain off, and let it stand till cold; then skim it, and take the jelly from the sediment.

Cullis, or Brown Gravy.

Lay over the bottom of a stew-pan as much lean veal as will cover it an inch thick; then cover the veal with thin slices of undressed gammon, two or three onions, two or three bay-leaves, some sweet herbs, two blades of mace and three cloves. Cover the stew-pan, and set it over a slow fire; but when the juices come out let the fire be a little quicker. When the meat is of a fine brown, fill the pan with good beef broth, boil and skim it, then simmer an hour; add a little water, mixed with as much flour as will make it properly thick; boil it half an hour, and strain it. This will keep a week.

Bechamel, or White Gravy.

Cut lean veal into small slices, and the same quantity of lean bacon or ham; put them into a stew-pan with a good piece of butter, an onion, a blade of mace, a few mushroom-buttons, a bit of thyme and a bay-leaf; fry the whole over a very slow fire, but not to brown it; thicken it with flour. Add an equal quantity of good veal or mutton broth, and cream. Let it boil gently one hour, stirring it all the time; strain it through a soup-strainer.

Apple Sauce for Pork.

Take sour apples, pare, core and quarter; put them in an earthen dish with just enough water to make a steam; when done mash through a colander; add a little butter; it should be as firm as potatoes; serve on the plate like potatoes.

A Cheap and Good Gravy.

Fry three onions in butter a nice brown; toast a large slice of bread till quite hard, and very brown, but not burnt. Set these, and any bit of meat, or bone of a leg of mutton, etc., and some herbs, on the fire, with water in proportion, and stew till the gravy is thick and rich; add salt and pepper; strain off, and keep cool.

Mayonnaise Dressing.

Put the uncooked yolk of an egg on a cold platter; beat well with a silver fork; add a small salt-spoonful of mustard powder, and two salt-spoonfuls of salt; work them well a minute before adding the oil; then mix in a little good oil, which must be poured in very slowly—a few drops at a time; alternate occasionally with a few drops of vinegar.

SAUCES AND DRESSINGS.

Dressing for Sandwiches.

One-half pound of nice butter, two tablespoonfuls of mixed mustard, three tablespoonfuls of salad oil, a little red or white pepper, a little salt, yolk of an egg; rub the butter to a cream, add the other ingredients and mix thoroughly; set away to cool; spread the bread with this mixture and put in the ham, chopped fine.

Curry Balls.

Take some bread crumbs, hard-boiled eggs (grated), butter and curry powder; pound the whole in a mortar, and moisten with the yolk of an egg, well beaten. Make into balls, and add them to stewed chicken or rabbit about five minutes before serving.

Vinaigrette, for Cold Fowl or Meat.

Chop mint, parsley, and shallot, mix with salt, oil and vinegar. Serve in a boat.

Benton Sauce, for Hot or Cold Roast Beef.

Grate, or scrape very fine, some horseradish, a little made mustard, some pounded white sugar, and four large spoonfuls of vinegar. Serve in a saucer.

SALADS.

CHICKEN SALAD—No. 1.

Boil a young, tender chicken, and when cold separate the meat from the bones; cut it into little square blocks or dice; do not mince it. Cut white tender stalks of celery into about three-quarter inch lengths, saving the outside green stalks for soup; mix the chicken and celery together, and then stir well into them a mixture in the proportion of three tablespoonfuls of vinegar to one tablespoonful of oil, with pepper, salt, and a little mustard to taste. Put this aside for an hour or two, or until just before serving; this is called marinating the chicken; it will absorb the vinegar. When about to serve, mix the celery and chicken with a Mayonnaise sauce, leaving a portion of the sauce to mask the top. Reserve several fresh ends or leaves of celery with which to garnish the dish. Stick a little boquet of these tops in the centre of the salad, then a row around it. From the centre to each of the four sides sprinkle rows of capers. Sometimes slices or little cut diamonds of hard-boiled eggs are used for garnishing. Chicken salad is often made with lettuce instead of celery. Marinate the chicken alone; add it to the small tender leaves (uncut) of the lettuce the last moment before serving; then pour Mayonnaise dressing over the top. Garnish with little centre heads of lettuce, capers, cold chopped red-beets, if you choose, or sliced hard-boiled eggs. Sometimes little strips of anchovy are added for a garnish. When on the table it should all be mixed together. Many may profit by this recipe for chicken salad; for it is astonishing how few understand making so common a dish. It is generally minced and mixed with hard-boiled eggs for a dressing.

Chicken Salad—No. 2.

To the whole of a boiled chicken add half its weight in finely-chopped celery, two hard-boiled eggs, one raw egg, three tablespoonfuls salt, pepper and made mustard, three teaspoonfuls salad oil, two teaspoonfuls of white sugar, and twelve teaspoonfuls of vinegar. Pour on the vinegar when ready to serve.

Cabbage and Celery Salad.

One-quarter head of cabbage, two bunches celery; chop very fine; add pepper and salt to one-half cup vinegar, two teaspoonfuls sugar, one teaspoonful cream, one teaspoonful mustard, one tablespoonful butter. Heat the dressing and mix with cabbage and celery; into this chop two hard-boiled eggs.

Cabbage Salad—No. 1.

Take one teacupful of sour cream that has no bitter taste, and beat into it two raw eggs; half a teaspoonful of raw mustard, rubbed smooth in cold vinegar; two-thirds of a teaspoonful of salt and a dash of pepper; put upon the stove or range and let it boil up, stirring it as soon as it begins to boil, to prevent the eggs from curdling; when thick as custard, take from the fire; add half a teacupful of strong vinegar, with a teaspoonful of mustard into it, let it cool, turn it over a dish of finely-chopped raw cabbage, and see if you have not a dainty dish to go with the Sunday's dinner of cold meat.

CABBAGE SALAD—NO. 2.

One cup vinegar, one teaspoonful white mustard seed, one tablespoonful butter, one beaten egg; shred the cabbage into slender strips, season with salt, pepper and the mustard seed. Heat the vinegar hot; add the butter and beaten egg and pour over the cabbage.

CREAM CABBAGE.

Cup milk, butter size walnut; one egg, three tablespoonfuls vinegar, teaspoonful dry mustard; pepper and salt to taste; chop raw cabbage fine; cook sauce (except vinegar, have that cold) and pour over cabbage.

DRESSING FOR CABBAGE.

Beat one egg and a small piece of butter; stir in vinegar; boil until it thickens; pour over the chopped cabbage; salt and pepper.

COLD SLAW.

Fill a dish with cabbage cut up fine; make a dressing of the yolks of four hard-boiled eggs, two tablespoonfuls of mixed mustard, one tablespoonful of sugar, and one teaspoonful of salt, and a little pepper, one-fourth of a pound of butter, one teacupful of cream; mix these ingredients thoroughly and boil a few minutes, having previously added half a teacupful of vinegar; after boiling pour over the cabbage while hot.

POTATO SALAD.

Boil four potatoes, let them get cold, peel and slice. Put a layer of sliced potatoes on a platter, add a small onion cut fine and a very little chopped celery, also a few capers. Cover with Mayonnaise dressing.

Lobster Salad—No. 1.

Four pounds chopped lobster, one-half bunch chopped celery; prepare a sauce of one cup vinegar, one teaspoonful mustard, one-half teaspoonful pepper, one-half teaspoonful salt, three tablespoonfuls melted butter. Pour this over the lobster and celery.

Lobster Salad—No. 2.

Make a salad and put some of the red part of the lobster to it. This forms a pretty contrast to the white and green of the vegetables. Do not use much oil, as shell fish absorbs the sharpness of vinegar. Serve in a dish, not a bowl.

Where salads are constantly used, if the ingredients are kept ready, much time and trouble will be saved.

The following proportions make a most excellent salad:

Four mustard-ladles of mustard.
Four salt-ladles of salt.
Three dessert-spoonfuls of essence of anchovies.
Four dessert-spoonfuls of the best mushroom catsup.
Three dessert-spoonfuls of the best sweet oil.
Twelve dessert-spoonfuls of vinegar.
The yolks of three eggs boiled hard.

When the salad vegetables are cleaned and put into a dish, pour over them a sufficient quantity of the above, and stir it well.

Ham Salad.

Line your dish thickly with lettuce-leaves, and fill centre with cold boiled ham, chopped. Add an equal quantity of finely-chopped celery, if that be preferred or more convenient than lettuce. This should be dressed with the following sauce: On one teaspoonful of mustard drop the yolk of one egg, adding one-fourth of a spoonful of salt; mix and beat very thoroughly, adding gradually a generous tablespoonful of fine olive oil or melted butter; keep up a vigorous beating, and pour in, a little at a time, a tablespoonful of vinegar. This sauce should be used at once and its success depends entirely upon its being thoroughly beaten. The salad may also be dressed with cucumber and beet pickles sliced fine with olives.

Beef Salad.

One cup beef, chopped fine, three hard-boiled eggs, chopped fine, one dessert-spoonful of mustard, teaspoonful oil, a little salt, red and black pepper and enough vinegar to make it pack nicely. Set in a cold place till ready to use, then turn into another dish.

French Salad.

Chop small three anchovies, a shallot, and some parsley; put them into a bowl with two tablespoonfuls of vinegar, one of oil, a little mustard and salt. When well mixed, add by degrees some cold roast or boiled meat in very thin slices; put in a few at a time, not exceeding two or three inches long. Shake them in the seasoning, and then add more; then cover the bowl close, and let the salad be prepared three hours before it is to be eaten. Garnish with parsley, and a few slices of the fat.

Tomato and Onion Salad.

Take a tomato, not over-ripe, and cut into slices as you would a cucumber; take a small onion and cut it up as fine as you can; sprinkle it over the tomato slices, add salt, pepper and vinegar at discretion, and you will have a salad which, as a relish, puts the cucumber to shame.

WATERCRESS SALAD.

Watercresses, as a salad, are best served simply with a sauce of lemon juice and olive oil poured over them in a salad bowl; but, if preferred, may be served with the addition of a little grated horseradish, sliced leeks and sliced hard-boiled eggs.

OYSTER SALAD.

Put one quart of oysters, in their own liquor, over the fire until they ruffle. Two teaspoonfuls dry mustard, one-half teaspoonful salt, one-quarter teaspoonful red pepper, one teaspoonful flour, one egg (the whites and yolks beaten separately). Take as much oil as you like and beat with the yolks, adding the oil little by little. Add the dry seasoning, then one gill vinegar. Put this in a skillet over the fire until it is a little thickened; whip the whites thoroughly and stir in; cut up the same bulk of celery and the oysters and pour into a dish; then pour over the dressing. When you cut your oysters up let them drain in a colander. Do not use the liquor of the oysters.

ADDITIONAL RECIPES.

EGGS.

To Boil Eggs.

Wash the shells clean in cold water before boiling; have a stew-pan of boiling water, into which put the eggs; keep it boiling—four minutes for very soft, five that the yolk only may be soft, six minutes will boil the yolk hard for eating. Eight minutes are required to boil eggs for salad or garnish. When done, take them from the boiling water into a basin of cold water, which will prevent the yolk turning dark or black.

Boiled eggs will become harder from the heat of the shell, if they lie a few minutes before breaking, if they are not to be served immediately, take them up a minute sooner than otherwise, and put them into a dish with a cover; in this way they will keep hot for ten or fifteen minutes, and become but little harder. If the water is kept fast boiling after the eggs are in, one minute less will do them than if otherwise.

A more delicate way of eggs in the shells is this: Have a stew-pan of pure water, boiling hot; put the eggs in, cover the stew-pan without putting it over the fire; five minutes will do them for those who like soft eggs, and a minute or two longer for those who like them harder. The whites of eggs boiled in this way is more like poached eggs, less firm than in the other manner.

The most healthful and delicate way of cooking eggs is to poach them thus: Have a clean stew-pan with boiling hot water, add to it a little salt; break the eggs, one at a time, into a cup, and from it slip them into boiling water; when the white is set and firm, which will be after about five minutes, take each up with a skimmer, and lay them into a dish over a pot of boiling water; cover the dish, when all are done, put a bit of butter, and, if liked, sprinkle pepper over them, and serve. In this way they may be kept hot and soft for a long time, so that you may do any number of them.

After boiling eggs as directed for garnishing, when they are quite cold, take off the shell, and cut them lengthwise in two; then cut each half in two or three pieces. This looks well over spinach or lettuce or boiled fish; or cut them in slices across; or the white may be cut in long strips, and the yolk in slices or quarters.

Poached Eggs.

Carefully break fresh eggs into a shallow pan of boiling water, have ready slices of buttered toast, and when the white part has set round the yolk, take them up in a skimmer and lay each one upon a slice of bread. They are seasoned at table.

Scrambled or Stirred Eggs.

Break eight or more eggs into a basin, add to them a tablespoonful of sweet butter cut into bits, and a teaspoonful of salt; make a little bit of butter hot in a frying-pan, pour in the eggs, and let them cook. Stir them with a silver spoon until they are just set without becoming hard or brown; serve with or without toast.

Rolled Eggs

Take one dozen eggs, one tablespoonful flour dissolved in a little milk; add one cup milk, a little salt; have heaping tablespoonful butter in pan, put in oven and brown. When brown take from oven and roll; serve hot, cut in slices.

Stuffed Eggs.

Cut hard-boiled eggs in halves; remove the yolks, chop and mix with them cold chicken or veal, and a little chopped onions, parsley, and a few soaked bread crumbs; season and add the uncooked yolk of an egg and fill in the cavity even; put the two halves together, roll in the beaten egg and bread crumbs, put in a wire egg basket and dip in boiling lard until slightly brown; serve with celery.

Pickled Eggs.

Boil them twenty minutes and place them into cold water to make the shells cool off easily; boil some beets very soft, peel and mash fine, and put them, with salt, pepper, cloves and nutmeg, into vinegar enough to cover the eggs. Put the eggs into a jar and pour the mixture over them.

Eggs and Sausages.

Boil four sausages for five minutes; when half cold cut them in half lengthwise, put a little butter or fat in frying-pan, and put the sausages in and fry gently; break four eggs into pan, cook gently, and serve. Raw sausages will do as well, only keep them whole, and cook slowly.

Egg Sauce.

Take a quarter of a pound of butter and braid it well into three even spoonfuls of flour; then turn on a scant pint of boiling water, chop well three boiled eggs, and stir in the butter as it goes to the table.

EGG DUMPLINGS.

Make a batter of a pint of milk, two well-beaten eggs, a teaspoonful of salt, and flour enough to make the batter as thick as for pound cake. Have a clean saucepan of hot water; let the water first boil and then drop in the batter by the teaspoonful; four or five minutes will boil sufficiently; take them out with skimmer, place on a dish and put a bit of butter and pepper over them, and serve with boiled or cold meats.

OMELET—No. 1.

Four eggs, one cup of milk, one tablespoonful of flour, a little salt. Bake or fry.

OMELET—No. 2.

Four eggs well beaten, as much milk as there is egg, and half tablespoonful flour to each egg; a little salt and pepper; fry as you do any omelet.

OMELET—No. 3.

Take as many eggs as required, and add three teaspoonfuls of milk and a pinch of salt to each egg. Beat lightly for three or four minutes. Melt a teaspoonful of butter in a hot pan and pour on the eggs. They will at once begin to bubble and rise up, and must be kept from sticking to the bottom of the pan with a knife. Cook two or three minutes. If desired beat finely-chopped ham or parsley with the eggs before cooking.

PUFF OMELET.

Beat up the yolks of six eggs. Mix with a small teacupful of milk and a little salt. Beat together a tablespoonful each of butter and flour till smooth. Add the mixture to the eggs and beat all well together. Pour into hot, buttered pan, and when it begins to thicken add the whites of the eggs well beaten. Sprinkle a very little salt on the top, and when stiff remove carefully to the dish.

Omelet au Naturel.

Break eight or ten eggs into a basin; add a small teaspoonful of salt and a little pepper, with a tablespoonful of cold water; beat the whole well with a spoon or whisk. In the meantime put some fresh sweet butter into an omelet-pan, and when it is nearly hot put in an omelet; whilst it is frying with a skimmer-spoon raise the edges from the pan, that it may be properly done. When the eggs are set, and one side is a fine brown, double it half over, and serve hot. These omelets should be put quite thin in the pan; the butter required for each will be about the size of a small egg.

French Omelet.

Break eight eggs into a basin, season with a small teaspoonful of salt and a little pepper, and, if liked, mace or nutmeg; add two tablespoonfuls of milk or cream, two ounces of butter broken in bits, and a little parsley cut small, if liked, also a finely-chopped shallot or white onion well washed. Beat these ingredients well together with a spoon; put an ounce of butter in a frying-pan; let it become boiling hot, and pour the omelet in about half an inch thick; as it is cooking, continue to stir it with a spoon, drawing it from the sides to the centre, that it may be evenly done; shake the pan now and then to free the omelet from it; let it fry gently; when it is a fine clear brown, turn it into a dish, and serve.

Ham Omelet.

Put a proper quantity of chopped ham into the frying-pan, pouring over it enough of eggs (which have previously been well beaten with a small cup of milk) to make a generous omelet; stir thoroughly, and, as soon as the egg stiffens, dish, and send smoking hot to the table.

Smoked Beef with Eggs.

Cut some smoked beef in thin shavings or chips, put them into a frying-pan, and nearly fill it with hot water; set it on the fire, and let it boil up once, then pour it off; add to the beef a good bit of lard, twice the size of an egg, for half a pound of the beef, shake a little pepper over, and let it fry for a few minutes over a quick fire; then break two or three or more eggs into it, stir them together until the eggs are done, then turn it on to a dish. Or, after frying the beef with a little wheat-flour dredged over, fry eggs, and serve with it the same as ham.

Eggs, a la Mode.

Remove the skin from a dozen tomatoes, medium size, cut them up in a saucepan, add a little butter, pepper and salt; when sufficiently boiled, beat up five or six eggs, and just before you serve turn them into the saucepan, with the tomato, and stir one way for two minutes, allowing them time to be well done.

To Keep Eggs.

To four quarts air-slacked lime, put two tablespoonfuls cream tartar, two of salt, and four quarts cold water. Put fresh eggs into a stone jar, and pour this mixture over them. This will keep nine dozen, and if fresh when laid down, they will keep many months. If the water settles away, so as to leave the upper layer uncovered, add more water. Cover close, and keep in a cool place.

ADDITIONAL RECIPES.

RARE-BITS, CHEESE CAKES, ETC.

Welsh Rare-bit—No. 1.

Cut or grate some good cheese, put a bit of butter and some made mustard to it; put it in a frying-pan over the fire, and stir it smooth; a little milk may be added to it; when it is hot and a smooth paste, spread it on slices of nicely-toasted bread, and serve hot.

Welsh Rare-bit—No. 2.

Cut your cheese into small bits, if soft, but if hard grate it; have ready a spirit-lamp and a deep, block-tin dish; put in the cheese, with a lump of butter, and set it over the lamp. Have ready the yolk of an egg, whipped with a half glass of Madeira and as much ale or beer; stir your cheese, when melted, till it is thoroughly mixed with the butter; then add gradually the egg and wine; keep stirring till it forms a smooth mass; season with cayenne or grated nutmeg. To be eaten with a thin, hot toast.

Roasted Cheese.

Grate three ounces of dry cheese, and mix it with the yolks of two eggs; put four ounces of grated bread, and three of butter; beat the whole together in a mortar with a dessert-spoonful of made mustard, a little salt, and some pepper; toast some slices of bread, cut off the outside crust, cut it in shapes, and spread the paste thick upon them, and put them in a Dutch oven; let them become hot and slightly browned; serve hot as possible.

VEAL CHEESE.

Take equal quantities of boiled veal and boiled tongue, sliced; pound each separately in a mortar, adding butter as you do so. Mix in a stone jar, press hard and pour on melted butter. Keep it covered in a dry place. To be eaten at tea in slices.

LEMON CHEESE CAKES.

Take two ounces of butter, two eggs, three tablespoonfuls of moist sugar, the grated rinds and juice of two lemons, and two stale biscuits (or hard crackers of any kind), also finely grated. Mix all together and then simmer over the fire for a few minutes in a saucepan. Have ready some patty-pans, lined with puff-paste. Put a very small quantity of the mixture into each, and bake for fifteen or twenty minutes in rather a quick oven. This quantity will make about one dozen and a half of cheese cakes.

CHEESE CAKES.

One-fourth pound butter, one pound sugar, six eggs, juice and rind of two lemons; simmer together and bake in pans. Serve as pastry.

VEGETABLES.

TO BOIL VEGETABLES.

Vegetables should be carefully examined for insects and thoroughly washed in cold water. Be sure the water boils when you put the vegetables over, but do not over-boil, as by so doing much of the flavor and crispness is lost. The younger the vegetable, the more quickly it is cooked.

BOILING POTATOES.

Not one housekeeper out of ten knows how to boil potatoes properly. The information contained in the following will be found invaluable: Wash clean the potatoes, and leave the skin on; boil the water and throw them in. As soon as boiled soft enough for a fork to be easily thrust through them, dash some cold water into the pot, let the potatoes remain two minutes, and then pour off the water. This done, half remove the pot-lid, and let the potatoes remain over a slow fire till the steam is evaporated; then peel, and set them on the table in an open dish. Potatoes of a good kind, thus cooked, will always be sweet, dry, and mealy. A covered dish is bad for potatoes, as it keeps the steam in, and makes them soft and watery.

Fancy Baked Potatoes.

Select large potatoes and of even size; bake and when done, cut a piece from an end and remove the inside, rub it through a fine sieve or mash thoroughly; put on the fire with half an ounce of butter and one ounce of grated cheese for every four potatoes; add boiling milk, pepper and salt, as for mashed potatoes; fill the potato shells and put them in a hot oven, and brown.

Fried Potatoes.

Cut a quart of cold boiled potatoes into cubes, prepare three tablespoonfuls chopped onion and one of chopped parsley. Fry the onions till done in three tablespoonfuls of butter, then add the potatoes, season with salt and pepper. Stir gently with a fork so as not to break them. When heated through, add the parsley and cook two minutes longer. Serve on a hot dish.

Stewed Potatoes.

Pare the potatoes and cut in slices; put them in hot water and rinse them; then put in saucepan with enough boiling water for gravy. When nearly done, season with pepper, salt and butter. Thicken with flour batter. Let it boil up two or three times before sending to the table.

Hashed Potatoes.

Peel and chop some cold boiled potatoes, put them into a stew-pan with a very little milk or water to moisten them, put to them a small bit of butter, and pepper and salt to taste; cover the stew-pan close, and set it over a gentle fire for fifteen or twenty minutes; stir them once or twice while cooking; serve hot for breakfast.

Mashed Potatoes.

Boil and peel the potatoes and break them into paste; then to two pounds add a quarter of a pint of milk, a little salt and two ounces of butter; stir all well over the fire. Either serve them in this manner or place them on a dish in a form and brown the top.

Broiled Potatoes.

Cut whole boiled Irish or sweet potatoes lengthwise into slices a quarter of an inch thick, and lay upon a gridiron over a hot fire; brown on both sides, sprinkle with pepper and salt and lay a bit of butter on each.

Saratoga Potatoes.

Slice potatoes as thin as possible, let them lie in the coldest water an hour or two, then dry with a cloth; have a good deal of lard boiling hot, drop in a few slices at a time, and as soon as they are browned, take out with a skimmer; when put in the dish for the table, sprinkle salt over them.

Lyonnaise Potatoes—No. 1.

Twelve potatoes parboiled, and when cold, sliced or cut into dice; one onion, chopped; butter or dripping for frying; chopped parsley, pepper and salt. Heat the butter in a frying-pan; put in the onion; fry one minute; then the potatoes, stir briskly and fry slowly five minutes; there should be butter enough to keep them from sticking to the bottom of the pan; and they should not brown; add the seasoning just before you take them up; drain perfectly dry by shaking them to and fro in a heated colander; serve in a hot dish.

Lyonnaise Potatoes—No. 2.

One pint of cold boiled potatoes cut into small pieces; season with salt and pepper, one spoonful of butter, one slice of onion cut very fine, one teaspoonful chopped parsley; add parsley to potatoes, fry onion brown in butter, then add potatoes and fry; use fork to turn them instead of knife.

Lyonnaise Potatoes—No. 3.

Put a pint of milk in a frying-pan; add a piece of butter the size of a butter-nut, some salt and pepper; let it boil; take a heaping teaspoonful of corn-starch, mix with a little cold milk, add, stirring till it thickens; have six or seven good-sized peeled potatoes (boiled or baked the day before), cut them in small pieces, put all together; cook fifteen minutes, stirring to prevent burning.

Potato Cakes.

Roast some potatoes in the oven; when done, skin and mash in a bowl with a small bit of butter warmed in a little milk; chop a shallot and a little parsley very fine, mix well with the potatoes, add pepper and salt, shape into cakes, egg and bread-crumb them, and fry a light brown.

Potato Croquettes.

Season cold mashed potatoes with pepper, salt and nutmeg; beat to a cream with a tablespoonful of melted butter to every cupful of potato. Add two or three beaten eggs and some minced parsley; roll into small balls; dip in beaten egg, then into bread crumbs, and fry in hot lard.

Riced Potatoes.

Have a flat dish and the colander hot. With a spoon rub mashed potato through the colander on to the hot dish. Be careful that the colander does not touch the potato on the dish. It is best to have only a few spoonfuls of the potato in at one time. When all has been pressed through, place the dish in the oven for five minutes.

Cale Cannon.

Boil three large potatoes with the skins on; bruise them to meal, and mix them with three cabbages, boiled, pressed from the water, and chopped; to which add half an ounce of butter, two spoonfuls of cream, pepper and salt. Heat and stir it over the fire, and send it to the table in the shape of a cake, or in a mould.

Turnips with Sauce.

Pare and cut into square pieces one-eighth inch thick; boil until tender in salted water; drain but do not mash them, and pour over them in your vegetable dish the following sauce: Take a tablespoonful of flour, tablespoonful of butter, and mix, beating to a cream, add salt-spoonful of salt, half salt-spoonful of pepper, a pint of milk, and half a pint of water; boil the milk and water, pour over the butter and flour, and cook the whole over a slow fire. This sauce can also be used for boiled onions.

Stewed Onions.

Peel six large onions; fry gently to a fine brown, but do not blacken them; then put them into a small stew-pan, with a little weak gravy, pepper and salt; cover and stew two hours gently. They should be lightly floured at first.

Boiled Onions.

Wash, peel, boil fifteen minutes, drain off the water and add boiling water; add salt and boil till thoroughly soft; then pour off the water and pour over them sweet milk. Stir flour and butter together, and when the milk boils stir in this thickening, adding salt and pepper to taste. Thus prepared the strong flavor of the onions is toned down. The water in which they are boiled should be abundant and soft. Old onions require two hours to boil.

Onion Ormoloo.

Peel ten or twelve large white onions, steep them an hour in cold water, then boil them soft. Mash them with an equal quantity of boiled white potatoes, adding half a pint of milk and two or three well-beaten eggs. Stir the mixture very hard, season it with nutmeg, pepper and salt, and bake it in a quick oven; when half done pour a little melted butter or gravy over the top.

Shallots.

Shallots, a species of onions, are an excellent spring dish. Strip off the outside skin and remove the green part; boil in salted water, and serve with drawn butter. They are also eaten raw, served with lettuce, radishes or watercresses.

Stewed Cabbage—No. 1.

Take off the outer leaves, clean, cut in four pieces, free from stump and stalk, and drop in boiling water, with a little salt; boil until tender, and drain. Put two ounces of butter, half a pint of milk, and a little flour, in a saucepan; lay in the cabbage, season with pepper and salt, and stew gently for a few minutes.

Stewed Cabbage—No. 2.

Slice a small, or half a large red cabbage, wash and put in a saucepan with pepper, salt and what water hangs to the cabbage but no more, and a piece of butter. Stew till quite tender, and when ready to serve add two or three teaspoonfuls of vinegar, and give one boil over the fire. Serve sausages on it or with cold meat.

Ladies' Cabbage.

Boil a firm, white cabbage, fifteen minutes; change the water and continue boiling until tender, when strain and set aside until perfectly cold; then chop fine, and add two beaten eggs, a tablespoonful of butter, three tablespoonfuls of rich milk or cream, a little pepper and salt; stir all well together, and bake in a buttered pudding dish until brown. This dish is digestible and palatable, much resembling cauliflower.

Hot Slaw.

Cut the cabbage into fine shreds; put in a saucepan with a cup of vinegar, a little water, salt and pepper; stew gently for a few minutes. For fried cabbage, add some butter and lard; cook brown.

Stuffed Cabbage.

Cut out the heart of a large, fresh cabbage; fill the vacancy with cooked chicken or veal, chopped very fine, highly seasoned, and rolled into balls with the yolk of an egg. Tie the cabbage firmly together and boil in a covered kettle two hours. This makes a delicious dish.

Summer Squash.

There are many varieties of this vegetable, but the general rules for cooking them are the same. Unless they are extremely tender, it is best to pare them, cutting away as little as possible besides the hard outer rind. Take out the seeds, quarter them, and lay the pieces in cold water. Boil about an hour. Drain well, pressing out all the water; mash soft and smooth, and season with butter, pepper and salt.

Winter Squash.

Prepare it the same as summer squash, but steam instead of boiling. Hubbard squash is very nice baked. Cut it in slices, take out the seeds, but do not peel; lay the slices in a dripping-pan and bake in a moderate oven. Steam one hour. Bake three-quarters of an hour.

Boiled Parsnips.

If young, scrape before cooking. If old, pare carefully, and if large, split. Put into boiling water, salted, and boil, if small and tender, from half to three-quarters of an hour; if full grown, more than an hour. When tender, drain and slice lengthwise, buttering well when they are dished.

Fried Parsnips.

For frying scrape and boil them, and cut them lengthwise in thick slices, dredge with flour, and fry brown on both sides in hot butter or lard; season with butter, pepper and salt.

To Mash Parsnips.

Boil them tender; scrape, then mash them into a stew-pan with a little cream, a good piece of butter and pepper and salt.

Fricassee of Parsnips.

Boil in milk till they are soft. Then cut them lengthwise into bits two or three inches long, and simmer in a white sauce, made of two spoonfuls of broth, a bit of mace, half a cupful of cream, a bit of butter, and some flour, pepper and salt.

VEGETABLES.

To Crisp Parsley.

When picked and washed very clean, put it into an oven, or on a sheet of paper, and keep it at a moderate distance from the fire; turn it till crisp.

Green Peas.

Shell green peas until you have a quart; half a peck in the shells will generally produce a quart of shelled peas. Put boiling water to cover them, add a teaspoonful of salt, cover the stew-pan, and boil fast for half an hour; then take one between your fingers; if it will mash easily, they are done; drain off the water, take them into a deep dish, put to them a teacup or less of sweet butter and a little pepper; a small teaspoonful of white sugar is a great improvement. Serve hot. Small young potatoes, nicely scraped, may be boiled and served with them, or in a separate dish with a little butter over.

To Boil Green Peas.

Wash after shelling them; boil with a spoonful of sugar in the water. Serve with scalded mint chopped; put a piece of butter to the peas after they are taken up.

To Stew Green Peas.

Put a quart of peas, a head of lettuce and an onion, both sliced, a bit of butter, pepper, salt, and no more water than hangs round the lettuce after washing. Stew them two hours very gently. When to be served, beat up an egg and stir it into them, or a bit of flour and butter. Some think a teaspoonful of white powdered sugar is an improvement. Gravy may be added, but it will diminish the flavor of the peas. Chop a bit of mint, and stew in them.

To Stew Old Peas.

Steep them in water all night, if not fine boilers; otherwise only half an hour; put them into water enough just to cover them, with a good bit of butter, or a piece of beef or pork. Stew them very gently till the peas are soft, and the meat is tender; if it is not salt meat, add salt and a little pepper. Serve them around the meat.

Succotash.

This is made of green corn and Lima, string or butter beans. Have a third more corn than beans, when the former has been cut from the cob and the beans shelled. Put into boiling water enough to cover them—no more—and stew gently together until tender, stirring now and then. Pour off nearly all the water, and add a large cupful of milk. Stew in this for an hour; then stir in a great lump of butter, a teaspoonful of flour wet with cold milk, pepper and salt to taste. Salt fat pork may be used instead of butter; cut it in slices and stew with the corn and beans. Succotash may also be made of dried corn and beans, but they must be soaked all night before using.

Egg-plant.

The long purple is best; the next best is the round, with prickles on the stem. Peel and slice them, spread salt on each separate piece, and lay in a colander to drain; let them lie one hour, parboil, drain, and dip in egg batter, or beaten eggs and bread crumbs, and fry, until thoroughly cooked, in pork-fat or butter. Egg-plants, unless well cooked are insipid. This is the usual way of cooking them, but they may be baked in the following manner: After they have been parboiled, mash, season with salt, pepper and butter; put this mixture in a deep earthen dish, sprinkle over some bread crumbs, and bake it a light brown.

Fricasseed Egg-plant.

Having peeled and sliced the egg-plants, boil them in water with a salt-spoonful of salt until they are thoroughly cooked. Drain off the water, pour in sufficient milk to cover the slices, and add a few bits of butter rolled in flour; let it simmer gently, shaking the pan over the fire till the sauce is thick, and stir in the beaten yolks of two or three eggs just before it is served.

Fried Egg-plant.

Peel the egg-plants, slice and sprinkle a little salt over them and let them so remain for half an hour; then wipe the slices dry; dip them into beaten yolks of egg, then into powdered cracker, and fry them to a light brown in boiling lard, seasoning them slightly with pepper while they are cooking. Another way is to parboil the egg-plants in a little soft water after they are peeled, then slice and dust them with common flour or corn-starch, and fry brown.

Egg Broccoli.

Take half a dozen heads of broccoli, cut off the small shoots or blossoms and lay them aside for frying; trim the stalks short and pare off the rough rind up to the head; wash them well, and lay them in salt water for an hour; then put them into plenty of boiling water (salted) and let them boil fast till quite tender. Put two ounces of butter into a saucepan, and stir it over a slow fire till it is melted; then add gradually six or eight well-beaten eggs, and stir the mixture until it is thick and smooth. Lay the broccoli in the centre of a large dish, pour the egg around it, and having fried the broccoli blossoms, arrange them in a circle near the edge of the dish.

STEWED ASPARAGUS.

Cut the asparagus in pieces half an inch in length, put them in boiling water with a little salt and cook them about ten minutes; then pour the water off, add milk and finish cooking; season well with butter, pepper and salt. String beans, lima beans or green peas may be cooked in the same way.

ASPARAGUS ON TOAST.

Tie the stalks in small bunches, boil them in a very little salted water about half an hour; toast as many slices of bread as there are bunches of asparagus, lay a bunch on each slice, add butter and one cupful of cream; thicken with a half teaspoonful of corn starch. When hot, pour over asparagus and toast.

ASPARAGUS OMELET.

Boil two pounds of tender fresh-cut asparagus in a very little water, with a small portion of salt; or better, steam the asparagus until it is tender without water; chop it very fine; mix with it the yolks of five eggs and the whites of three well-beaten eggs, and two tablespoonfuls of sweet cream. Fry and serve hot.

SPINACH.

Spinach requires a great deal of water to free it from the grit with which it is covered from its low growth. The stalks should be broken off, the spinach well washed and put in a saucepan with a little salt; cover with hot water. A very large quantity of uncooked spinach is needed to make a dish, as it wastes away considerably in cooking. Boil about one-half hour, or until the leaves are tender. When done, pour in a colander and press out the water; cut up fine and season well with butter, pepper and salt, and set in the oven a few minutes. Serve with boiled eggs cut in slices.

CAULIFLOWER—No. 1.

Pick off the outside leaves and cut the stalks close to the bottom of the flower; wash and put in cold water about half an hour; unless very large, do not divide them; put in boiling water, slightly salted; when tender, take up, drain and put butter among the leaves, or pour egg sauce over them.

CAULIFLOWER—No. 2.

Soak it head down in cold water for an hour to draw out any insects that may harbor in it; cut off all the superfluous leaves and put it into boiling salted water; boil until tender; take up and drain in a colander; pour over it gravy made of boiling milk, with flour and butter mixed together stirred into it. Serve with slices of lemon.

FRIED CAULIFLOWER.

Prepare and boil the cauliflower as directed. Then divide it equally, into small tufts, and spread it on a dish to cool. Prepare a sufficient quantity of batter made in the proportion of a tablespoonful of flour, and two tablespoonfuls of milk to each egg; dip each tuft of cauliflower twice in this batter, and fry them a light brown. Broccoli may also be fried in this manner.

CAULIFLOWER IN WHITE SAUCE.

Half boil it; then cut it into handsome pieces, and lay them in a stew-pan with a little broth, a bit of mace, a little salt, and a dust of white pepper; simmer half an hour; then add a little cream, butter and flour; shake, and simmer a few minutes, and serve.

Boiled Carrots.

Carrots require a good deal of boiling when old; when young, wipe off the skin after they are boiled; when old, boil them with salt meat, but first scrape them.

Stewed Carrots.

Half boil, then nicely scrape, and slice them into a stew-pan. Put to them half a teacupful of any weak broth, some pepper and salt, and half a cupful of cream; simmer them till they are very tender, but not broken. Before serving, rub a very little flour with a bit of butter, and warm up with them. If approved, chopped parsley may be added ten minutes before serving.

Stewed Celery.

Trim and cut to the same length a number of heads of celery; split them in two, lengthwise; tie them in bundles with thread, and parboil them for ten minutes in salted water; drain them and arrange them in a saucepan over slices of bacon with a bundle of sweet herbs, a couple of onions, pepper and salt to taste, and a blade of mace; add enough stock just to cover the contents; and set the saucepan to simmer gently till the celery is quite tender. Having removed the string, place the celery neatly on a dish; take some of the stock in which it has been stewed, remove all fat from it, add a small piece of fresh butter, pour it over the celery, and serve.

How to Boil and Dress Macaroni.

Put in an iron pot or stew-pan two quarts of water; .et it boil; add two teaspoonfuls of salt, one ounce of butter; then add one pound of macaroni; boil till tender; let it be rather firm to the touch; it is then ready for use, either for soup, pudding, or to be dressed with cheese. Drain it in a colander; put it back in the pan, add four ounces of cheese or more, a little butter, salt and pepper; toss it well together and serve. It will be found light and nutritious.

To Dress Artichokes.

Trim a few of the outside leaves off, and cut the stalk even. If young, half an hour will boil them. They are better for being gathered two or three days first. Serve them with melted butter in as many small cups as there are artichokes, having clipped off the sharp points of the leaves.

Artichoke Bottoms.

If dried, they must be soaked, then stewed in weak gravy, and served with or without force-meat in each. Or they may be boiled in milk, and served with cream sauce; or added to ragouts, French pies, etc.

To Stew Cucumbers.

Slice them thick; or halve and divide them into two lengths; strew over them some salt and pepper, and sliced onions; add a bit of butter. Simmer very slowly. Before serving, if it lacks richness, put in some more butter and a little flour; or, only a little flour if it is rich enough. Another way is to slice the onions, and cut the cucumbers large; flour them, and fry in some butter; then pour on some good broth or gravy, and stew them till done enough. Skim off the fat.

Baked Tomatoes.

Take large, smooth tomatoes, wipe them and cut a thin slice from the blossom end, take out the seeds and fill each tomato with a force-meat, made of bread crumbs, some salt pork chopped very fine, seasoned with salpicant; put a bit of butter in each, and fit on the top; place them in a deep dish and bake about half an hour.

Stewed Tomatoes.

Loosen the skins by pouring scalding water upon them; peel and cut them up. Stew in a saucepan (tin or porcelain) half an hour, then add salt and pepper to taste, and a tablespoonful of butter. Stew gently fifteen minutes longer, and serve. Thicken with a little grated bread. A minced onion—a small one—improves the flavor.

Fried Tomatoes.

Put scalding water on the tomatoes and let them stand a few minutes; turn it off and pare them; salt and pepper them and dust a little flour on one side; have the butter hot and lay them in it; fry slowly about fifteen minutes, then turn and fry for the same length of time; a few minutes before they are done add the cream to suit the taste.

Scalloped Tomatoes.

One can tomatoes; put a layer into an earthen dish; strew bits of butter over it with salt and pepper; then put a layer of rolled crackers, then tomato and so on until the dish is filled. Bake three-fourths of an hour.

Salsify or Oyster Plant.

Cut off the tops close to the roots, scrape, wash and slice them lengthwise or round; steam until tender in salted water; drain and put in a saucepan; cover with milk; to one pint of salsify add a tablespoonful of butter rolled in flour; season with salt and pepper; let it stew a few minutes and add a little vinegar.

Artificial Oysters.

Grate as many ears of green corn as will make one pint of pulp; add one teacupful of flour, one-half teacupful of butter, one egg; pepper and salt to suit your taste. To be dropped in butter and fried.

Sea Kale.

Pick it over carefully, tie it up in bunches, and let it lie in cold water an hour. Put into salted boiling water, and cook about half an hour, drain and season with butter, pepper and salt, or lay it on toasted bread, and pour rich drawn butter over it.

French Beans.

String and cut them into four or eight pieces; the latter looks best. Lay them in salt and water, and when the saucepan boils, put them in with some salt. As soon as they are done, serve them immediately, to preserve the green color. Or when half done, drain the water off, and put into them two spoonfuls of broth strained; add a little cream, butter and flour, to taste.

Lima Beans.

Put a pint of shelled beans in just enough salted boiling water to cover them, boil till tender, then drain off the water and add a cup of cream, a little butter, pepper and salt. Simmer a few minutes and serve.

Sweet Corn.

If some of the tenderest and nicest of the husks are put into a kettle in which corn on the cob is cooked, the flavor of the corn will be improved. Corn is sometimes cooked with the inner husks on, and these are removed just before serving it.

Stewed Green Corn.

Cut from the cob and stew fifteen minutes in boiling water. Turn off most of this, cover with cold milk, and stew, until very tender, adding, before taking up, a large lump of butter cut in bits and rolled in flour. Season with pepper and salt to taste. Boil five minutes and serve. Cold boiled corn may be used instead.

Green Corn Fritters.

Grate the corn and allow to every cupful, one egg, a tablespoonful of milk, and a little salt and butter; stir all together and thicken with a little flour. They may be fried in hot lard or cooked on a griddle the same as batter cakes.

To Can Corn.

For every eight quarts of corn cut from the cob, take one ounce of tartaric acid, cook together and can. Another way is to use glass cans. Cut the corn from the cob, press it into the cans till the milk flows over. Put on the tops, screw down tight. Place them in a boiler with sticks on the bottom, pour in cold water enough to about two-thirds cover them. Boil five hours. When about half cooked, remove a can at a time, tighten the tops and replace.

ADDITIONAL RECIPES.

ADDITIONAL RECIPES.

PICKLES.

Chow-chow.

Two quarts each of green tomatoes, white onions, pickled beans, one dozen each of green cucumbers and peppers, and one-half of a large cabbage. Season with mustard, celery seeds and whatever else one may desire. Cover mixture with vinegar and boil two hours, stirring continually; add two tablespoonfuls olive oil while hot.

Mixed Pickles.

Five heads cauliflower, two hundred cucumbers, two quarts nasturtiums, two quarts onions and twelve green peppers. Put the cauliflower, onions and cucumbers into salt water for twenty-four hours. Use whole spices.

Pickled Cucumbers.

To one gallon cucumbers take one teacupful salt, with sufficient water to cover; pour boiling hot water over them for three mornings; the fourth morning scald them in equal parts of cider vinegar and water, with a little alum added. Then drop them into cold vinegar with brown sugar, mustard seed, cinnamon, peppers, horseradish, mace and a few bay-leaves. Seal them up for future use.

To Salt Cucumbers.

To one pail of cucumbers take two quarts of salt.

Ripe Cucumber Pickle, or Russian Bear.

Take large and ripe cucumbers before they become soft; cut in rings, pare, divide in smaller pieces, and remove the seeds; cook the pieces very slightly in water salted just enough to flavor well; drain and put in a stone jar. Prepare a vinegar as follows: Two pounds of sugar to two quarts of vinegar, a few slices of onion, some cayenne pepper, whole allspice, whole cloves, cinnamon according to one's judgment and taste. Much cooking injures the pickle very much; the pieces should be firm and admit a silver fork with difficulty, when taken from the fire.

To Pickle Cucumbers and Sliced Onions.

Cut them in slices, and sprinkle salt over them. Next day drain them for five or six hours; then put them into a stone jar, pour boiling vinegar over them, and keep them in a warm place. The slices should be thick. Repeat the boiling vinegar, and stop them up again instantly; and so on till green; the last time put in pepper. Keep in small stone jars.

Pickled Onions.

In the month of September, choose the small white round onions, take off the brown skin, have ready a very nice tin stew-pan of boiling water, and throw in as many onions as will cover the top; as soon as they look clear on the outside, take them up as quick as possible with a skimmer, and lay them on a clean cloth, cover them close with another, and scald some more, and so on. Let them lie to be cold, then put them in a jar, or glass, or wide-mouth bottles, and pour over them the best vinegar, just hot, but not boiling. When cold, cover them. Should the outer skin shrivel, peel it off. They must look quite clear.

Pickled Red Cabbage.

Slice it into a colander, and sprinkle each layer with salt; let it drain two days, then put it into a jar, and pour boiling vinegar enough to cover, and put in a few slices of red beet-root. Observe to choose the purple-red cabbage. Those who like the flavor of spice will boil it with the vinegar. Cauliflower cut in bunches, and thrown in after being salted, will look of a beautiful red.

Virginia Damson Pickles.

To five pound damsons allow five pounds of sugar and two and one-half pints vinegar. Take the vinegar and put to it two ounces mace, one ounce cinnamon and one ounce cloves. Let it come to a boil and pour over the fruit and sugar; cover close. Turn off and scald the syrup for six successive days; the seventh day let fruit, spices, and all come to a boil. It will keep for years.

Pickled Crab-apples.

To one quart of fruit add one quart of sugar, and vinegar enough just to cover. Spice with ground cloves to your taste. Put your fruit into the vinegar, and stir till they are soft; or, better, steam them first, and pour the vinegar and sugar on them when hot.

Tomato Sauce for Hot or Cold Meats.

Put tomatoes, when perfectly ripe, into an earthen jar, and set it in an oven, when the bread is drawn, till they are quite soft; then separate the skins from the pulp, and mix this with capsicum-vinegar, and a few cloves of garlic pounded, which must both be proportioned to the quantity of fruit. Add powdered ginger and salt to your taste. Use white-wine vinegar and cayenne.

Tomato Pickle.

Eight pounds skinned tomatoes and four of brown sugar. Put them in a preserving kettle, and stir often to prevent burning. Boil to the thickness of molasses, then add one quart of good cider-vinegar, one teaspoonful of mace, one teaspoonful of cloves, and boil five minutes longer.

Spiced Tomatoes.

One peck of green sliced tomatoes, and six good-sized onions; sprinkle a coffee cup of salt through them and press down with a weight for twenty-four hours; drain off this brine and take one quart of vinegar and two quarts of water, and boil the tomatoes in it about ten or fifteen minutes, or until tender. Then take two quarts of vinegar, four of sugar, two tablespoonfuls each of cinnamon, cloves and ginger, a little mace, one teaspoonful black pepper; let them come to a boil, and then add the tomatoes; then boil fifteen minutes, or till tender.

Cauliflower Pickle.

Cut the cauliflowers into little flowerets of equal size. Throw them into boiling salted water. Place them at the back of the range, and when they are just about to boil take them off and drain them. Put them into jars. Boil about fifteen minutes enough vinegar to cover them, seasoning it with one ounce of nutmeg, one ounce of mustard seed, and half an ounce of mace to three quarts of vinegar. Pour this hot over the cauliflowers, adding a little sweet oil the last thing to cover the top. Cover them while warm with a bladder or fine leather over their corks, or seal them in glass cans.

Picollilly.

Four quarts each of cut cucumbers, beans and cabbage. Two quarts each of cut peppers and onions, and four quarts each of celery and nasturtions. Pour on boiling vinegar, flavored strongly with mustard, mustard seed and ground cloves.

Pickled Apples.

Take sweet apples, fully ripe, core and quarter them. Take two quarts of vinegar, two pounds of sugar, one-half ounce of mace, one of cloves and one of cinnamon, with a spoonful of allspice. (These spices should not be ground.) Let it boil together ten minutes. Then put in enough of the apples to cover the surface of the syrup and let them boil until clear. Skim them and lay on a platter; put fresh apples to cook, until you have as many as your syrup will cover when placed in a jar. These, after a few days, sometimes need to be brought again to boiling point, and then will keep any length of time.

Celery Chowder.

One gallon green tomatoes, chopped, and one cabbage; sprinkle over a teacupful of salt, and spread on a large platter; let it stand over night and drain off; scald in vinegar; when almost done, add one teaspoonful each of ground cloves, white mustard seed and brown sugar, and two of celery seed. Place in a stone jar for use.

Pickled Peppers.

Cut out the stem of the peppers in a circle, and wash out in cold water; then fill each with a mixture of finely-chopped cabbage, horseradish, cucumbers and mustard seed; then replace the pieces cut from the top and sew around with coarse thread. Pack in stone jars and cover with cold vinegar.

Pickled Butternuts.

Gather them the last week in June. Make and skim a brine of salt and water, strong enough to bear up an egg. When cold, pour it on the nuts, and let them lie in it for twelve days. Drain and lay them in a jar, and pour over them the best cider-vinegar, which has been previously boiled with peppercorns, cloves, allspice, white mustard seed, ginger, mace and horseradish. The vinegar must be cold when poured on; cover close, and keep one year before using. Walnuts are pickled the same way, and the vinegar may be used as catsup, for it is very nice.

Pickled Oysters.

Scald one hundred large oysters in their own liquor and lay them on a platter; when cold add to the liquid one quart of vinegar, two tablespoonfuls of salt, whole spice and mace; when it comes to a boil add one lemon; pour over the oysters; place in glass jars.

French Pickles.

One peck green tomatoes and six large onions, sliced; mix these, throw over them a teacupful of salt and let them stand over night; next day drain thoroughly and boil fifteen minutes in one quart of vinegar mixed with two quarts of water. Mix together four quarts of vinegar, two pounds of brown sugar, half a pound white mustard seed, two tablespoonfuls allspice (ground), the same of cinnamon, cloves, ginger and ground mustard; put in the tomatoes and boil all together fifteen minutes.

Okra and Tomatoes.

Cut the okra in thin slices, and pare and slice the tomatoes. Have one pint of tomatoes to two of okra. Put them in a stew-pan with a teaspoonful of salt and a little pepper. Stew fifteen minutes, then turn into a deep dish; add a tablespoonful of butter. Cover with bread or cracker crumbs, dot with butter and bake half an hour.

Lemon Pickle.

Peel very thinly six lemons, take off the white, cut the pulp into slices and remove the seeds. Put the peel and pulp into a jar, sprinkle with two ounces of salt; cover the jar and let it stand three days, then boil in a quart of vinegar six cloves, three blades of mace, two or three shallots and two ounces of bruised mustard seed; pour it boiling hot over the lemons in the jar, and when cold tie over; in a month strain and bottle the liquor and use the lemon as pickle. This is a nice sauce for veal cutlets and minced veal.

Pickled French Beans.

Gather them before they become stringy; without taking off the ends, put them into a very strong brine until they become yellow; drain the liquor from them and wipe them dry with a cloth. Put them into a stone jar by the fire, and pour boiling vinegar upon them every twenty-four hours; keep covered to prevent the escape of the steam; in four or five days they will become green.

Pickled Nasturtiums.

Gather them young; lay them in salt and water one night. Drain; then cover with hot vinegar, boiled with a little black and Jamaica pepper. A couple of capsicums put into the jar will be a great improvement.

Chili Sauce.

Twelve ripe tomatoes, four ripe peppers, two onions, two tablespoonfuls salt, two tablespoonfuls sugar, three teacups vinegar and a little cinnamon; peel the tomatoes and chop them fine; also the peppers and onions, and boil all together one hour. Canned tomatoes may be used if fresh ones are not at hand.

To Pickle Walnuts.

When they will bear a pin to go into them, put them in a brine of salt and water, boiled, and strong enough to bear an egg on it, being quite cold first. It must be well skimmed while boiling. Let them soak six days; then change the brine and let them stand six more; then drain them, and pour over them in a jar a pickle of the best white-wine vinegar, with a good quantity of pepper, pimento, ginger, mace, cloves, mustard seed and horseradish, all boiled together, but cold. To every hundred of walnuts put six spoonfuls of mustard seed and two or three heads of garlic or shallot, but the latter is least strong. Thus done, they will be good for several years, if close covered. The air will soften them. They will not be fit to eat under six months. When the walnuts are used, boil up the pickle with half a pound of anchovies to a gallon, and a teaspoonful of cayenne, and you will have a very good catsup.

Sweet Pickles.

Seven pounds fruit, three pounds sugar, one pint vinegar, one ounce each of cloves and cinnamon, tied in a thin muslin bag.

Tomato Catsup—No. 1.

One-half bushel ripe tomatoes cut in halves; sprinkle with salt and leave them over night. Drain off the juice, add one pint of water, and stew slowly in a large preserving-kettle till quite soft. Then put through a colander to free from skins. Return to the kettle and add one cupful of salt, one-half ounce cayenne pepper, one ounce powdered cloves, one ounce each of nutmeg and mace. Simmer slowly for two or three hours, and add, when nearly cooked, one bottle of cooking wine. When quite cold, bottle and cork tight.

Tomato Catsup—No. 2.

Boil one bushel of tomatoes in a granite ware kettle until soft, press them through a sieve; then add half a gallon of vinegar, two ounces of cloves, one and a half pint of salt, one ounce cayenne pepper, five heads of garlic skinned or chopped, two ounces of whole pepper, one pound of allspice, five ounces of mace, and five ounces of celery seed. Mix all together, and boil until it is reduced one-half. Strain and bottle it. Black pepper may be used instead of cayenne, and onions instead of garlic.

Grape Catsup.

Take five pounds of grapes and one pint of vinegar; cook until you can strain through a sieve; to the juice add two pounds of sugar, one tablespoonful of cinnamon, half a teaspoonful of salt, one of black pepper and one of cloves. Cook down to two quarts

Mushroom Catsup—No. 1.

Take the largest broad mushrooms, break them into an earthen pan, strew over salt, and stir them now and then for three days. Then let them stand for twelve days; strain and boil the liquor with Jamaica and black peppers, mace, ginger, a clove or two, and some mustard seed. When cold, bottle it, and secure the corks as above, leaving the spice in. At the end of three months strain the liquor, and boil with fresh spice, which put into the bottles; and in a cool place it will keep two or three years.

Mushroom Catsup—No. 2.

Take a stew-pan full of the large flap mushrooms, that are not worm-eaten, and the skin and fringe of those you have pickled; throw a handful of salt among them and set them by a slow fire; they will produce a great deal of liquor, which u must strain; then put to it four ounces of shallots, two cloves of garlic, a good deal of pepper, ginger, mace, cloves, and a few bay-leaves: boil slowly, and skim very well. When cold, bottle, and cork close. In two months boil it up again with a little fresh spice, and a stick of horseradish, and it will then keep a year, which mushroom catsup rarely does, if not boiled a second time.

Walnut Catsup.

Boil or simmer a gallon of the expressed juice of walnuts when they are tender, and skim it well; then put in two pounds of anchovies, bones and liquor, two pounds of shallots, one ounce each of cloves, mace and pepper, and one clove of garlic. Let all simmer till the shallots sink; then put the liquor in a pan till cold, bottle, and divide the spice to each. Cork closely, and tie a bladder over. It will keep twenty years in the greatest perfection, but it is not fit for use the first year. Be very careful to express the juice at home; for it is generally adulterated, if bought. Some people make liquor of the outside shell, when the nut is ripe; but neither the flavor nor color is then so fine; and the shells being generally taken off by dirty hands, there is much objection to this mode.

India Pickle.

Lay a pound of white ginger in water one night; then scrape, slice, and lay it in salt in a pan till the other ingredients shall be ready. Peel, slice, and salt a pound of garlic three days; then put it in the sun to dry. Salt, and dry long pepper in the same way. Prepare the various vegetables as follows: Quarter small white cabbages, salt three days, squeeze, and set them in the sun to dry. Cauliflowers cut in their branches; take off the green from radishes; cut celery in three-inch lengths; also young French beans whole, after being stringed; likewise, shoots of elder, which will look like bamboo. Apples and cucumbers of the least seedy sort; cut them in slices, or quarters, if not too large. All must be salted, drained, and dried in the sun, except the latter, over which you must pour boiling vinegar, and in twelve hours drain them, but no salt must be used. Put the spice, garlic, a quarter of a pound of mustard seed, and as much vinegar as you think enough for the quantity you are to pickle, into a large stone jar, and one ounce of turmeric to be ready when the vegetables shall be dried. When they are ready observe the following directions: Put some of them into a two-quart stone jar, and pour over them one quart of boiling vinegar. Next day take out those vegetables; and when drained, put them into a large stock jar, and boiling the vinegar, pour it over some more of the vegetables; let them lie a night, and do as above. Thus proceed till you have cleansed each set from the dust which must inevitably fall on them by being so long in doing; then, to every gallon of vinegar put two ounces of flour of mustard, mixing, by degrees, with a little of it boiling hot. The whole of the vinegar should have been previously scalded, but set to be cool before it was put to the spice. Stop the jar tight.

Pickled Peaches—No. 1.

Twelve pounds peaches, seven pounds sugar, three pints vinegar; scald the sugar and vinegar, and when hot put in the fruit. Let it remain until heated through; spice to taste with cinnamon and cloves. Cover tight.

Pickled Peaches—No. 2.

Seven pounds peaches, three or four pounds brown sugar, one quart vinegar, two tablespoonfuls whole cloves, two tablespoonfuls allspice, one tablespoonful mace. Boil together and pour over the peaches. Let them stand twenty-four hours, and repeat the boiling three or four times.

Pickled Plums.

One peck plums, seven pounds sugar, half pint vinegar; dissolve together the sugar and vinegar, and add the plums; boil three hours, stirring it all the time, and take out the stones while boiling; add two tablespoonfuls allspice, two of ground cloves.

Pickled Pears.

To one peck of pears take seven pounds sugar. Boil the fruit in the syrup without the vinegar.

Pickled Cherries.

To twelve pounds of fruit put seven pounds of sugar and one pint of vinegar; scald and pour upon the fruit three or four mornings in succession; the last morning boil the juice thick.

Pickled Blackberries.

Twelve pounds blackberries, three pounds sugar, two quarts vinegar and two ounces cloves; scald all together; leave twenty-four hours; drain off the syrup and scald; leave twenty-four hours and scald all together.

Raspberry Vinegar.

Put a pound of fine raspberries into a china bowl, and pour upon it a quart of the best white-wine vinegar; next day strain the liquor on a pound of fresh raspberries; the following day do the same, but do not squeeze the fruit, only drain the liquor as dry as you can from it.

Shallot Vinegar.

Split six or eight shallots; put them into a quart bottle, and fill it up with vinegar; shake often; stop it, and in a month it will be fit for use.

Sugar Vinegar.

To every gallon of spring water put two pounds of the very coarsest sugar; boil and skim thoroughly; then put one quart of cold water to every gallon of hot. When cool, put into it a toast spread with yeast. Stir it nine days; then barrel, and set it in a place where the sun will lie on it, with a bit of slate on the bunghole. Observe the caution about the barrel, as in gooseberry vinegar. Make in March; it will be ready in six months.

Wine Vinegar.

The raisins must not be pressed, but drained from the liquor; lay them in a tub, in a heap, to heat. In three or four days add fifteen gallons of water to every hundred weight. Let the mash be well beaten, and stirred often, for forty-eight hours; then strain and press them in a hair bag. Put the liquor into a barrel, with a toast covered with yeast. Mind that the cask be full, and set over a tub to work. When it ceases to ferment, cover the bung-hole with a piece of slate. Keep it in a warm place.

Gooseberry Vinegar.

Boil spring water, and when cold, put to every three quarts a quart of bruised gooseberries in a large tub. Let them remain sixty hours, stirring often; then strain through a hair bag, and to each gallon of liquor add a pound of the coarsest sugar. Put it into a barrel and a toast and yeast; cover the bung-hole with a bit of slate, etc., as above. Set the barrel in the sun, observing that the barrel be well painted, and the iron hoops all firm. The greater quantity of sugar and fruit, the stronger the vinegar; and as this is particularly useful for pickles, it might be well to make it of double the strength for that purpose.

Nasturtiums for Capers.

Keep them a few days after they are gathered; then pour boiling vinegar over them, and, when cold, cover. They will not be fit to eat for some months; but are then finely flavored and by many preferred to capers.

ADDITIONAL RECIPES.

YEAST.

Hop Yeast.

Tie two ounces of hops in a thin bag, and boil them in three quarts of water; moisten with cold water a sufficient quantity of flour, and stir in the hop yeast while boiling hot; add a tablespoonful of salt; let it stand until it is lukewarm, and then add a pint of old yeast; when it is light, cover it, and stand it in a cool place for use.

Potato Yeast—No. 1.

Boil a quarter of a peck of potatoes, mash them fine, and thin them a little with the water in which they have been boiled; add some salt and a tablespoonful of brown sugar; when lukewarm, stir in about half a pint or more of old yeast, let it rise, then cover it closely, and put it in a cool place.

Potato Yeast—No. 2.

One teacupful of grated raw potato, one tablespoonful of salt, one-half teacupful of sugar, mix and pour over it two quarts of boiling water; when lukewarm add half of a yeast cake or some yeast to raise it; let it stand until light, when it is better to be kept in a cool place tightly covered. It will keep longer in winter than summer.

Augusta's Yeast.

Two teaspoonfuls pressed hops, one-half cup salt, one cup sugar, one cup flour; three large potatoes boiled with the hops, and put hot with the other ingredients; strain the hop water and pour it over all. Set it in a warm place to rise.

Yeast Cakes.

Make the yeast as directed above, and when it has become quite light, stir in as much corn meal as it will take to roll out in cakes, and place them on a cloth in a dry place, taking care to turn them every day. At the end of a week, or ten days, they may be put into a bag, and should be kept in a dry place. When used, soak a cake in some milk-warm water, mash it up smooth, and use it the same as the other yeast.

BREAD AND BISCUITS.

Yeast Bread.

Six quarts of flour, two quarts of warm water, a tablespoonful of salt, three tablespoonfuls of lard. Put the flour into a deep pan, heap it round the sides, leaving a hollow in the centre, and put into it a quart of warm water, the salt, lard and yeast; have ready three pints more of warm water, and with as much of it as may be necessary, make the whole of it into a rather soft dough, kneading it well with both hands. When it is smooth and shining, strew a little flour on it, lay a thickly-folded cloth over the pan, and set it in a warm place by the fire, for four or five hours in cold weather, or all night; then knead it again; cover it over, and set it to rise again. This bread can also be made of rye or graham flour.

Margaret's Wheat Bread.

Make the sponge at night with one pint of warm water, one coffee-cupful of potato yeast, a little salt, a little sugar and about a quart of flour; let it stand over night; when light, in the morning, put six quarts of flour into a pan, make a hole in the centre, pour in the sponge, together with a pint and a half of warm milk; mix and let it stand until light, then mix again, kneading a good deal; allow it to stand until light again; mix and put into the bread pans; when light set it in the oven. A coffee-cupful of mashed potatoes stirred into the sponge improves it.

WHEAT BREAD—No. 1.

One quart lukewarm water, salt, one-half cup yeast, one-half cup sugar, two large spoonfuls molasses, one large spoonful shortening, eight and a half cups flour. Do not knead it. Stir it with a spoon to a moderately stiff batter; let it stand over night. In the morning put it in pans, and let it rise; then bake. This makes two loaves.

WHEAT BREAD—No. 2.

One cake yeast, one cup sugar, one quart of milk, one tablespoonful salt, flour to make a thin dough. Let it rise, then stir down and put in pans; let it rise again, then bake.

WHEAT AND INDIAN BREAD.

Put three pints of water over the fire; when it is boiling hot, add a large tablespoonful of salt, stir into it sweet white corn meal until it is a thick batter; continue to stir it for ten minutes, that it may not burn, then turn it into a dish; stir into it a quart of cold water; when it is cool enough to bear your hand in it, pour it into a bowl to which are seven pounds of wheat-flour, heaped around the sides so as to leave a hollow in the centre; add to it a gill of baker's yeast, and half a teaspoonful of saleratus, dissolved in a little hot water, then work the whole into a smooth dough; work it or knead for nearly an hour, then strew a little flour over it, lay a thickly-folded cloth over, and set in a warm place for five or six hours in summer, or mix at night in winter; when light, work it down, set it to rise for an hour, then heat the oven, work the bread down, and divide it into loaves, and bake, according to their size, in a quick oven; when taken from the oven, turn them over in the pans, and set them to become cold; if the crust is hard, wrap them in a towel as soon as taken from the oven.

Unfermented Bread.

To make good unfermented bread, graham flour should be mixed with water, or milk, and a little salt, and baked in small loaves, in cast iron bread-pans, or cast iron "gem pans." The oven and pans should be hot, the dough made of the ordinary consistence, and the pans half full. The heat coagulates the gluten on the outer surface of the dough, thereby preventing the escape of steam and causing the bread to rise in a moment. If the oven is sufficiently hot, the bread bakes before the steam escapes, and is light and wholesome.

Quick Bread.

With one quart of flour mix two teaspoonfuls of baking powder and half a teaspoonful of salt; add sufficient milk or water to make a soft dough; mould it into loaves, and bake at once in a hot oven. This bread may be made of graham flour with the addition of half a cup of molasses.

Hoyleton Bread.

Five cups of Indian meal, seven cups of wheat flour, two cups of rye meal, four cups of buttermilk, two cups of sweet milk, one-half cup of molasses, two teaspoonfuls of salt, two teaspoonfuls of soda. Put it into a three-quart pail that has a cover; let it stand near the fire thirty minutes with the cover off, to rise, then put on the cover, and bake or steam four hours.

Corn Biscuits.

One pound of Indian meal, three-quarters of a pound of wheat flour, two ounces of butter, six eggs, one and one-half ounces of baking powder, one quart of sweet milk and a little salt. Bake in patty pans in a quick oven.

German Bread.

One pint of milk well boiled, one teacupful of sugar, two tablespoonfuls of nice lard or butter, two-thirds of a teacupful of baker's yeast. Make a rising with the milk and yeast; when light, mix in the sugar and shortening, with flour enough to make as soft a dough as can be handled. Flour the paste-board well, roll out about one-half inch thick; put this quantity into two large pans; make about a dozen indentures with the finger on the top; put a small piece of butter in each; and sift over the whole one tablespoonful of sugar, mixed with one teaspoonful of cinnamon. Let this stand for a second rising; when perfectly light, bake in a quick oven fifteen or twenty minutes.

Corn Bread.

One quart of sour milk, two tablespoonfuls of saleratus, four ounces of butter, three eggs, three tablespoonfuls of flour, and corn meal sufficient to make a stiff batter.

Mississippi Corn Bread.

One pint of buttermilk, two eggs, one pint of Indian meal, two tablespoonfuls of melted butter, a little salt, one teaspoonful of soda.

Graham Bread.

Two cups of sweet milk, two cups of sour or buttermilk, one-half cup of molasses, one teaspoonful of soda. Salt, and stir in flour to thicken.

Boston Brown Bread.

One-half cup of flour, one cup of Indian meal, two cups of rye flour, two-thirds cup of molasses, two teaspoonfuls of cream tartar, one teaspoonful of soda—mix soft with cold water or milk; tablespoonful of salt. Steam three hours.

Good Brown Bread.

Two teacupfuls of Indian meal, one cup of flour, one cup of buttermilk or sour milk, one cup of sweet milk, one teaspoonful of soda, one teacupful of molasses, one-half teaspoonful of salt. Steam three hours and bake one-half hour.

Biscuits.

Two quarts of flour, two cups of sour cream or milk, two cups of buttermilk, six teaspoonfuls of cream tartar, four teaspoonfuls of soda and a little salt.

Cream Biscuits.

One quart of flour, three teaspoonfuls of cream tartar, two teaspoonfuls of soda, one teacupful of cream, and one teacupful of buttermilk.

German Biscuits.

Take one quart of milk, boil it and then let it cool to a blood heat; add flour enough to make a sponge, same as for bread, and one teacupful of malt yeast; let this stand over night; in the morning take a small teacupful of butter, partly melted, add to it two small teacupfuls of rolled sugar; after beating these a little, add four eggs, then beat the butter, sugar and eggs thoroughly, adding a teaspoonful of salt; add all to the sponge, beating well when mixing.

Graham Biscuits.

Stir with a spoon tepid water into graham flour until stiff enough to form into a dough as soft as can be kneaded; roll out when sufficiently kneaded to be well mixed, and cut into cakes three-quarters of an inch in thickness. Lay them in baking pans so they will not touch each other, and bake in a quick oven, letting them remain long enough to become brown and crisp, which, with a good heat, will require about twenty-five minutes, or taking them out when just done through, as one prefers; if not sufficiently baked they will be heavy at the bottom. Put them on a grate or colander to cool, that they may not steam and become heavy. This bread is excellent for growing children and for brain-workers. None of its nutritive qualities are diminished by fermentation, and eaten with good cow's milk and some sub-acid fruit it forms perfect food.

Crackers.

One pint of water, one teacupful of butter, one teaspoonful of soda, two of cream of tartar, and flour enough to make as stiff as biscuit. Let them stand in the oven until dried through. They do not need pounding.

ADDITIONAL RECIPES.

ADDITIONAL RECIPES

BREAKFAST AND TEA CAKES.

MUFFINS—No. 1.

One pint of milk, piece of butter the size of an egg, one-half cup of yeast, two eggs, and flour enough to make a stiff batter; put the milk on to boil and put the butter into it; when the milk is nearly cool add the eggs beaten, the yeast and flour; let it rise six hours; bake in muffin rings.

MUFFINS—No. 2.

Three cups of milk, one tablespoonful of melted butter, two eggs, beaten stiff, three tablespoonfuls of yeast, one tablespoonful of white sugar, one teaspoonful of salt and one-quarter teaspoonful of soda; flour to make a pretty stiff batter. Make all the ingredients, except the eggs, into a sponge, and set it to rise over night; half an hour before breakfast add the eggs and the soda (dissolved in hot water), beaten all together hard; part into muffin rings; let them stand on the hearth ten minutes, and bake about twenty minutes in a brisk oven.

RYE AND INDIAN MUFFINS.

Two cups of Indian meal, two cups of rye flour, half a cup of yeast. Let it rise over night; in the morning add one teaspoonful of soda, half a cup of molasses, a little salt, and bake.

French Muffins.

One quart of milk, four eggs, one-half cup of sugar, one teaspoonful of salt, one cup of yeast; make a stiff batter; in the morning add one cup of half lard and half butter, one teaspoonful of soda; stir this in and let it rise; when light, put into muffin rings, without stirring, and bake.

Saratoga Graham Muffins.

Three cups of sour milk, one-half cup of molasses, three small teaspoonfuls of soda, a little salt. Put the molasses in the sour milk and add the soda and salt. Mix in one quart of graham flour, and bake in muffin rings. This makes a delicious muffin.

Water Muffins.

One quart of flour, half teacupful of yeast, tablespoonful of salt, warm water enough to make a thick batter, beat it with a spoon. Let it rise eight hours. Bake in muffin rings half full, and bake them fifteen or twenty minutes

Graham Muffins.

Six cups of graham meal, two cups of flour, two teaspoonfuls of salt, two-thirds cup of molasses, one teaspoonful of soda; mix with sour milk. Bake in muffin rings.

Mrs. H.'s Muffins.

One pint of sour milk, teaspoonful of soda, one egg, and flour to make a thick batter.

Breakfast Muffins.

Two eggs, well beaten, one cup of sugar, one lump of butter the size of an egg, one pint of milk, one quart of flour and three teaspoonfuls of baking powder Bake in a quick oven.

Mrs. D's Muffins.

Melt half a teacupful of butter in a pint and a half of milk; add a little salt, a gill of yeast, and four eggs; stir in flour enough to make a batter rather stiffer than for griddle cakes; if kept in a moderately warm place it will rise sufficiently in eight or nine hours.

Hominy Muffins.

Having washed a pint of small hominy through two or three waters, pour boiling water over it and cover; let it soak several hours, and then put it into a thick saucepan with half a pint of boiling water, and let it boil until soft enough to wash; drain it and mix well with a pint of white corn meal or wheat flour, a little salt, a pint and a half of milk, and two tablespoonfuls of yeast. Cover and set in a warm place until very light, with the surface covered with bubbles; butter muffin rings, set them on a hot griddle, pour into each a portion of the mixture, and bake brown on both sides. Pull open with the fingers and butter while hot.

Rice Muffins.

Boil soft and dry one-half cup of rice, stir in three spoonfuls of sugar, piece of butter the size of an egg, a little salt, one pint of sweet milk, one cup of yeast and two quarts of flour. Let it rise all night. If sour in the morning, add a little soda dissolved in milk, and bake in muffin rings.

New England Pancakes.

Mix a pint of milk, five spoonfuls of fine flour, seven yolks and four whites of eggs, and a very little salt; fry them very thin in fresh butter, and between each strew sugar and cinnamon. Serve six or eight at once.

Brown, or Graham Pancakes.

Beat one egg and stir into a cupful of sour milk or cream with one small teaspoonful of soda; add one teaspoonful of sugar, a pinch of salt, and then stir rapidly or beat with a fork, sufficient graham flour to make a stiff batter; drop in a pan with boiling lard and turn quickly as pancakes. They will be light and crisp; and are delicious with omelet and good coffee.

Bread Pancakes, with Water.

Soak pieces of stale bread till quite soft; drain them through a sieve, and rub the bread through a colander. To one quart of this add three eggs and milk to make a thick batter. Bake on a griddle.

Soda Pancakes.

One pint of milk, two teaspoonfuls of cream of tartar, one teaspoonful of soda, flour to make a thin batter. Fry on a griddle.

Corn Griddles, to Eat with Meat.

Twelve ears of sweet corn, grate off the grains, two eggs, pepper, salt, and a very little butter, half a teacup of flour, half teacup of milk. Stir well together, and fry on a griddle.

Ground Rice Pancakes.

Boil a quart of milk; rub smooth a teacupful of ground rice in a gill or two of cold milk, and stir it into the boiling milk; add a little salt, and while it is scalding hot stir in flour enough to make the right thickness for baking. When cool, add a teacup of yeast and four eggs. Let it rise light.

Flap Jacks.

Half coffee-cup scalded Indian meal, one pint of sour milk, teaspoonful soda, flour to thicken.

Rice Pancakes.

Put a teacupful of rice into two teacupfuls of water, and boil until the water is nearly absorbed; then add a pint and a half of milk, and boil slowly until the rice is very soft. Fry on a griddle.

Buckwheat Cakes.

One quart of buckwheat flour, one teaspoonful of salt; stir in warm water enough to make a thin batter; beat in thoroughly four level tablespoonfuls of home-made yeast. Set the batter in a warm place. Stir in a teaspoonful of soda in the morning.

Sally Lunn—No. 1.

Six cups of light dough, one-half cup of milk, one-half cup of butter, two eggs and two spoonfuls of white sugar; add flour enough to make it the consistency of thick batter; mix well and pour into greased bake pans. Let them set in a warm place one-half hour, and bake by a slow fire.

Sally Lunn—No. 2.

Six cups of flour, two cups of milk, two-thirds cup of sugar, two teaspoonfuls of butter, four eggs, four teaspoonfuls of cream of tartar, two teaspoonfuls of soda. Eat while hot.

Rice Cakes.

Mix together half a pound of very soft boiled rice, one-fourth pound of butter, one quart of milk, six eggs, and enough flour to form a thin batter.

Susan's Rye Drop Cakes.

One cup of Indian meal, one cup of rye meal, one-half cup of yeast, a little molasses. Let them rise, add a little soda, if sour, a little salt, and bake in a quick oven.

Rye Drop Cakes.

One quart of milk, two eggs, piece of butter the size of an egg, half a teacup of white sugar, two teaspoonfuls of cream of tartar, one teaspoonful of soda; rye meal to make a stiff batter. Fill your pans half full, and bake half an hour.

Pan Doddlings.

Three teacupfuls of fine rye meal, three teacupfuls of Indian meal, one egg, three tablespoonfuls of molasses; add a little salt, allspice and sufficient sweet milk to form a batter stiff enough to drop from a spoon. Fry them in hot lard until a nice brown.

Graham Gems.

Two cupfuls of milk, one tablespoonful of butter, two tablespoonfuls of molasses, one teaspoonful of salt; add flour enough to make a stiff batter, three teaspoonfuls of baking powder. Drop into hot gem pans, and bake in a quick oven.

Breakfast Gems.

One cup of sweet milk, one and one-half cups of flour, one egg, one teaspoonful of salt, one teaspoonful of baking powder, beaten together five minutes. Bake in hot gem pans in a hot oven about fifteen minutes.

Rye Cakes.

One pint of scalding hot milk, one-half cup of Indian meal, one-half cup of sugar, one cup of rye meal, two cups of flour; cool, and then add a little salt, one-half a cup of yeast. Let this rise over night. In the morning add one-half teaspoonful of saleratus and two eggs.

Fried Mush.

The night before, stir into two quarts of boiling water a little salt and one pound of farina; boil for ten minutes, and pour it into a shallow dish to cool; next morning cut it into slices, and fry in lard light brown. This is far superior to corn meal mush.

Little Milk Cakes.

Place on a table or slab one pound of flour, half a teaspoonful of salt, two of sugar, three of fresh yeast, two ounces of butter, and one egg; have some new milk, pour in a gill, mix all together, adding more milk to form a nice dough; then put some flour in a cloth, put the dough in, and lay it in a warm place; let it rise for about two hours; cut it in pieces the size of eggs, roll them even, and mark the top with a sharp knife; egg over and bake quick. Serve hot or cold.

Johnny Cake.

One cup of Indian meal, two cups of flour, sifted together with three tablespoonfuls of baking powder, one cup of sugar, two eggs, one tablespoonful of lard melted in warm water, a pinch of salt, and sufficient water to mix.

Connecticut Corn Cakes.

Mix in the following order one cup of fine sifted "golden" corn meal, one cup of sifted flour, half cup sugar, one beaten egg, one cup of sour milk or cream, two tablespoonfuls of butter (one if cream is used), teaspoonful of soda dissolved in the milk, a little salt. Drop from the spoon into greased patty pans, and bake in a hot oven fifteen minutes. These are nice split open and toasted for breakfast, or to accompany Boston baked beans.

Corn Cakes.

Boil a pint of milk and pour it upon five tablespoonfuls of corn meal, stirring all the time. Add three well-beaten eggs, a piece of butter, half the size of an egg, and a little salt. Wet four tablespoonfuls of flour in a little cold milk and mix all together. Stir the mixture just before putting it into the pans, which must be well buttered and slightly warmed. Bake twenty or thirty minutes.

Dixie Corn Cakes.

Two cups of Indian corn meal, one cup of flour, two teaspoonfuls of cream of tartar, one of soda, a little salt, resift, rub in a tablespoonful of lard, two of sugar; mix with enough milk and water to make a thick batter. Bake twenty-five minutes in a quick oven, either in shallow pans or moulds.

Boston Corn Cakes.

Two eggs, three-fourths coffee-cup of sugar, two cups of sour milk, two cups of Indian meal, one cup of flour, one-half teaspoonful of soda and salt.

Round Lake Corn Cakes.

One cup each of flour, sugar, Indian meal and milk, two eggs, one tablespoonful of butter and one and a half teaspoonfuls of baking powder.

Kentucky Corn Meal Gems.

Take two cups of Indian meal, one cup of flour, one pint of sour milk, two eggs, one tablespoonful of white sugar, a piece of butter the size of a nutmeg, a pinch of salt, one teaspoonful of soda; if buttermilk is used no butter is needed. Mix thoroughly, and bake in gem irons twenty-five minutes.

Georgia Indian Cake.

One cup of milk one teaspoonful of sugar, one egg, butter half the size of an egg, one cup of Indian meal, one and one-half cups of flour, one teaspoonful of cream of tartar, one-half teaspoonful of soda, a little salt.

Indian Meal Puffs.

Into one quart of boiling milk stir eight spoonfuls of Indian meal, and four spoonfuls of sugar. Boil five minutes, stirring constantly; when cool add six well-beaten eggs. Bake in buttered cups half an hour.

Rye and Indian Johnny Cakes.

Two cups of rye, two cups of Indian meal, a small teaspoonful of saleratus, a little salt, sufficient sour milk to make a stiff batter. Bake in cakes on a griddle; split open and butter them. Send to the table hot.

Parker House Rolls.

Rub a tablespoonful of lard into two quarts of flour; make a sponge with one pint of cold boiled milk, one-half cup of yeast, one-half cup of sugar; let it stand until light, and knead twice; roll out one-half inch thick, cut with a biscuit-cutter, then fold one side over upon the other. Rub a little butter on the top before baking.

Delmonico Rolls.

Warm one ounce of butter in a pint of milk; put to it a spoonful and a half of yeast of small beer and a little salt; put two pounds of flour in a pan and mix with the above; let it rise an hour. Knead well and bake in a hot oven.

BRENTFORD ROLLS.

Mix well two pounds of flour, a little salt, two ounces of sifted sugar, four ounces of butter and two eggs beaten with two teaspoonfuls of yeast, and about a pint of milk. Knead the dough well, and set it to rise before the fire. Make twelve rolls, butter tin plates and set them before the fire to rise until they become the proper size. Bake half an hour.

FLANNEL ROLLS.

One cup of sweet milk, whites of two eggs, two-thirds cup of butter, flour to make a thick batter, one-half cup of yeast, two tablespoonfuls of sugar. Let it rise over night. Add the eggs and butter in the morning.

CINCINNATI ROLLS.

Take three-quarts and a pint of flour; make a hole in the centre of the flour and put in about a teacupful of milk warmed like new milk, and a coffee-cupful of potato yeast; mix and let it rise three or four hours. If to be made for the evening the sponge should be set about 9 o'clock in the morning; then add one pint more of warm milk, knead and let it stand three hours, then mix in a little sugar and salt and one-half pound of butter.

FRENCH ROLLS.

Rub an ounce of butter into a pound of flour; mix one egg beaten, a little sweet yeast and as much milk as will make a dough of a middling stiffness. Beat it well, but do not knead. Let it rise and bake on time.

THE SUPERB ROLLS.

One quart of milk, one cup of butter, two eggs. Let the dough rise once, take it out, knead it over and let it rise again; after this roll it out, cut it out with a tumbler, double together, roll, fashion, and let it rise in the pans half an hour before baking.

Unique Rolls.

One pint of new milk, one cup of yeast, one egg, a teaspoonful of flour; make into a stiff batter. Let it rise over night, but do not put in the saleratus until morning. Make the batter so stiff that you can form them into rolls without adding any more flour. Let it rise, after being formed into rolls, as long as possible, allowing thirty minutes to bake.

Dutch Rolls.

One quart of flour, two eggs, half pint of milk, one teaspoonful of butter; one gill of yeast; pour this into the flour. It must be mixed softer than bread, and if not moist enough add some more milk. Let it rise before baking.

Rusks.

One pint of dough, one cup of milk, two cups of white sugar, the whites of two eggs, two tablespoonfuls of lard, one of butter. Dissolve all but the eggs on the stove. Beat the eggs, and then add flour enough so it can be rolled easily and cut.

Barrington Rusks.

One cup of sugar, one cup of yeast, one cup of flour; mix over night; in the morning add half cup of sugar, and half cup of butter, rubbed together, two eggs, reserving the white of one, beaten to a stiff froth with a little sugar, to spread over the tops of the rusks.

Buns.

Mix one pound and a half of dried flour with half a pound of sugar; melt a pound and two ounces of butter in a little warm water; add six spoonfuls of rose-water, and knead the above into a light dough, with half a pint of yeast.

Light Dough Dumplings.

One pound of raised dough, made into small balls the size of eggs; boil in plenty of water, and serve with butter and sugar, or with sauce. Two ounces of chopped suet added to the above, or, to vary the taste, add a few currants, a little sugar, grated nutmeg or lemon peel.

Breakfast Waffles.

One quart of sweet milk, four well-beaten eggs, two tablespoonfuls of butter, a teaspoonful of soda dissolved in the milk and strained, and two of cream of tartar sifted with the flour. Make the batter as thick as pound cake batter.

Mrs. Bleeker's Waffles.

One quart of milk, a little sour if possible; a piece of butter the size of an egg; a piece of lard the same size; four eggs. Mix well with flour enough to make a stiff batter. If the milk is a little sour, enough soda to cover a five-cent piece will be sufficient to raise the waffles; but if it is fresh a teaspoonful of soda must be used; a teaspoonful of salt. Bake as quickly as possible.

Rice Waffles.

One cup of boiled rice, one pint of milk, two eggs, lard the size of a walnut, half teaspoonful of soda, one teaspoonful of cream of tartar, one teaspoonful of salt. Flour for a thin batter.

Corn Omelet.

Boil twelve ears of young corn twenty minutes. When done and cold, grate fine and season with salt; stir the yolks of five eggs into one gill of cream or milk; after being well mixed stir it into the corn; then beat the whites to a stiff froth and stir all together. Have your butter or lard hot, and then pour in your mixture and fry quickly. Serve hot.

Fritters.

Make them of any plain batter for pancakes, by dropping a small quantity into the pan; put pared apples, sliced and cored, into the batter, and fry some of it with each slice. Currants, or sliced lemon as thin as paper, make an agreeable change. Any sort of sweet meat or ripe fruit, may be made into fritters.

Spanish Fritters.

Cut the crumb of a French roll into lengths, as thick as your finger, in any shape you choose. Soak in some cream or milk, nutmeg, sugar, pounded cinnamon and an egg. When well soaked fry to a nice brown. Serve with butter, wine and sugar-sauce.

Potato Fritters.

Boil two large potatoes, and scrape them fine; beat four yolks and three whites of eggs, and add to the above one large spoonful of cream, another of sweet wine, a squeeze of lemon, and a little nutmeg. Beat this batter half an hour at least. Will be extremely light.

Apple Fritters.

Peel and slice crosswise, a quarter of an inch thick, some apples; remove the core, and dip them one after the other in the following batter: Put in a basin about two ounces of flour, a little salt, two teaspoonfuls of melted butter, and the yolk of an egg, moistened by degrees with water, stirring all the while with a spoon, till forming a smooth consistency, to the thickness of cream, then beat the white of the egg till firm, mixing it with the batter; it is then ready to fry. Use any fruit for fritters.

CORN FRITTERS.

One teacupful of sweet milk, three eggs, one pint of grated green corn, a little salt, and as much flour as will form a batter. Beat the eggs, the yolks and whites separately. To the yolks add the corn, salt, milk, and flour enough to make a batter. Beat the whole very hard and then stir in the whites, and drop a spoonful at a time into hot lard, and fry on both sides a delicate brown.

TO MAKE TOAST.

Cut slices from a loaf of wheat bread; let them be smooth, even, and half an inch thick; have a bright fire, and toast them quickly; when both sides are a fine brown, lay the slices on a hot plate, and put a tin cover over till served.

MILK TOAST.

Having toasted the bread nicely, spread it with sweet butter; make some milk hot, add a small bit of butter and a little salt to it, then pour it over the toast and serve. Or lay toasted bread in a deep plate or dish; to a pint of milk put a teaspoonful of salt and a teacupful of butter, make it boiling hot, then pour it over the toast. Some persons work a small teaspoonful of flour with the butter, and stir it into the milk when it is boiling hot; stir it for a few minutes, then pour it over the toast.

SOFT TOAST.

Some invalids like this very much indeed, and nearly all do when it is nicely made. Toast well, but not too brown, a couple of thin slices of bread; put them on a warm plate and pour over boiling water; cover quickly with another plate of the same size, and drain the water off; remove the upper plate, butter the toast, put it in the oven one minute, and then cover again with a hot plate and serve at once.

FRENCH TOAST.

Stir two eggs beaten very light into one pint of milk; slice some nice light bread, dip into the egg, place in a pan of hot butter and fry brown; boil up the milk, pour over and serve hot.

BROILED AND DEVILED TOAST.

Toast a round of bread, cut a quarter of an inch thick; mix in a plate one ounce of butter, half a teaspoonful of cayenne, one teaspoonful of mustard, one teaspoonful of catsup; spread it over the toast, and serve very hot. Broiled sausages may be served on it.

WELSH RARE-BIT ON TOAST.

Lay large slices of wheat bread browned delicately upon a large platter, and pour over the following cream when to the consistency of thick cream: One coffee-cup of sweet milk, one-half tablespoonful of flour, two tablespoonfuls of grated cheese; let the milk boil, stir in briskly the cheese and flour, after mixing it carefully in one-half cup of milk.

CHEESE TOAST.

Mix some fine butter, made mustard and salt, into a mass; spread it on fresh-made thin toasts, and grate or scrape cheese upon them.

Anchovy Toast.

Bone and skin six or eight anchovies; pound them to a mass with an ounce of fine butter till the color is equal, and then spread it on toast or rusks.

Stewed Cheese.

Grate two ounces of cheese, put it into a basin, and mix with it a small teacupful of cream, and an egg beaten and strained. Put into a small saucepan an ounce of butter, or less if the cheese be very fat; let it melt; then stir in the other ingredients, and boil until well incorporated. Serve hot, either a little browned or not.

Roast Cheese.

Grate three ounces of cheese, mix it with the yolks of two eggs, four ounces of grated bread, and three ounces of butter; beat the whole well in a mortar, with a dessert-spoonful of mustard, and a little salt and pepper. Toast some bread, cut it into proper pieces, lay the paste thick upon them, put them into an oven, covered with a dish, till hot through; remove the dish, and let the cheese brown a little. Serve as hot as possible.

Cheese Cakes.

Strain the whey from the curd of two quarts of milk; when rather dry, crumble it through a coarse sieve, and mix with six ounces of fresh butter, one ounce of pounded blanched almonds, a little orange-flower water, half a glass of raisin wine, a grated biscuit, four ounces of currants, some nutmeg and cinnamon in fine powder, and beat all the above with three eggs, and half a pint of cream, till quite light. Then fill the patty-pans three parts full.

Cheese Omelette.

Into a bowl break eight fresh eggs. Season with salt and pepper, and add half a gill of water. Beat well with a beater, and add grated cheese and small lumps of butter. Melt some butter in a pan, and fry the omelette quickly a delicate brown. Fold over and serve very hot. More or less cheese may be added, according to taste.

Pop Overs.

Four cups of flour, four eggs, four cups of milk, piece of butter the size of two nutmegs, half a teaspoonful of salt; melt the butter.

Oatmeal.

Soak the meal over night in just water enough to moisten it thoroughly. In the morning put it in a dish with a tight cover and set it into boiling water. As it swells and seems to become dry, pour over it a little cold water; this will need to be done quite frequently during the first two hours. Steam three hours, keeping the kettle in which the dish is, well covered. The mush may be stirred occasionally.

CAKE.

The following is a table of weights and measures, which will be found useful in connection with these recipes:

One quart of flour	one pound
Two cupfuls of butter	one pound
One generous pint of liquid	one pound
Two cups of granulated sugar	one pound
Two heaping cupfuls of powdered sugar,	one pound
One pint of finely-chopped meat	one pound

The cup used is the common kitchen cup, holding half a pint.

Molasses Cookies.

Two cups of molasses, one-half cup of lard, one tablespoonful of ginger and cloves, and one teaspoonful of soda. Enough flour to roll properly.

Ginger Snaps.

Two cups of molasses, one-quarter cup of brown sugar, one large cup of butter, one-half cup of sour milk, two teaspoonfuls of saleratus, three teaspoonfuls of ginger. Melt the molasses and butter together, and pour hot upon one quart of flour; then add ginger and saleratus. Mix the saleratus with the sour milk.

Graham Ginger Cookies.

One cup of molasses, one cup of sugar, one full cup of shortening, one-fourth cup of water, one tablespoonful of ginger, one teaspoonful of soda and a pinch of salt. Add equal portions of graham and white flour enough to make a dough to roll nicely.

Ginger Cookies.

One cup each of lard, brown sugar and molasses, one tablespoonful of ginger, two teaspoonfuls of soda dissolved in eight tablespoonfuls of hot water. Roll very thin.

Sugar Cookies—No. 1.

Three eggs, two cups of sugar, one cup of butter, five cups of flour and a small teaspoonful of cold water. Dissolve the soda in the water.

Sugar Cookies—No. 2.

One cup of butter, two cups of sugar, three eggs, one teaspoonful of sour milk, one teaspoonful of cream of tartar, and a small half teaspoonful of soda.

Preserved Ginger Cake.

One cup each of butter, brown sugar and molasses, two eggs, four and a half cups of flour, one tablespoonful each of ginger and cinnamon, four tablespoonfuls of brandy, one grated nutmeg, one teaspoonful of soda dissolved in a little warm water, one cup of finely-chopped raisins and one preserved ginger-root cut in strips. Beat the butter to a cream, then beat in the sugar, molasses, brandy and spices; then the eggs well beaten; stir the soda (dissolved) in the molasses; put two teaspoonfuls of baking powder in the flour; have two tins well buttered and pour in the mixture about two inches thick, then sprinkle a layer of the fruit, then the mixture and add more fruit. Keep a layer of the mixture for the top. Bake in a moderate oven for an hour.

Wilson's Ginger Cake.

One-half cup each of butter and lard, one cup each of molasses, brown sugar and sweet milk, three cups of flour, two teaspoonfuls of baking powder, two eggs, one teaspoonful of both ginger and cinnamon, and one-half teaspoonful of salt. Mix the shortening, molasses and sugar well together, then the eggs, well beaten, and the milk and spices. Put the baking powder and salt in the flour and sift it in, beating all well together before baking.

Soft Ginger Bread—No. 1.

One pint of molasses, one cup of butter, one-half cup of milk, one-half cup of water, two teaspoonfuls of soda, one egg, four cups of flour and a little ginger. First mix the soda with the molasses, then add the rest.

Soft Ginger Bread—No. 2.

One cup of molasses, one cup of butter, one cup of sour milk, one egg, one teaspoonful of soda, two teaspoonfuls of cream of tartar.

Graham Cake.

One quart of graham flour, three tablespoonfuls of sugar, one tablespoonful of butter, one teaspoonful of soda, two teaspoonfuls of cream of tartar, and enough sweet milk to make a stiff batter. Drop with a spoon upon flat tins, or bake in patty pans.

Bread Cake.

Four cups of bread dough, two cups of butter, two teacupfuls of sugar, three eggs, one glass of wine, one teaspoonful of soda and a little nutmeg. Mix very thoroughly.

Fool Cake.

One cup of sugar, one-half cup of butter, one cup of sour milk, one egg, one teaspoonful of soda and a little salt. To be eaten warm for supper, with or without butter.

Soda Cake—No. 1.

Three cups of sugar, one cup of butter, six eggs, four cups of flour, one cup of milk, one-half teaspoonful of soda, one teaspoonful of cream of tartar.

Soda Cake—No. 2.

Two cups of sugar, one cup of sweet milk, one cup of butter, four cups of flour, four eggs, one teaspoonful of cream of tartar, one-half teaspoonful of soda.

French Cake.

Two and a half cups of sugar, one-half cup of butter, one cup of sour milk, four cups of flour, three eggs, one teaspoonful of soda, two teaspoonfuls of cream of tartar.

Burwick Cake.

Beat six eggs, yolks and whites together, two minutes; add three cups of sugar and beat five minutes; put two cups of flour with two teaspoonfuls of cream of tartar, and beat two minutes; add one cup of cold water, one teaspoonful of saleratus dissolved in it, and beat one minute; the grated rind and half the juice of one lemon, a little salt, and two more cups of flour, and beat one minute. Observe the time exactly in beating. Bake in rather deep pans.

Cream Cake—No. 1.

One cup of sugar, one cup of sour cream, two cups of sifted flour, two eggs, one teaspoonful of cream of tartar, half a teaspoonful of soda and half a teaspoonful of salt. Flavor with essence of almond.

Cream Cake—No. 2.

Mix a quart of flour, a pint or more of sweet cream to wet it well, a teaspoonful of saleratus dissolved in a little sour cream, and bake.

Cream Cake—No. 3.

One cup of sugar, one tablespoonful of butter, three eggs, one-half cup of sweet milk, one teaspoonful of cream of tartar, one-half teaspoonful of soda, a little salt, one and one-half cups of flour. For the inside take one cup of milk, one egg, one tablespoonful of corn starch. Sweeten and flavor to taste.

Cream Cake—No. 4.

Two cups of sugar, one cup of butter, one cup of sweet milk, three cups of. flour, four eggs, three teaspoonfuls of baking powder. Bake in jelly tins. *Filling*—One cup of sweet milk put on to boil, adding sugar to taste, beat one egg and two teaspoonfuls of corn starch together, and when the milk has come to a boil, stir in the eggs; flavor with vanilla and set away to cool; then put between layers of the cake.

Washington and Domestic Cake.

Two pounds of sugar, one and one-half pounds of butter, four and one-half pounds of flour, one and one-half pounds of lard, five eggs, one pint of milk, half an ounce of ammonia, and mace.

Seed Cakes.

One and one-quarter pounds of sugar, three-quarters of a pound of butter, three-quarters of a pound of lard, two and one-quarter pounds of flour, three eggs, one and one-half gills of milk, one-quarter ounce of saleratus, one tablespoonful of caraway seeds.

Jumbles—No. 1.

Two pounds of sugar, two pounds of butter, three pounds of flour, six eggs, one pinch of saleratus, and oil of lemon.

Jumbles—No. 2.

One cup of butter, two cups of sugar, three eggs, one tablespoonful of sour milk, one teaspoonful of cream of tartar, a little soda and caraway seeds.

Noodles.

Two cups of white sugar, one cup of butter, three and a half cups of flour, half cup of milk, one teaspoonful of cream of tartar, half teaspoonful of soda, four eggs. Drop with a spoon on a buttered tin pan. Sift nutmeg and sugar on the top.

Fancy Cake.

Eight eggs, seven ounces of sugar, seven ounces of flour, one-quarter pound of butter, and oil of lemon.

Walnut Macaroons.

Half a pint of brown sugar, half a pint of walnut meats chopped, three even tablespoonfuls of flour, one-third teaspoonful of salt, and two eggs; beat the eggs, add the sugar, salt, flour, and then walnuts. Drop the mixture on buttered paper some distance apart, and bake till brown.

Almond Macaroons—No. 1.

Blanch four ounces of almonds, and pound; beat the whites of four eggs to a froth, then mix it, and a pound of sugar, sifted, with the almonds, to a paste. Lay a sheet of wafer-paper on a tin, and put it on in different little cakes, the shape of macaroons.

ALMOND MACAROONS—No. 2.

One pound of almonds, one and three-quarters pounds of sugar, ten to twelve whites of eggs. Prepare the almonds by blanching them in boiling water the day before using them. Strip off the skin, and, when perfectly cold, pound them, a few at a time, and occasionally add a little rose water. Beat the eggs to a stiff froth, add the sugar and then the almonds. Drop with a teaspoon upon buttered sheets in tins; sift fine sugar over and bake in a slow oven.

PINEAPPLE CAKE.

One cupful of butter, two cupfuls of pulverized sugar, two cupfuls of flour, seven eggs, two tablespoonfuls of baking powder, two tablespoonfuls of water, a large pinch of salt. Work the butter to a very light cream, add the sugar, then the well-beaten yolks, the whites beaten to a very stiff froth, the water, and lastly the flour, baking powder and salt sifted well together. Bake in jelly-cake pans, in a hot oven. Spread pineapple marmalade between the cakes.

ROUND CAKE.

One pound of flour, one pound of sugar, three-quarters of a pound of butter, twelve eggs, one-half teaspoonful of soda.

LADIES' CAKE.

Two cups of sugar, one cup of butter, one cup of sweet milk, whites of eight eggs, one teaspoonful of soda, one teaspoonful of cream of tartar.

KISSES—No. 1.

The proportions are the whites of six eggs to one pound of powdered sugar. Have your eggs perfectly fresh, and beat with a wire egg-spoon until stiff; add a few drops of vanilla flavoring, and sift the sugar slowly into the egg, stirring it well in; when all the sugar is in, beat the mixture lightly and steadily for about an hour, or until it is so stiff as to remain in any form you stir. Place thick white paper on an oven slide, sprinkle sugar on and chop the mixture in little heaps with a spoon. Bake in rather a cool oven until a light fawn color.

Kisses—No. 2.

Beat the whites of four eggs to a stiff froth; stir in one-half pound of sugar, lemon or rose water; beat well together until very light; lay the mixture in little heaps on white paper; put the paper on wood one-half inch thick; put them in a hot oven; as soon as they look yellowish, take them out. When cool, put two of them together.

Kisses—No. 3.

Seven eggs, one pound of the finest white sugar; flavor with lemon; add the sugar and lemon, when the eggs are beaten to a stiff froth. Butter a white paper and put in pans, and drop the kisses on with a teaspoon. Bake in a slow oven thirty minutes.

Kisses—No. 4.

White of one egg beaten well; add slowly fine sugar enough to make quite stiff, and two tablespoonfuls of corn starch. Flavor to taste.

Cup Cake.

One cup of butter, two cups of sugar, three cups of flour, one cup of milk, one teaspoonful of soda, two teaspoonfuls of cream of tartar, whites of three eggs.

Minnehaha Cake.

Two eggs, two teaspoonfuls of baking powder, one cup of sugar, one-half cup of butter, one-half cup of milk, one and one-half cups of flour. Beat the sugar with the butter. Bake in jelly-cake tins. *Filling*—Boil one cup of granulated sugar in water enough to moisten it, until it becomes ropy. Then place it in a basin of cold water to cool. Beat the white of one egg to a stiff froth, pour into the syrup and beat until cool; then add one cup of stoned raisins.

White Mountain Cake.

One cup of milk, one cup of butter, three cups of sugar, five cups of flour, six eggs, one teaspoonful of soda and two teaspoonfuls of cream of tartar. Dissolve the soda in the milk; stir the cream of tartar in the flour. Bake in jelly-cake tins. *Filling*—One pound of sugar and the whites of four eggs. Spread each cake with the icing when nearly cold.

Mountain Cake.

Two coffee-cups of sugar, one teacup of butter, one teacup of sweet milk, four teacups of flour, four eggs, one teaspoonful of soda, two teaspoonfuls of cream of tartar.

Cocoanut Cake—No. 1.

Two cups of sugar, three cups of flour, three eggs (leaving out the whites of two of them), one cup of milk, two tablespoonfuls of butter, two teaspoonfuls of cream of tartar and one of soda; bake as jelly cake. Prepare frosting with the whites of two eggs, and sugar. Lay it upon each layer of cake and sprinkle grated cocoanut upon the frosting, reserving the largest amount for the top of the cake.

Cocoanut Cake—No: 2.

One-half cup of butter, one and one-half cups of sugar, one-half cup of sweet milk, two cups of flour, three eggs, one-half teaspoonful of soda and one teaspoonful of cream of tartar.

Cocoanut Cake—No. 3.

One and one-quarter cups of sugar, one and one-half cups of flour, one cup of cocoanut grated, five tablespoonfuls of butter, four tablespoonfuls of sweet milk, one teaspoonful of cream of tartar, one-quarter teaspoonful of soda, whites of five eggs. Flavor with essence of lemon.

Tea Cakes.

Rub four ounces of butter into eight ounces of flour; mix eight ounces of currants, and six of fine sugar, two yolks and one white of eggs. Roll the paste the thickness of a cracker, and cut with a wineglass. You may beat the other white, and wash over them, and either dust sugar, or not, as you like.

Cocoanut Jelly Cake.

One cup of sugar, two tablespoonfuls of butter, two eggs, one-half cup of milk, one teaspoonful of cream of tartar, one-half teaspoonful of soda, two cups of flour. *For Preparing Cocoanut*—One cup of milk scalded and poured over the cocoanut. When cold add the white of one egg, well beaten, and three tablespoonfuls of sugar.

Cocoanut Drops.

One pound of cocoanut, three-quarters of a pound of sugar and three eggs.

Delicate Cake—No. 1.

One cup of sugar, one and one-quarter cups of flour, four tablespoonfuls of soft butter, one-quarter of a cup of sweet milk, whites of four eggs, one-quarter of a teaspoonful of soda, one-half teaspoonful of cream of tartar in the flour, and essence of lemon. Bake forty minutes.

Delicate Cake—No. 2.

One and one-half cups of sugar, one cup of butter, two-thirds cup of milk, whites of six eggs, three wine cups of flour and three teaspoonfuls of baking powder.

Delicate Cake—No. 3.

One pound of sugar, three-quarters of a pound of butter, one pound of flour, whites of ten eggs.

Sponge Cake—No. 1.

One cup of sugar, three eggs, one cup of flour, one teaspoonful of baking powder and one teaspoonful of vinegar. Bake twenty-five minutes.

Sponge Cake—No. 2.

The weight of nine eggs in sugar and six eggs in flour; beat the yolks and sugar together, with juice and rind of one large fresh lemon; add the whites of eggs beaten stiffly, and the flour last thing; stir as little as possible after the flour is added.

Sponge Cake—No. 3.

Weight of eight eggs in sugar and four eggs in flour, and a little pinch of salt; beat the yolks of the eggs ten minutes, then beat the sugar and yolks fifteen minutes, and let some one beat the whites to a stiff froth; at the end of the twenty-five minutes put the stiff whites into the yolks and sugar, and stir the flour in slowly. Bake in a very evenly heated oven, not too hot; it must not bake too quickly nor stand to dry out. The grated rind and juice of one lemon may be used if desired.

White Sponge Cake.

Whites of ten eggs, one and one-half heaping cups of sugar, one heaping cup of flour, one heaping teaspoonful of cream of tartar, and a pinch of salt. Beat the eggs to a stiff froth, then add the sugar and beat lively for ten or fifteen minutes; add salt. Then stir the flour and cream of tartar together, and add carefully to the eggs and sugar. Put it in the oven at once.

Roll Sponge Cake.

One cup of flour, three eggs, one cup of sugar, one and one-half teaspoonfuls of baking powder.

Sponge Drops.

Beat to a froth three eggs and one teacup of sugar; stir into this one heaping coffee-cup of flour, in which one teaspoonful of cream of tartar and half a teaspoonful of saleratus are thoroughly mixed. Flavor with lemon. Butter tin sheets with washed butter, and drop in teaspoonfuls about three inches apart. Bake instantly in very quick oven. Watch closely, as they will burn easily. Serve with ice cream.

Coffee Cake—No. 1.

One and one-half cups of sugar, one and one-half cups of molasses, one cup of butter, one egg, one teaspoonful of soda and one-half a teaspoonful of cream of tartar, four cups of flour, one nutmeg, two teaspoonfuls of powdered cloves, one pound of raisins, one cup of cold strong coffee. Makes two loaves.

Coffee Cake—No. 2.

One cup of brown sugar, one-half cup of butter, one teaspoonful of all kinds of spices, one cup of chopped raisins, one cup of currants, one-quarter pound of citron, one cup of strong coffee, with milk and sugar in it, three eggs, two cups of flour. Mix well, and bake in a deep dish one hour in a moderate oven.

Gold Cake—No. 1.

One-half cup of butter, one cup of sugar, one and one-half cups of sweet milk, the yolks of six eggs, one-half teaspoonful of soda, one ounce of cream of tartar and two cups of flour.

Gold Cake—No. 2.

One cup of yellow sugar, the yolks of three eggs, one-half cup of water, one-half cup of butter, two even cups of flour; flavor with vanilla or rose water. Cream the butter, add the sugar, then the eggs and water; two teaspoonfuls of baking powder in the flour. Bake fifty minutes, in a moderate oven.

Jumbles.

Two cups of sugar, one cup of butter, two eggs, two even teaspoonfuls of baking powder. Roll them, sprinkle with sugar, cut a piece out of the centre and bake in a quick oven.

Nut Cake.

One cup of butter, two cups of white sugar, four cups of flour, one cup of sweet milk, the whites of eight eggs, three teaspoonfuls of baking powder and two cups of walnut meats.

Hickory Nut Cake.

One cup of meats (broken), one and one-half cups of sugar, one-half cup of butter, two cups of flour, three-fourths cup of sweet milk, two teaspoonfuls of baking powder, the whites of four eggs well beaten; add the meats last.

Christmas Cake.

Two cups of butter, three cups of sugar, one-half cup of milk, one-half cup of water, a piece of soda as big as a bean, and caraway seeds.

Feather Cake.

Two cups of sugar, three cups of flour, one small cup of butter, one cup of milk, three eggs, three teaspoonfuls of baking powder, and one teaspoonful of lemon juice.

Butternut Cake.

One cup of sugar, one-half cup of butter, one-half cup of milk, one cup of chopped butternut meats, one cup of raisins, two eggs, two cups of flour.

Lemon Cake—No. 1.

One teacup of butter, three teacups of white sugar, five eggs, one cup of milk, one teaspoonful of saleratus; grate the peel of one lemon and add the juice of the same, four cups of flour.

Lemon Cake—No. 2.

One cup of white sugar, three tablespoonfuls of melted butter; beat together until smooth; four eggs, whites and yolks beaten separately; add to the butter and sugar; three tablespoonfuls of sweet milk, two teaspoonfuls of baking powder sifted into one cup of flour; the rind of one lemon grated; beat until quite light. Bake in a quick oven.

LEMON LAYER.

One grated lemon, two eggs, piece of butter the size of an egg, one cup of sugar; put them on the stove, melt together, and, when cool (not cold), spread between the layers of the cake.

WHITE CITRON CAKE.

One cup of butter, two cups of sugar, three cups of sifted flour, three teaspoonfuls of baking powder, mixed in the flour, one teaspoonful of water, four eggs, whites and yolks beaten separately, one-half pound of citron cut in long strips; beat the butter to a cream; add the sugar and beat until melted; then add the eggs, milk and flour mixed well together; quickly bake in two shallow pans thirty minutes.

WHITE FRUIT CAKE—No. 1.

One cup of butter, one and one-half cups of white sugar, the whites of six eggs, one wine-glass of white wine, one and one-quarter pounds of citron, cut fine, one-half pound of chopped almonds, one teaspoonful of prepared cocoanut, three cups of sifted flour, three teaspoonfuls of baking powder; beat the butter to a cream; then add the sugar and wine; beat the eggs to a stiff froth; after adding the wine add the fruit and eggs; sift the baking powder in the flour; mix well. Bake in two loaves for forty minutes in a quick oven.

WHITE FRUIT CAKE—No. 2.

One cup of butter, two cups of sugar, one cup of sweet milk, two and one-half cups of flour, whites of seven eggs, two even teaspoonfuls of baking powder, one pound each of raisins, figs, dates and blanched almonds, and one-quarter pound of citron; cut all fine. Beat all well before adding fruit. **Stir the fruit in** last, with a sifting of flour over it. **Bake slowly.**

Fruit Cake—No. 1.

Twelve eggs, one pound of flour, one pound of sugar, one pound of butter, two pounds of raisins, two pounds of currants, one pound of citron, two tablespoonfuls of cinnamon, four nutmegs, one cup of sweet milk, one cup of molasses, one teaspoonful of cream of tartar, one teaspoonful of soda, one gill of brandy. Bake two hours or more.

Fruit Cake—No. 2.

One pound of flour, one pound of sugar, one pound of butter, two pounds of raisins, two pounds of currants, one-half pound of citron, six eggs, one teaspoonful of soda, one teaspoonful of sour cream, one gill of brandy, one nutmeg, one teaspoonful of cloves, one teaspoonful of cinnamon, one cup of molasses. This will make a loaf large enough for a six quart pan. Bake three hours in a slow oven.

Water Melon Cake.

Take one-half cup of white sugar, whites of four fresh eggs, half a cup of sour milk, half a cup of butter, two cups of flour; cream the butter and sugar, then add the milk with not quite a half teaspoonful of soda; stir in the flour, then a little egg, and so on, till all the ingredients are added. The eggs must be beaten till very light. This completes half the recipe. Then take one and one-half cups of pink sugar, one-half cup of butter, one-half cup of sour milk, not quite half a teaspoonful of soda, and two cups of flour; flavor the pink with anything you wish. Rose water is much used. Seed a quarter of a pound of raisins; rub them well in flour. After both kinds are ready, spread well the bottom and side of your pan with white dough; fill up with pink, leaving enough white to cover the top.

Wedding Cake—No. 1.

Two pounds of butter, two pounds of brown sugar, two pounds of flour, twenty eggs, one quart of brandy, one pint of molasses, fifteen pounds of raisins, six pounds of currants, three pounds of citron, one pound of hard shelled almonds chopped, cloves, cinnamon, allspice and mace to suit taste.

Wedding Cake—No. 2.

Six cups of butter, three pints of sugar, six pounds of raisins, six pounds of currants, two pounds of citron, two pounds of shelled almonds, one pint of brandy, one tablespoonful of all kinds of spices, twenty eggs, three quarts of browned flour; beat the butter and sugar together; add the spices, fruits, nuts and brandy; then add your eggs, well beaten, and the browned flour sifted. This quantity will make three large loaves, and will keep for years. Bake in a moderate oven four hours.

Banana Cake.

One heaping tablespoonful of butter, two cups of sugar, three and three-fourths cups of flour, one cup of milk, two teaspoonfuls of baking powder. Flavor with vanilla. *Filling*—To the whites of three eggs take nine teaspoonfuls of fine sugar, flavor with vanilla; cut the cake in four layers, and spread with icing; cover thick with sliced banana. Take one banana for one cake and bake in one loaf.

Lady Fingers.

Two eggs, one half cup of pastry flour, scant half cup of powdered sugar. Have the bottom of two baking pans lined with buttered paper. Beat the yolks of the eggs, and sugar to a froth. Beat the whites to a stiff dry froth, and add to the yolks and sugar; add the flour and stir quickly; pour the mixture into the pastry bag and press it through on the paper in any size you wish; sprinkle powdered sugar over them, and bake sixteen minutes in a slow oven.

DOMINOES.

Make a plain cake; bake in a sheet about an inch thick. Cut it into square pieces and frost the top and sides. When the frosting is hard take a fine brush and mark the lines and spots with melted chocolate.

GATEAUX MADELEINES.

One pound of sugar, sixteen eggs, half pound of butter, and three-quarters of a pound of best flour. Beat the eggs and the sugar together in a bowl; when done mix in the flour, then the butter. Put the paste in small mounds, and bake in a warm oven.

GENEVA CAKES—FANCY.

Rub two cupfuls of sugar and one and a half cups of butter to a cream; add eight eggs, two at a time, beating five minutes between each addition; add one teaspoonful of baking powder sifted through one and a quarter pints of flour, one teaspoonful of extract of lemon. Mix into a smooth batter; drop into fancy shaped patty-pans, and just before putting in the oven, cover the tops with coarsely-chopped almonds or hickory nut meats. Bake in a moderate oven half an hour. If made in one loaf, bake an hour.

POUND CAKE.

One pound of flour, one pound of sugar, one pound of butter, eight eggs, one teaspoonful of rose water and half a nutmeg.

Chocolate Cake—No. 1.

One cup of butter, two cups of sugar, three eggs, four-fifths of a cup of milk, three cups of flour. *Paste*—Two ounces of grated chocolate, one-half cup of milk, one cup of sugar.

Chocolate Cake—No. 2.

One small cup of butter, one cup of sweet milk, two cups of sugar, three and one-half cups of flour, four eggs, three teaspoonfuls of baking powder. *Chocolate for Cake*—Six tablespoonfuls of bakers' chocolate, grated fine; scald with milk enough to make a paste to spread easily, and flavor with vanilla.

Chocolate Cake—No. 3.

Five eggs, reserving the whites of two for frosting; one cup of butter, two cups of sugar, scant cup of sweet milk, three and one-quarter cups of flour, two teaspoonfuls of baking powder. For the frosting take the whites of the two eggs, and beat to a stiff froth; add one and a half cups of powdered sugar, six tablespoonfuls of powdered chocolate, and two teaspoonfuls of vanilla.

Romeo and Juliet Cake.

Juliet—One cup of white sugar, whites of six eggs, well beaten; one tablespoonful of butter, one and one-half cups of flour, one heaping teaspoonful of baking powder, four tablespoonfuls of sweet milk. *Romeo*—One cup of sugar, one tablespoonful of butter, yolks of six eggs, one cup of flour, four tablespoonfuls of sweet milk, one heaping teaspoonful of baking powder. Bake in separate tins. Beat the whites of two eggs to a stiff froth, add the grated rind and juice of lemon; thicken this with pulverized sugar, and spread between the cakes.

Pork Cake.

Chop one pound of salt pork, pour on one pint of boiling water, two pounds of raisins, two pounds of currants, one-half pound of citron, two cups of molasses, two cups of sugar, flour enough to make a thick batter, one tablespoonful of baking powder, one teacupful of wine, all kinds of spice. Bake in a slow oven.

Barnard Cake.

One cup of butter, three cups of sugar, four and one-half cups of flour, four eggs, one cup of sour milk; the juice and a little of the rind of a lemon, and one teaspoonful of saleratus.

Shrewsbury Cakes.

One-quarter of a pound of butter, one-quarter of a pound of sugar, six ounces of flour, one teaspoonful of pounded cinnamon and mace, one egg. Beat the sugar and butter to a cream, then add the egg and spice; then stir in very gradually the flour; roll out the paste as thin as possible, and cut into cookies and bake. A teaspoonful of water will prevent the mixture sticking to the board.

Jelly Cake.

One cup of sugar, one-half cup of sweet milk, one-half cup of butter, two cups of flour, two eggs, one teaspoonful of cream of tartar, one-half teaspoonful of soda.

Roll Jelly Cake.

Mix half a teaspoonful of baking powder in one cup of flour; add one cup of sugar and four eggs. Bake in a shallow pan in a moderate oven, turn out on a clean towel, having cakes "upside down;" spread with jelly and roll quickly while warm.

LAYER CAKE.

One cup of sugar, one tablespoonful of butter; mix thoroughly; one egg beaten, three-quarters of a cup of sweet milk, one and one-half cups of flour, two teaspoonfuls of baking powder. Flavor to taste and bake quickly.

SILVER CAKE—No. 1.

The whites of eight eggs, one cup of butter, two cups of sugar, three cups of flour, one-half cup of sweet milk, one teaspoonful of cream of tartar, one-half teaspoonful of soda.

SILVER CAKE—No. 2.

One cup of pulverized sugar, one-half cup of butter, the whites of three eggs, one-half cup of milk, one and one-half cups of flour; use almond flavoring; beat the butter to a cream, then beat in the sugar; add the flavoring; put two teaspoonfuls of baking powder into the flour; mix quickly and well. Bake in a rather quick oven half an hour.

WASHINGTON CAKE.

Stir together until quite white, one pound of sugar, three-quarters of a pound of butter, four eggs, beaten well; stir in gradually one and one-half pounds of flour; dissolve one teaspoonful of saleratus in a teacup of milk; add a glass of wine, one teaspoonful of rose water, one-half a nutmeg and one pound of stoned raisins just before it is baked.

MRS. BURNHAM'S FIG CAKE.

One cup of sugar, one cup of flour, half a cup of butter, half a cup of sweet milk, half a cup of corn starch, two teaspoonfuls of baking powder, mixed in flour, whites of four eggs, well whipped and stirred in last. Bake the cake in round tins for layer. *Filling*—Three-fourths of a pound of figs, chopped fine, one cup of sugar in five tablespoonfuls of hot water. Bring to a boil and turn over the figs. When cool spread between the layers of the cake. Make three layers of cake and two of figs.

Angel's Food.

The whites of ten eggs, one and one-half cupfuls of pulverized sugar, sifted, one cupful of best flour, sifted before measured, one teaspoonful of baking powder sifted into the flour, one teaspoonful of almond flavoring. Beat the whites of the eggs to a stiff froth; beat the sugar into the eggs; add flavoring and flour; beat until very light. Bake in a ring made for this cake forty minutes in a moderate oven. Line the ring with note paper, but do not crease it.

Marble Cake—No. 1.

Light Part—One and one-half cups of white sugar, half cup of butter, half cup of sweet milk, half tablespoonful of soda, one teaspoonful of cream of tartar, adding the whites of four eggs, two and a half cups of sifted flour; beat very light. *Dark Part*—Two cups of brown sugar, half cup of butter, half cup of sour milk, half teaspoonful of soda, one teaspoonful of cream of tartar, two and a half cups of sifted flour; add the yolks of four eggs together with cinnamon, cloves and nutmeg, of each one teaspoonful.

Marble Cake—No. 2.

Dark Part—One cup of brown sugar, one-half cup of butter, yolks of seven eggs, one nutmeg, one tablespoonful each of cinnamon, cloves, allspice and pepper, one teaspoonful of soda, one-quarter of a cup of sour milk. *Light Part*—Two cups of white sugar, one cup of butter, whites of seven eggs, half cup of sweet milk, three teaspoonfuls of baking powder, and flour enough to make it the consistency of cup cake. Put the dark mixture on the bottom of the pan, then a layer of white, and so on, having the top a layer of the dark.

PINK MARBLE CAKE.

One cup of flour, one-half cup of corn starch, one-half cup of butter, whites of four eggs, one cup of red sugar sand, one-half cup of sweet milk, three-quarters of a teaspoonful of baking powder. Flavor to taste.

CREAM PUFFS.

One cup of water, half a cup of butter, boiled together; stir in while boiling one cup of flour, dry; then take from the fire and allow it to cool; add three eggs, not beaten; mix well and drop on buttered tins, and bake twenty-five minutes. Avoid opening the oven. *Cream*—One cup of milk, one egg, half a cup of sugar, three tablespoonfuls of flour; beat the eggs and sugar together, add flour, and stir them in the milk while boiling; flavor with vanilla. When cold, open and fill.

QUEEN CAKE.

Two cupfuls of butter, two and a half cups of sugar, one and one-half pints of flour, eight eggs, one teaspoonful of baking powder, one wine-glass each of wine, brandy and cream, teaspoonful each of extract of nutmeg, rose and lemon. One cup of currants, mashed and picked, cup of raisins, stoned and cut in two, one cup of citron cut in small, thin slices. Bake carefully in well-prepared tins in a moderate, steady oven one and one-half hours.

Midnight Cake.

One and one-half cups of butter, one pint of dark sugar, half pint of molasses, one-half pint of brandy, one-half pint of wine, one tablespoonful of all kinds of spices, ten eggs, two pounds of raisins, two pounds of currants, one pound of citron, three pints of browned flour, one teaspoonful of soda in the molasses, two teaspoonfuls of baking powder sifted into the flour. Beat the butter to a cream, stir in the sugar, then the molasses, then the brandy, wine and spices, raisins stoned and chopped fine, currants, citron and eggs well beaten. Brown your flour, sift it and stir in the cake; add baking powder. Bake in two deep pans in a moderate oven for four hours.

Puff Cake.

Two cups of white sugar, one cup of sweet milk, half cup of butter, three cups of flour, two eggs, one teaspoonful of baking powder.

Puff Overs.

One pint of milk, one pint of flour, two eggs, a little salt, one teaspoonful of baking powder; pour patty tins half full. Bake in a hot oven.

White Cake.

One-quarter of a pound of white sugar, one-half pound of flour, rub into the sugar one ounce of butter, one egg, one lemon, and milk to soften.

Crullers.

Dissolve one teaspoonful of saleratus in four tablespoonfuls of milk; four tablespoonfuls of melted butter, one teaspoonful of salt. Beat four eggs with six tablespoonfuls of rolled sugar. Flavor with nutmeg. Add flour to make stiff enough to roll out easily

Spice Cake.

One cup of sugar, one cup of sweet milk, one-half cup of butter, spice of all kinds.

Fried Cakes—No. 1.

One quart of milk, one-half pound of butter, six eggs, two pounds of sugar, one pound of raisins, one teaspoonful of soda, flour to make a stiff batter. Beat well and drop in hot lard.

Fried Cakes—No. 2.

Two cups of sugar, one cup of milk, four tablespoonfuls of soda cream, one and one-half teaspoonfuls of soda and three eggs. Mix soft and fry in hot lard.

Doughnuts—No. 1.

Twelve eggs, three-fourths of a pound of butter, two pounds of sugar, one pint of sour cream, one teaspoonful of saleratus; season to your taste; flour sufficient to roll them out. Fry in lard.

Doughnuts—No. 2.

One quart of flour, two teaspoonfuls of cream of tartar, one teaspoonful of soda, two eggs, one and a half cups of sugar, two cups of milk, half cup of butter, a little salt.

Frosting—No. 1.

One and one-quarter pounds of sifted loaf sugar, the whites of five eggs, half an ounce of pulverized gum arabic, and lemon to the taste.

Frosting—No. 2.

Allow the whites of two eggs to each half pound of sugar, add a little lemon or orange juice, and whip till you can turn the bowl upside down without dropping, or till it flakes. Some people add a little starch.

Frosting—No. 3.

Beat the whites of two eggs or more, according to the quantity wanted, and add pulverized sugar till quite thick; add a little powdered starch, and lay on the cake, immediately after it is baked, with a broad knife, returning to the oven for a moment, leaving the oven door open.

Frosting—No. 4.

Soak one teaspoonful of gelatine in one tablespoonful of cold water half an hour; dissolve in two tablespoonfuls of hot water; add one cup of powdered sugar and stir until smooth.

Icing for Cake.

The white of an egg and one-quarter of a pound of powdered sugar. Beat the egg stiff, and add by degrees the sugar. Flavor with lemon juice. This makes it whiter and smoother, and improves it much.

Whip Churn for Creams.

Whip churns cost but little, and are very useful. It is a tin cylinder with a dasher. By placing this in a bowl of cream you can bring the cream to a strong froth in five minutes. Very rich or poor cream will not whip well; when too rich, it turns to butter; when too poor the froth becomes thin. If you have thick rich cream, add a little milk. The cream should always be used cold.

ADDITIONAL RECIPES.

PASTRY AND MEAT PIES.

Puff Paste.

One quart of flour, one pint of butter, one tablespoonful of salt, one and one-fourth cupfuls of ice water. Do not use any more water than specified. Before using the butter, mix well in cold water, to get all the salt out, and let it harden. Roll it out, and put half of the butter over it in small pieces; turn in the ends and roll it thin; do this twice, and touch it no more than can be avoided; use the last half of the butter for the last time you roll it. Then put on ice for at least an hour before using it. If it sticks, put it on a tin sheet before putting on the ice. The least flour you use in rolling, the nicer will be your paste. Bake in a quicker oven than for a short crust, and lay a paper over the top to keep it from scorching.

A Less Rich Paste.

Weigh a pound of flour, and a quarter of a pound of butter, rub them together, and mix into a paste with a little water, and an egg well beaten. Roll, and fold it three or four times.

New England Pie Crust.

One coffee-cup of lard, three coffee-cups of sifted flour and a little salt. In winter soften the lard (but not in summer), cut it well into the flour with a knife, stir quickly, mix with cold water into a moderately stiff dough, handling as little as possible; this quantity is sufficient for four common-sized pies (covered). Take a new slice of paste each time for top-crust, using the trimmings, etc., for under-crust.

French Pie Paste.

Into two quarts of very cold water put half a pound of butter, and let it remain thirty minutes; when the time has expired, remove it from the water and rub it lightly into a pound of flour with two eggs; wet it with half a pint of the water in which the butter was placed, two teaspoonfuls of salt, and knead it; roll it out thin, and fold it for five consecutive times. Let it stand half an hour, and bake.

Common Paste.

Rub half a pound of butter and one spoonful of lard into a quart of flour; add a little salt, and cold water enough to make a dough; flour your moulding board and roll out the dough. Be sure and not mould it, but handle as little as possible.

Pie Crust—No. 1.

One cup of water, one cup of lard and one quart of flour.

Pie Crust—No. 2.

Three-quarters of a pound each of butter and lard mixed with one pound of flour; stir with a spoon, and add milk enough to make the pastry just stiff enough to roll; salt to taste, and roll out in as little additional flour as possible.

Dedham Cream Pie.

Bake your paste, not too rich, in a common pie plate first. Boil one pint of milk; when boiling stir in half a cup of flour, one cup of sugar and the yolks of two eggs; beat well together. Cook long enough not to have a raw taste; add the juice and grated rind of one lemon and a little salt; beat the whites of the two eggs, with a cup of sugar, to a stiff froth; spread over the pie when filled, and brown in the oven.

LEMON CREAM PIE.

One cup of sugar, one cup of water, one raw potato grated; the juice and grated rind of one lemon; bake in pastry top and bottom. This will make one pie.

CREAM PIE—No. 1.

Place a pint of milk where it will heat; then beat together one cup of white sugar, one-half cup of flour with two eggs, and stir into the milk when nearly boiling. Stir rapidly until it is cooked thoroughly, then add essence of lemon, and pour upon the crust, which should be baked before the cream is put in. This will make two pies. If you wish it extra, make a frosting of the whites of two eggs and three tablespoonfuls of sugar; spread this evenly over the pies, and set in the oven to brown slightly.

CREAM PIE—No. 2.

Three eggs, one cup of sugar, one and one-half cups of flour, one tablespoonful of sweet milk, one teaspoonful of cream of tartar, half a teaspoonful of soda; beat thoroughly together five or ten minutes, and bake in two round tin plates in a quick oven. When wanted for the table split them open, and spread the cream between. For the cream take one pint of milk, half a cup of sugar, two eggs, half a teaspoonful of vanilla, one tablespoonful of flour, one small pinch of salt; when the milk begins to boil add the eggs with the other ingredients; boil a few minutes, stirring constantly.

Cream Pie—No. 3.

One full pint of sweet milk, place in a pan of water until at boiling point; one tablespoonful of flour or corn starch, stirred in half a cup of cold milk; yolks of two eggs stirred in with the flour and milk; sweeten to the taste, and add a little salt; then pour the milk on one cupful of grated cocoanut; add to the other ingredients while hot; then let it stand until it thickens; when the crust (which should be baked by itself) is cool, pour in the above; put in a meringue on the top of whipped cream; or, if you choose, use the whites of the eggs, beaten with the cream. Flavor with half a teaspoonful of vanilla.

Pumpkin Pie.

Pare the pumpkin and take out the seeds without scraping the inside; stew and strain through a sieve. To every quart of milk add five eggs, and stir the pumpkin into the milk and eggs until to the proper consistency; sweeten with sugar or the best syrup; molasses makes it too strong. Add some salt, powdered cinnamon, powdered ginger and the grated peel of lemon. Bake in either deep or shallow dishes in a hot oven.

Rhubarb Pie.

Wipe the rhubarb, peel and cut in small pieces, and put it in a stew-pan, allowing half a pound of sugar to each pound of rhubarb, but no water. Stew it slowly. When done, turn it into a dish and set it away to cool. Line the plates with paste, put in the sauce, and cover with an upper-crust. For tarts, put strips across instead of an upper-crust.

MARLBORO PIE.

One cup of stewed and sifted apples, one cup of sugar, one cup of milk, two tablespoonfuls of melted butter, and the yolks of three eggs; whip the whites of the eggs, and put on top as for orange pie.

EGGLESS SQUASH PIE.

Stew the squash till very dry; press through a colander; to each pint of squash allow one tablespoonful each of butter and cinnamon, one cup of sugar, one teaspoonful of ginger, a little salt, and a few crackers rolled very fine. Add milk according to judgment.

SQUASH PIE.

Pare the squash and remove the seeds; stew until soft and dry; then pulp it through a colander. Stir into the pulp enough sweet milk to make it thick as batter. Spice with ginger, cinnamon, nutmeg or other seasoning to taste; sweeten with sugar and add four beaten eggs for each quart of milk. Fill a pie plate lined with crust and bake one hour.

LEMON PIE—NO. 1.

One cup of hot water, one tablespoonful of corn starch, one cup of white sugar, one tablespoonful of butter, the juice and grated rind of one lemon. Cook for a few minutes, add one egg, and bake with a top and bottom crust.

LEMON PIE—NO. 2.

The juice and grated rind of one lemon, one cup of white sugar, the yolks of two eggs, three tablespoonfuls of sifted flour and sufficient milk to fill a plate. Make it with under-crust but not the upper-crust. Bake till nearly done, and then add a frosting made of the beaten whites of two eggs, and two tablespoonfuls of powdered sugar, and set back in the oven and brown slightly.

Lemon Pie—No. 3.

One cup of water, three-quarters of a cup of sugar, yolks of two eggs, a piece of butter the size of a walnut, and one slice of bread broken without the crust. Grate one lemon, mixing the juice with the grated rind; bake with only an under-crust. When done, beat the whites of the eggs with four tablespoonfuls of pulverized sugar and a few drops of lemon, and spread over the top. Then return to the oven to brown slightly.

Lemon Pie—No. 4.

Grate the yellow rind of one lemon, then take off the inside skin and chop the pulp after taking out the seeds; add the grated rind, one tablespoonful of flour, one teacup of sugar, one cup of water, one egg and a tablespoonful of butter melted. Bake without an upper-crust.

Lemon Fruit Pie.

One cup of raisins, stoned and chopped fine, the juice and pulp of one lemon, one cup of sugar, one egg, and three tablespoonfuls of water. Bake with two crusts. This is very nice and as rich as mince pie, but more quickly prepared.

Lemon Custard Pie.

One lemon, one cup of water, yolks of three eggs, one cup of sugar, two tablespoonfuls of flour. Peel the lemon and pulverize half the peel. When the pie is about done beat the whites of the eggs to a froth, and add two tablespoonfuls of sugar; pour over the pie and let it stand a few moments in the oven.

MINCE MEAT—No. 1.

Six pounds of beef, eight pounds of suet, one heart, sixteen pounds of apples, nine pounds of brown sugar, three quarts of molasses, two and a half ounces of salt, one ounce of pepper, one gallon of sweet cider, eight pounds of raisins, four pounds of currants, three pounds of citron, one-quarter of a pound of cloves, one-quarter of a pound of cinnamon, one-quarter of a pound of nutmeg, one gallon of brandy, one gallon of wine. Mix all well together except the wine and brandy. Scald the mixture well, and then add the wine and brandy, and, when cold, cover with a cloth dipped in molasses. Keep in a cool place.

MINCE MEAT—No. 2.

One bowl of chopped meat, one bowl of chopped suet, two bowls of chopped apples, one bowl of sugar, one bowl of raisins, one bowl of currants, two bowls of cider, one-half bowl of citron, one teaspoonful of salt and one lemon chopped fine; nutmeg, cinnamon and cloves to taste. Wine or brandy may be used, if desired.

MOCK MINCE PIE—No. 1.

Two-thirds of a cup of rolled crackers, one cup of sugar, one cup of molasses, one-half cup of vinegar, one and one-half cups of boiling water, one cup of chopped raisins, butter the size of an egg, salt, one teaspoonful of cinnamon, and one teaspoonful each of cloves and nutmeg. After this has come to a boil and cooled stir in two eggs.

Mock Mince Pie—No. 2.

Six soda crackers, one-half cup of butter, one cup of molasses, one cup of currants. three cups of warm water, one cup of vinegar, two cups of raisins. Cook all together and spice to taste.

Mock Mince Pie—No. 3.

Four Boston crackers rolled fine; pour on a cup of boiling water, and add one cup of sugar, one cup of molasses, one-half cup of vinegar, two eggs, two teaspoonfuls of extract of lemon, one-half teaspoonful of cloves and one teaspoonful of cinnamon. Boil until it thickens. This will make two pies.

Orange Pie—No. 1.

The rind and juice of one orange, the yolks of three eggs, one-half cup of water, one tablespoonful of flour; when nearly done beat the whites, add three tablespoonfuls of sugar, and spread over the pie; return to the oven and brown.

Orange Pie—No. 2.

Cut into small pieces the inside of one orange, add the yolks of two eggs, one cup of sugar, one cup of milk, and one tablespoonful of flour. Bake the pie, then spread over the top the whites of the eggs beaten with two tablespoonfuls of sugar; return to the oven to brown.

Cocoanut Pie—No. 1.

One large or two small cocoanuts, four eggs, three and one-half cups of sugar, one small cup of butter, one cup of milk or enough for two pies. Rub the sugar and butter to a cream.

Cocoanut Pie—No. 2.

One good-sized cocoanut peeled and grated, one quart of milk sweetened like custard, a piece of butter the size of a walnut in each pie; four eggs to the quart.

Pineapple Pie.

Pare and grate large pineapples, and to every teacupful of grated pineapple add half a teacupful of fine white sugar; turn the pineapple and sugar into dishes lined with paste, put a strip of the paste around the dish, cover the pie with paste, wet and press together the edges of the paste; cut a slit in the centre of the cover, through which the vapor may escape. Bake thirty minutes.

Banana Pie.

Slice raw bananas, add butter, sugar, allspice and vinegar or boiled cider or diluted jelly; bake with two crusts. Cold boiled sweet potatoes may be used instead of bananas, and are very nice.

Custard Pie without Eggs.

Place a quantity of new milk, as much as desired, over a slow fire, and allow it to heat slowly until it boils, taking pains not to scorch it, as that imparts a disagreeable taste. For every quart of milk take four tablespoonfuls of flour, beat it well with cold milk to prevent it from being lumpy, and as soon as the milk boils, pour in the thickening, and stir it well until it boils again; then remove it instantly from the fire. Sweeten to suit the taste, and flavor with nutmeg or cinnamon, and it is ready for use, either cold or hot. Prepare the crust as usual for custard pies, fill them with the above preparation, and bake them an hour in an oven moderately hot. When sufficiently cooked, they will resemble, in appearance, a genuine egg pie, and will scarcely be distinguished by the taste. Custards may be made the same way, and if baked until the whey starts from them, they will be nearly equal to those prepared with eggs. Rice and other puddings may be made without eggs, by boiling and thickening the milk in this way, and if they are well baked, will prove excellent.

Apple Custard Pie.

Take nice sweet apples, jam and grate them, add good sweet milk until you have a batter as thick as for pumpkin pies; add one beaten egg and two tablespoonfuls of sugar to each pie. Bake slowly.

Delicate Pie.

The grated rind and juice of one lemon, one cup of powdered sugar, yolks of three eggs, five tablespoonfuls of flour, two-thirds of a cup of water; take the whites of the eggs and three tablespoonfuls of sugar and beat to a froth, and turn it upon the pie when baked. Set it in the oven again and let it remain three minutes.

Tomato Pie.

Take ripe tomatoes, peel and slice. Sprinkle over a little salt, and let them stand a few minutes; pour off the juice, and add sugar, half a cup of cream, one egg, nutmeg, and cover with a rich paste, and bake in a moderate oven over half an hour. This makes an excellent and much approved pie.

Orange Tartlets, or Puffs.

Line small patty-pans, or roll out some paste, if for puffs. When baked, put in orange marmalade made with apple jelly.

Lemon Tart.

Pare, rather thick, the rinds of four lemons, and boil tender in two waters, and beat fine. Add to it four ounces of blanched almonds, cut thin, four ounces of lump sugar, the juice of the lemons, and a little grated peel. Simmer to a syrup. When cold turn it into a shallow tin tart dish, lined with a rich thin puff paste, and lay bars of the same over. As soon as the paste is baked, turn it out.

Orange Tart.

Squeeze, pulp, and boil two nice oranges tender; use double their weight of sugar. Beat both together to a paste, and then add the juice and pulp of the fruit, and the size of a walnut of fresh butter, and beat all together. Choose a very shallow dish, line it with a light puff crust, and lay the paste of orange in it. You may ice it.

Bread Pie.

Soak one slice of very light bread in a pint of rich milk. When it is quite soft, beat it smooth; add one egg well beaten, and four tablespoonfuls of sugar. Flavor with nutmeg. Bake in a rich crust.

Raspberry Tarts with Cream.

Roll out some thin puff paste, and lay it in a patty-pan of any size you choose. Put in raspberries, strew over them fine sugar, cover them with a thin lid, and then bake. Cut it open, and have ready the following mixture warm: Half a pint of cream, the yolks of two or three eggs well beaten, and a little sugar, and when this is added to the tart, return it to the oven for five or six minutes.

Francatelli Puff Paste.

One pound of flour, one pound of butter, the yolk of an egg, a teaspoonful of salt, and about half a pint of water. Place the flour on the pastry board, spread it out in the centre so as to form a well, in which place the salt, a small piece of butter, the yolk of an egg, and about two-thirds of the quantity of water required to mix the paste; spread out the fingers of the right hand, and mix the ingredients together gradually with the tips of the fingers, adding a little more water if necessary; when the whole is thoroughly incorporated together, sprinkle a few drops of water over it, and work the paste to and fro on the board for two minutes, after which it should be rather soft to the touch, and present a perfectly smooth appearance. The paste, thus far prepared, must now be spread out on the board with the hands, and after the butter has been pressed in a cloth, to extract any milk it may contain, it should be placed in the centre of the paste, and partially spread, by pressing on it with the cloth; the four sides should then be folded over so as entirely to cover the butter; a little flour must next be shaken under and over it, and the paste must be shaped in a square form, measuring about ten inches each way, by pressing it out with the hand; it should then be placed in a clean baking-pan, laid on some broken ice, and a deep sautapan also filled with ice should be placed upon it; by these means the paste will be kept cool and firm. About ten minutes after the paste has been made, take it from the ice and place it on the board, shake a little flour over and under it, and then roll it out about two feet long and ten inches wide; observing that the paste must be kept square at both ends, as much of the success depends on due attention being paid to the turning and folding. The paste should then be laid in three equal folds, and after these have been rolled over to cause them to adhere together, the paste must next be turned round in the opposite direction and rolled out again in the same manner as before; it should then be put back on the ice, and after allowing it to rest for about ten or fifteen minutes, roll it out again, or, as it is technically termed, give it two more turns; the paste must now be put back on the ice, and again rolled twice or three times, as the case may require, preparatory to its being cut out for whatever purpose it may be intended. In the summer season it is impossible to insure success in making puff paste, unless ice be used to further that end, it being a matter of the first necessity that it should be kept cool and firm: two requisites that tend materially to facilitate the working of the paste, and also contribute very considerably to give to it that extraordinary degree of elasticity, when exposed to the heat of the oven, so well known to experienced pastry cooks. A piece of puff paste a quarter of an inch thick, when baked, will rise to the height of two inches, thus increasing in volume eight times. To effect this properly, it is necessary to procure three oblong tin-pans, of the following dimensions: the first should measure 20 inches by 16, depth 3 inches; the second, 18 inches by 14, depth 2 inches; and the third, 16 inches by 12, depth 3 inches. Place some broken ice in the largest, then set the second-sized tin on this, with the puff paste in it; lastly, put the smallest pan, also filled with ice, on the top of the paste: by this method puff paste may be easily made to perfection during the hottest days of summer. In winter, the use of ice may, of course, be dispensed with. In extreme cold weather, when the butter is very hard, it will be necessary to press it in cloth or on the board, to give it more expansion, and thus facilitate its incorporation with the paste. Care must be taken, in mixing the paste, not to make it too stiff, especially in summer, as, in that case, it becomes not only troublesome to work, but it also affects its elasticity in baking.

Pastry Custard, or Cream.

Four ounces of flour, four ounces of sugar, six yolks of eggs, two ounces of butter, one pint of cream or milk, one ounce of ratafias, a spoonful of orange-flower water, and a very little salt; mix the flour, sugar and salt with two whole eggs, in a stew-pan with a wooden spoon; then add the cream and the butter, and stir the whole over the fire till it boils; it must then be well worked together, so as to make it smooth. Withdraw the spoon, and after putting the lid on the stew-pan, place the cream in the oven or over a slow fire, that it may continue to simmer very gently for about twenty minutes; the cream must then be put out into a basin, and the bruised ratafias, the yolks of the eggs, and the orange-flower water may be added; after which put four ounces of butter into a small stew-pan over the fire, and as soon as it begins to fritter and has acquired a light-brown color (which gives to it the sweet flavor of nuts), add this also to the cream, and let the whole be well mixed. This cream may be used to garnish various kinds of pastry.

Meat Pies.

There are few articles of cookery more generally liked than meat pies, if properly made; and they may be made of a great variety of things. Some are best eaten when cold, and in that case there should be no suet put into the force-meat that is used with them.

If the pie is either made of meat that will take more cooking to make it extremely tender than the baking of the crust will allow, or if it is to be served in an earthen pie form, observe the following preparation: Take three pounds of the very nicest of beef that has fat and lean; wash it, and season it with salt, pepper, mace, and allspice, in fine powder, rubbing them well in. Set it by the side of a slow fire, in a stewpot that will just hold it. Put to it a piece of butter of about the weight of two ounces, and cover it quite close, and let it just simmer in its own steam until it begins to shrink. When it is cold, add more seasoning, force-meat, and eggs; and if it is in a dish, put some gravy to it before baking. But if it is only in crust, do not put the gravy with it until after it is cold and in jelly. Force-meat may be put both under and over the meat, if preferred to balls.

Veal Patties.

Mince some veal that is not quite done, with a little parsley, lemon peel, a scrape of nutmeg, and a bit of salt; add a little cream and gravy just to moisten the meat. If you have any ham, scrape a little, and add to it. Do not warm it until the patties are baked.

Turkey Patties.

Mince some of the white meat, and mix with it grated lemon, nutmeg, salt, a very little white pepper, cream, and a very little bit of butter warmed. Fill the patties.

Patties Resembling Mince Pies.

Chop the kidney and fat of cold veal, apple, orange and lemon peel candied, and fresh currants, a little wine, two or three cloves, a little brandy, and a bit of sugar. Bake as before.

A Good Mince for Patties.

Two ounces of ham, four ounces of chicken or veal, one egg boiled hard, three cloves, a blade of mace, pepper and salt, in fine powder. Just before you serve, warm the above with four spoonfuls of rich gravy, the same of cream, and an ounce of butter. Fill as usual.

Sweet Patties.

Chop the meat of a boiled calf's foot, of which you use the liquor for jelly, two apples, one ounce of orange and lemon peel candied, and some fresh peel and juice; mix with them half a nutmeg grated, the yolk of an egg, a spoonful of brandy, and four ounces of currants, washed and dried. Bake in small patty-pans.

Rabbit Pie.

Cut two rabbits, and a pound of fat and lean pork that has lain a week or two in pickle, into small bits; lay them, when seasoned with pepper and salt, into a dish. Parboil the livers, and chop them in a bowl, with their weight of fat pork and bearded oysters, some pepper, salt, mace, and sweet herbs, chopped fine. Make this into small balls, and distribute in the dish with some artichoke bottoms cut in dice. Grate half a small nutmeg over, and add half a pint of port wine and the same of water. Cover with a tolerably thick crust. Bake it an hour in a quick, but not violently heated oven.

Giblet Pie.

After very nicely cleaning goose or duck giblets, stew them with a small quantity of water, onion, black pepper, and a bunch of sweet herbs, until nearly done. Let them grow cold, and if not enough to fill the dish, lay a beef, veal, or two or three mutton steaks, at the bottom. Put the liquor of the stew to bake with the above, and when the pie is baked, pour into it a large teacupful of cream. Sliced potatoes added to it are much liked.

Crust for Venison Pasty.

To two quarts of fine flour use two pounds and a half of butter, and four eggs. Mix into paste with warm water, and work it smooth and to a good consistency. Put a paste round the inside, but not to the bottom of the dish, and let the cover be pretty thick, to bear the long continuance in the oven.

Beefsteak Pie.

Season the beefsteak with pepper and salt and a little shallot, minced very fine. Roll each slice with a good piece of fat, and fill your dish. Put some crust on the edge, and only an inch below it, and a cup of water or broth in the dish. Cover with rather a thick crust, and set in a moderate oven. Bake two hours.

Beefsteak and Oyster Pie.

Prepare the steaks as above, without rolling; and put layers of them and of oysters. Stew the liquor and beards of the oysters with a bit of lemon peel, mace and a sprig of parsley. When the pie is baked, boil with the above three spoonfuls of cream, and an ounce of butter rubbed in flour. Strain it, and put into the dish. Bake two hours.

Veal Pie.

Take some of the middle or scrag of a small neck; season it, and either put to it, or not, a few slices of lean bacon or ham. If it is wanted of a high relish, add mace, cayenne and nutmeg to the salt and pepper, and also force-meat and eggs; and, if you choose, mushrooms and sweet-breads cut into small bits. Have a rich gravy ready to pour in after baking. It will be very good without any of the latter additions. Bake two hours.

COLD VEAL OR CHICKEN PIE.

Lay a crust into a shallow tart-dish and fill it with the following mixture: Shred cold veal or fowl, and half the quantity of ham, mostly lean; put to it a little cream; season it with white pepper, salt, a grate or two of nutmeg, and a bit of garlic or shallot, minced as fine as possible. Cover with crust, and turn it out of the dish when baked; or bake the crust with a piece of bread to keep it hollow, and warm the mince with a little cream, and pour in.

PUDDINGS.

The outside of a boiled pudding often tastes disagreeable, which comes by the cloth not being nicely washed, and kept in a dry place. It should be dipped in boiling water, squeezed dry, and floured when to be used. If bread it should be tied loose, if batter, tight over. The water should boil quick when the pudding is put in, and it should be moved about for a minute, lest the ingredients should not mix. A pan of cold water should be ready, and the pudding dipped in as soon as it comes out of the pot, and then it will not adhere to the cloth. Very good puddings may be made without eggs, but they must have as little milk as will mix, and must boil three or four hours. Batter pudding should be strained through a coarse sieve when all is mixed. In others, the eggs separately. The pans and basins must be always buttered for a baked pudding. A few spoonfuls of fresh small beer, or one of yeast, will answer instead of eggs. Snow is an excellent substitute for eggs, either in puddings or pancakes. Two large spoonfuls will supply the place of eggs.

Green Corn Pudding.

Take a dozen ears and grate them; add a teacupful of milk, a spoonful of butter, a teaspoonful of salt, and some grated nutmeg; mix well together; put in a pan, place in a hot oven, and bake for an hour.

COCOANUT PUDDING.

Remove the shell and the brown skin from the meat; grate fine and mix with it three ounces of white sugar and half the grated peel of a lemon; add milk for two pies, put it into tins lined with paste, and bake it not too brown.

COCOANUT BREAD PUDDING.

Soak one-half cup of dessicated cocoanut in boiling hot milk for half an hour or more; then add it to usual bread-pudding preparation (the quantity of the bread being about three times as much as the cocoanut). Enrich and flavor to suit. This you will find to be a very pleasant and economical dessert.

BAKED SPONGE PUDDING.

Three eggs, their weight each in butter, sugar and flour; beat the eggs very light, add the butter beaten to a cream, sugar and flour; this will make four large cups; fill them half full, and bake in a moderate oven ten minutes. Serve with sauce.

OLD FASHIONED INDIAN PUDDING.

One quart of milk, with three handfuls of Indian meal stirred in while the milk is hot; let it cool, and add one egg; molasses to sweeten; butter half the size of an egg; cinnamon and salt to your taste. Bake three-quarters of an hour.

FLOUR SUET PUDDING.

Three cups of flour, one cup of suet, one cup of molasses, one cup of milk, one cup of fruit, one-half teaspoonful of soda, one teaspoonful of cinnamon, allspice and cloves. Steam three hours. Serve with sauce.

SUET PUDDING—No. 1.

Quarter of a pound of suet, quarter of a pound of raisins, stoned, quarter of a pound of currants, two tablespoonfuls of molasses, one pint of milk, two teaspoonfuls of baking powder, and flour to thicken. Steam three or four hours.

SUET PUDDING—No. 2.

A cup of suet chopped fine, three cups of flour; mix flour and suet well together; add one cup of molasses, one cup of milk, a cup of raisins, a cup of currants, half a teaspoonful of soda, one teaspoonful of cream of tartar; it should be well spiced. Put into a pudding boiler, allowing plenty of room to rise; boil three hours. Serve with wine sauce.

SUET PUDDING—No. 3.

One cup of flour, one cup of milk, one egg, one ounce of suet; mix well, and add dried fruit in any quantity you wish; boil two hours. Eat with liquid sauce. *Sauce*—White of one egg; thicken with sugar and a little butter, beaten to a froth; add a cup of boiling water, stirring all the time; wine, or flavoring to taste.

BLUE BERRY PUDDING.

One teacupful of sugar, one teacupful of sweet milk, two teacupfuls of flour, one tablespoonful of butter, one tablespoonful of baking powder, one egg, two cups of blue berries. Bake in a moderately warm oven, and serve with the following sauce: One good cupful of sugar, half a cup of butter, one heaping teaspoonful of corn starch beaten until white; add one cup of boiling water; let it boil up, and add one cup of wine.

Orange Pudding.

Pare six nice oranges and cut in small pieces into a deep dish with their juice, sprinkling sugar over them. Then take one pint of sweet milk, one tablespoonful of corn starch, the yolks of two eggs, three tablespoonfuls of sugar and thicken the milk, boiling it well and pour over the oranges. When cool, beat to a stiff froth the whites of two eggs, and frost it and brown in the oven.

Batter Pudding.

One pint of milk, four eggs, the yolks and whites beaten separately; ten tablespoonfuls of sifted flour and a little salt; beat in the whites of the eggs the last thing before baking. Bake half an hour.

Poverty Pudding.

One cup of molasses, half cup of milk, half cup of shortening, three cups of flour, one teaspoonful of allspice, one cup of raisins, half teaspoonful of soda, one teaspoonful of cream of tartar. Steam three hours.

Apple Snow.

Take a pint of stewed and sifted apples, whites of two eggs beaten to a stiff froth, and beat the whole well together. Sweeten to taste.

Baked Indian Pudding.

One quart of milk, one teacup of Indian meal, one egg, a pinch of salt; sweeten to taste with white sugar; take part of the milk and cook, with the meal; when done add balance of milk and then the egg, a piece of butter the size of a walnut. Bake three-quarters of an hour.

A Swiss Pudding.

Put layers of crumbs of bread and sliced apples, with sugar between, till the dish be as full as it will hold; let the crumbs be the uppermost layer. Then pour melted butter over it and bake.

Arrow-root Pudding.

Mix a dessert-spoonful of the powder in two of cold milk. Pour upon it a pint of boiling milk, in which have been dissolved, four ounces of butter and two of sugar, stirring all the time. Add a little nutmeg and five eggs. Bake half an hour in a dish lined with paste, then turn it out. Preserved fruits of any kind, laid at the bottom, eat well. If you wish it to look clear, substitute water for milk.

Corn Meal Pudding.

Boil one quart of milk, set it off the stove, and stir in one cup of Indian meal, one cup of molasses and sugar (half of each), one egg and a little salt. Bake one hour.

Fig Pudding—No. 1.

One cup of molasses, one cup of chopped suet, one cup of milk, three and a quarter cups of flour, two eggs, one teaspoonful of soda, one teaspoonful of cinnamon, half a teaspoonful of nutmeg, one pint of figs. Mix together the molasses, suet, spice and the figs cut fine. Dissolve the soda with a tablespoonful of hot water and mix with the milk; add to other ingredients. Beat the eggs light and stir into the mixture. Add the flour and beat thoroughly. Butter two small or one large mould. Turn the mixture into the mould or moulds and steam five hours. Serve with cream or wine sauce. Date pudding is made in the same way, using a pint of dates instead of the figs.

Fig Pudding—No. 2.

One-half pound of figs, one quarter of a pound of suet, one egg, one cup of flour. Chop the figs and suet together, add the flour and one cup of bread crumbs; sugar to taste, and milk to make a batter. Put in a cloth and boil three hours. Serve with sauce.

Cottage Pudding.

One cup of sugar, one cup of milk, half cup of melted butter, one egg, two small teaspoonfuls of cream of tartar, one teaspoonful of soda, one pint of sifted flour. Bake three quarters of an hour. Serve with sauce.

Snow Pudding.

Soak half a box of gelatine in half a pint of cold water for half an hour, then add half a pint of boiling water, juice of one lemon, and two cups of sugar; strain and let cool; when nearly cold add the whites of three eggs beaten to a stiff froth, then beat all well again. Put into a dish and let it cool on the ice. *Sauce*—Make a thin boiled custard of the yolks when the sauce is served. Put it around the sides of the dish after the pudding is dished.

Strawberry Pudding.

One quart of milk, four eggs (the yolks only); boil with corn starch enough to make it of the consistency of boiled custard. One quart of ripe strawberries, one coffee-cup of white sugar; put these in the bottom of a good-sized pudding dish. When the custard is cold pour it over the berries. Beat the whites of the eggs to a stiff froth, and add two heaping tablespoonfuls of pulverized sugar; pour this on top of the custard and set in the oven a few minutes to brown.

Delmonico Pudding.

One quart of sweet milk, boiled; five eggs, the yolks beaten with five tablespoonfuls of sugar and three tablespoonfuls of corn starch; mix with enough cold milk to make it free from lumps, then stir it into the boiled milk until it thickens and pour into a dish; cover with the whites of five eggs beaten to a stiff froth and sweetened. Brown slightly, and flavor with vanilla.

Plum Pudding.

The same proportions of flour and suet, and half the quantity of fruit, with spice, lemon, a glass of wine, or not, and one egg, and milk, will make an excellent pudding if long boiled.

English Plum Pudding.

One pound of beef suet, cut fine; one pound of raisins, stoned; one-half pound of currants and six eggs, well beaten; one gill of cream, one teacupful of bread crumbs, eight tablespoonfuls of flour, two tablespoonfuls of brandy, one teacupful of sugar, one-half teacupful of molasses, grated citron, lemon peel, and such spices as you choose, to taste. Boil not less than five hours.

English Christmas Plum Pudding.

One pound of raisins, one pound of currants, one pound of suet, one pound of flour, six eggs, half a pound of brown sugar, one nutmeg, one pint of milk, one teaspoonful of salt; mix these ingredients thoroughly; place them in a strong pudding-cloth, which has been wet and covered with flour; tie up the cloth, not leaving much room for the pudding to swell. Serve with rich sauce after boiling five hours.

Saratoga Plum Pudding.

In a large bowl or tray put eight eggs beaten separately, one pint of sugar, one grated nutmeg, one quart of milk; stir in one quart of seeded raisins, one pint of currants, half a pint of citron cut up (the fruit well floured), a heaping quart of stale bread crumbs, and a quart of nicely-chopped beef suet; add enough flour to make the fruit stick well together; dip a pudding bag in boiling hot water, dredge on inside a thick coating of flour, put in the pudding and tie tightly, allowing room to swell, and boil from two to three hours in a good-sized pot, filling as the water wastes with boiling water. Put an earthen plate in the bottom of the pot for the pudding to rest on. This will prevent any possible sticking to the kettle. Serve on a large flat dish with sauce made thus: Cream half a pound of sweet butter, stir in three-fourths of a pound of brown sugar, and the beaten yolk of an egg; simmer a few moments on a slow fire, stirring constantly; when near boiling add half a pint of bottled grape juice; grate nutmeg over the top and serve. This recipe furnishes enough for twenty people. It is good when warmed over by steaming.

President's Pudding.

Two thirds of a cup of sugar, two tablespoonfuls of butter, yolks of four eggs, well beaten; crumb fine, half a loaf of bakers' bread, add the rind and juice of one large lemon and one teaspoonful of vanilla; mix all together, then put half in the bottom of a pudding dish, spread on this a very little of preserves or fresh fruit, then put in the remainder of the mixture. Bake half an hour. Whip the whites of four eggs, half a cup of fine sugar and a teaspoonful of vanilla pour over and brown.

CRUMB PUDDING.

Half a pint of bread crumbs, three pints of milk, the yolks of four eggs, one and one-half cups of sugar; flavor with lemon. *Frosting*—Whites of four eggs, four tablespoonfuls of sugar, flavor with vanilla. Pour over the pudding when done, and place in an oven to brown.

TROY PUDDING.

One cup of beef suet (chopped very fine), one cup of molasses, one cup of sweet milk, one cup of stoned raisins, three cups of flour, one teaspoonful of soda, one teaspoonful of salt. Steam three hours. *Sauce*— One cup of sugar, one tablespoonful of butter beaten to a cream, and one teacup of boiling water. Let it stand in boiling water ten minutes.

BAKED DUMPLINGS.

These differ from boiled ones in the formation of the pastry. In baked puddings or dumplings use butter, or part butter and part lard for the crust; in boiled puddings—apple or plum—suet is substituted, because they are lighter made this way.

BIRDS' NEST PUDDING.

Pare six or eight large apples (spitzenbergs or greenings are best), and remove the core by cutting from the end down into the middle, so as to leave the apple whole except where the core has been removed; place them as near together as they can stand, with the open part upward in a deep pie-dish; next make a thin batter, using one quart of sweet milk, three eggs, with sufficient flour, and pour it into the dish around the apples, also filling the cavities in them. Bake in a quick oven. Eat them with butter and sugar.

Plain Fruit Pudding.

Take one and a half cups of flour, one cup of bread crumbs, one cup of raisins, half a cup of currants, two nutmegs, one cup of suet chopped fine, two tablespoonfuls of sugar, four eggs, a wine glass of brandy, a wine glass of syrup, and a little milk if necessary. Mix very thoroughly; tie it in a cloth as tight as possible, and boil fast for five or six hours. Serve with wine sauce.

Tapioca Pudding—No. 1.

Put a teacupful of tapioca and a teaspoonful of salt into a pint and a half of water and let it stand a couple of hours, where it will be quite warm and not cook. Peel six tart apples, take out the cores and fill them with sugar, in which is grated a little nutmeg and lemon peel, and put them in a pudding dish. Over these pour the tapioca, first mixing with it a tablespoonful of melted butter and a little cold milk. Bake one hour. Eat with sauce.

Tapioca Pudding—No. 2.

Put three tablespoonfuls of tapioca to soak over night in lukewarm water; in the morning pour on this one quart of milk, and set it on the stove till it comes to a boil, add a pinch of salt and four or five tablespoonfuls of white sugar, the yolks of three eggs, which, when you pour in, cools it; let it come to a boil again, or until it thickens, stirring all the time, then pour it in your pudding dish; then beat the whites of the three eggs to a froth, add four tablespoonfuls of powdered sugar, and spread over the top; put it in the oven and bake a light brown.

Tapioca Pudding—No. 3.

Six teaspoonfuls of tapioca, soaked two hours in one pint of water; then put it into a buttered pudding dish, and a custard made of one quart of milk, three eggs, one cup of sugar, well beaten and poured over the tapioca; add one-half of a cup of raisins, one teaspoonful of cinnamon, and one of extract of lemon. Bake one hour.

Little Bread Puddings.

One pint of bread crumbs, and one pint of milk; let the crumbs soak till soft. Beat two eggs and add two spoonfuls of sugar and a little melted butter; flavor with lemon; add a few currants well floured; pour the mixture into buttered round tins; grate a little nutmeg over each, and bake twenty minutes. Eat with warm sauce.

Apples, a la Cremone.

Choose such apples as will look clear when dressed; pare, and cut into pieces a sufficient quantity to weigh a pound and a half; strew over them a pound of good sugar, and several long strips of lemon peel, and cover them close in a bowl. Next day put the apples, piece by piece, into a small preserving-pan, with the sugar, etc., and two large spoonfuls of strong cider. Simmer gently, and as the pieces of apple become clear, take them out. When cold, build a wall with them on a small oval dish, and place the lemon-peel on the top. Pour the syrup into the middle. Serve cream to eat with it. The peel of an orange, cut very thin, does as well as lemon.

Batter Pudding.

One quart of milk, fourteen tablespoonfuls of flour, six eggs; mix the flour and milk together, let it be well beaten, and then add the eggs after they are whipped to a froth. Boil it two hours, and eat with a rich sauce.

Apple Pudding.

Pare and chop fine some of the best cooking apples; butter a pudding dish, cover the bottom and sides half an inch thick with grated bread and small lumps of butter, then add a layer of apple, with sugar and grated nutmeg sprinkled over, another layer of crumbs and butter, then a layer of apples, until the dish is filled, and pour over the whole a cup of milk, and bake it. Eaten with sauce.

Baked Apple Pudding.

Six apples well stewed, quarter of a pound of butter, half of it stirred into the apple while hot, and sugar to your taste. When cold add six eggs, well beaten, to the apple. Pound and sift six crackers, butter your dish, and put in a layer of cracker, and a layer of your prepared apple, and thus until you have filled your dish; let the cracker be the upper layer, and put the remainder of your butter in small bits upon it. Bake in two shallow dishes for half an hour.

Baked Vermicelli Pudding.

Simmer four ounces of vermicelli in a pint of new milk ten minutes; then put to it half a pint of cream, a teaspoonful of ground cinnamon, four ounces of butter, warmed, the same of white sugar, and the yolks of four eggs well beaten. Bake in a dish without a lining.

Delicate Pudding.

One quart of milk; while boiling, stir in one pint of flour after it is sifted, six eggs, six tablespoonfuls of white sugar, one spoonful of butter, grated peel and juice of two lemons. All the ingredients must be well beaten together before they are stirred into the milk; stir one way, without stopping, till it has boiled for a minute or two; take it off and turn into your pudding dish. It is to be eaten cold, with sugar and cream if you like.

Poverty Pudding.

Soak your bread in milk the night before using; when ready, butter your pudding dish, and place in a layer of the bread. Have a dozen apples pared and sliced, and place a layer of apples on the bread, another layer of bread, then of apples, and so on, till your dish is filled; let the last layer be bread, and bake it an hour. To be eaten with sauce.

Macaroni Pudding.

Simmer an ounce or two of the pipe sort in a pint of milk, and a bit of lemon and cinnamon, till tender; put it into a dish, with milk, two or three eggs, but only one white, sugar, nutmeg, a spoonful of peach-water, and half a glass of raisin wine. Bake with a paste round the edges. A layer of orange marmalade or raspberry jam, in a macaroni pudding, for change, is a great improvement, in which case omit the almond water, or ratafia, which you would otherwise flavor it with.

Brown Bread Pudding.

Half a pound of stale brown bread grated, same of currants, same of shred suet; sugar and nutmeg;

mix with four eggs, a spoonful of brandy, and two spoonfuls of cream. Boil in a cloth or basin that exactly holds it, three or four hours. Serve with sweet sauce.

Quaking Pudding.

Scald a quart of cream. When almost cold, put to it four eggs well beaten, a spoonful and a half of flour, some nutmeg and sugar. Tie it close in a buttered cloth, boil it an hour, and turn it out with care, lest it should crack. Melted butter, a little wine, and sugar.

Rice Pudding with Fruit.

Swell the rice with a very little milk over the fire; then mix fruit of any kind with it (currants, gooseberries scalded, pared and quartered apples, raisins, or black currants), with one egg into the rice to bind it; boil it well, and serve with sugar.

Frosted Rice Pudding.

One quart of milk, one-half cup of rice. Boil the rice in the milk until thoroughly cooked, the yolks of four eggs, beaten and put in when the rice is done. Beat up with eggs, sugar and a little salt, sufficient to season nicely. Pour into a buttered dish, beat the whites of the eggs with four tablespoonfuls of powdered sugar, flavor with lemon spread on the top, and put in the oven until a light brown.

Porcupine Pudding.

Boil half a pint of rice in new milk until perfectly tender, and not too dry; then add six eggs beaten, a spoonful of ratafia, as much sugar as shall be sufficient, and some grated fresh lemon; mix well, and boil in a mould one hour and a half. Turn it on a hot dish, and stick it thick with almonds cut in sixths. Serve with a rich custard around it. It is equally good cold.

Rice Meringue.

Simmer for several hours on the back of the stove one cupful of rice in one quart of milk; do not let it boil. When quite soft, add the yolks of four eggs and half a cup of sugar. Boil up once and remove from the fire When cold, add the juice and grated rind of one lemon. Pour into a dish and cover with a meringue made of the whites of the eggs beaten with four tablespoonfuls of sugar. Set in the oven for a few minutes to harden, and serve cold.

Rice Pudding without Eggs.

Two quarts of milk, half a teacup of rice, a little less than a teacup of sugar, the same quantity of raisins, and a teaspoonful of cinnamon. Wash the rice and put it with the rest of the ingredients into the milk; bake rather slowly from two to three hours; stir two or three times the first hour of baking. If properly done this pudding is delicious.

Royal Pudding.

Three-quarters of a cup of sago, washed and put into one quart of milk; put it into a saucepan, and stand in boiling water on the range until the sago has well swelled. While hot put in two tablespoonfuls of butter with one cup of white sugar. When cool add the well-beaten yolks of four eggs, put in a pudding dish, and bake from half to three-quarters of an hour, then remove it from the oven and place it to cool. Beat the whites of the eggs with two tablespoonfuls of powdered loaf sugar, till they are a mass of froth; spread your pudding with either raspberry or strawberry jam, and then put on the frosting; put in the oven for two minutes to slightly brown. If made in summer, be sure and keep the whites of the eggs on ice till you are ready to use them, and beat them in the coldest place you can find, as it will make a much richer frosting.

Boiled Custard Pudding

Eight eggs to one quart of milk, five spoonfuls of flour; boil three-quarters of an hour. To be served as soon as done, and with sauce.

Maizena Pudding.

Four tablespoonfuls of maizena, stirred into two eggs, and milk enough to make it smooth. Set a quart of milk to boil, and just before it boils stir in the above, constantly stirring the same way till it thickens; remove from the fire and flavor. To be cold, and eaten with milk, cream and sugar. It is very nice to admit the eggs, and take six tablespoonfuls of maizena to a quart of milk (stirring the same way), and eaten warm with wine sauce.

Dorchester Corn Pudding.

Twelve ears of sweet corn grated to one quart of sweet milk; add a quarter of a pound of good butter, quarter of a pound of sugar and four eggs; bake it from three to four hours.

Cabinet Pudding.

Dissolve one-half box of gelatine in enough water to cover. When dissolved, make a custard of three pints of milk and cream, mixed. Beat six eggs very smooth, one teaspoonful of corn starch and two cups of sugar into the cream, before adding to the boiling milk. Take a mould holding two quarts and arrange in layers, half a pound of lady fingers, half a pound of macaroons, half a pound of sliced citron, moistened with wine or milk. Stir the dissolved gelatine and custard together, fill the mould with it, pack in ice and salt and let it freeze. To be eaten with wine sauce.

Marblehead Apple Pudding.

Eight tablespoonfuls of apple, after it is stewed and strained through a sieve, five eggs, half a pound of sugar, half a pound of butter (cream the butter and sugar together and add the eggs), the peel of an orange or lemon grated, with the juice and one nutmeg. To be baked in a dish lined with paste.

Pea Pudding for Corned Beef or Pork.

Pick and wash a pint of split peas, and put them in a bag, not tied too closely, and let them cook until quite tender; take them out and sift through a sieve; mix with an egg, a bit of pepper, and a little butter; stir well together; flour the bag, put in the mixture, and tie very close; then put in the pudding with your meat one hour before the meat is served.

Norfolk Dumplings.

With a pint of milk, two well-beaten eggs, and a little salt, mix as much flour as will make a thick batter. Drop a spoonful at a time into a stew-pan of boiling water. Three minutes will do them. Take them up in a sieve to drain, and serve quickly with cold butter. The water must not cease boiling while they are cooking.

Light or German Puddings or Puffs.

Melt three ounces of butter in a pint of cream and let it stand till nearly cold; then mix two ounces of fine flour, and two ounces of sugar, four yolks and two whites of eggs, and a little rose or orange-flower water. Bake in little cups, buttered, half an hour. They should be served the moment they are done, and only when going to be eaten, or they will not be light. Turn out of the cups, and serve with white wine and sugar.

Yorkshire Pudding.

Mix five spoonfuls of flour with a quart of milk, and three eggs well beaten. Butter the pan. When brown by baking under the meat, turn the other side upwards, and brown that. It should be made in a square pan, and cut into pieces to come to the table. Set it over a chafing dish at first, and stir it some minutes.

Green-bean Pudding.

Boil and blanch old beans, chop them fine, with very little pepper and salt, some cream, and the yolk of an egg. A little spinach juice will give a finer color, but it is as good without. Boil it in a basin that will just hold it, an hour, and pour parsley and butter over.

Almond Pudding.

Beat half a pound of sweet and a few bitter almonds with a spoonful of water; then mix four ounces of butter, four eggs, two spoonfuls of cream, warm with the butter, one of brandy, a little nutmeg, and sugar to taste. Butter some cups, half fill, and bake the puddings. Serve with pudding-sauce.

Orange Pudding.

Grate the rind of a nice orange, put to it six ounces of fresh butter, six or eight ounces of lump sugar pounded, mix them all in a bowl, and add as you do it the whole of eight eggs well beaten and strained; scrape a raw apple, and mix with the rest; put a paste at the bottom and sides of the dish, and over the orange mixture put cross bars of paste. Half an hour will bake it.

Steak or Kidney Pudding.

If kidney, split and soak it, and season that or the meat. Make a paste of suet, flour and milk; roll and line a basin with it, put the kidney or steaks in, cover with paste, and pinch round the edge. Cover with a cloth and boil three hours.

Beefsteak Pudding.

Prepare some fine steaks, roll them with fat between, and if you like add a little shredded onion. Lay a paste of suet in a basin, and put in the rolls of steaks; cover the basin with a paste, and pinch the edges to keep the gravy in. Cover with a cloth tied close, and let the pudding boil slowly three hours.

Baked Beefsteak Pudding.

Make a batter of milk, two eggs and flour, or, which is much better, potatoes boiled or mashed through a colander; lay a little of it at the bottom of the dish; then put in the steaks, prepared as above, and very well seasoned; pour the remainder of the batter over them and bake it.

Mutton Pudding.

Season with salt, pepper, and a bit of onion; lay one layer of the steaks at the bottom of the dish, and pour a batter of potatoes, boiled and pressed through a colander and mixed with milk, and an egg over them; then putting in the rest of the steaks and batter, bake it.

A Pretty Supper Dish.

Having first washed a teacupful of rice, boil it in milk till tender; strain off the milk, lay the rice in little heaps on a dish, strew over them some finely-powdered sugar and cinnamon, and put warm wine and a little butter into the dish.

What to do with Stale Bread.

Stale bread may be made into very palatable dishes in several ways. 1. Cut into pieces of the same size or shape; soak them in milk prepared as for custard with eggs, sugar and spice; fry in butter or lard a delicate brown. Serve with any kind of sweet sauce. 2. Cut in slices, toast nicely; dip into hot salted water; butter liberally; lay the slices one on another in a deep dish; cover closely and set for a few minutes in a hot oven; serve. This makes a very appetizing dish. 3. Slice, and dip in a mixture made by stirring an egg or two well beaten into milk; fry in butter and serve when hot; this makes what is sometimes called French toast. 4. Put slices of stale bread into a flat pan and dry slowly in the oven till very crisp. Crumble them into milk and serve as bread and milk. Or roll them fine and use as cracker crumbs. Stale bread is a very pleasant addition to almost all kinds of hash. Everybody knows how to make bread puddings with eggs and milk. With the suggestions above the young housekeeper will never need to waste a crumb.

ADDITIONAL RECIPES.

ADDITIONAL RECIPES.

SAUCES FOR PUDDINGS.

WINE SAUCE—NO. 1.

A teacupful of sugar, with butter the size of an egg worked into it; add half a teacupful of boiling water, and set it over a kettle of boiling water ten minutes; just before going to the table, add a wine-glass of wine and the whites of two eggs whipped to a froth; nutmeg or other flavoring may be used instead of the wine, if preferred.

WINE SAUCE—NO. 2.

Two teacups of sugar, one teacup of butter, stir to a cream; beat two eggs very light and stir all together; add one teacup of wine; mix and set on top of a tea-kettle of boiling water. It must not be put on the stove nor boil.

WINE SAUCE—NO. 3.

One pint bowl of white sugar, not quite a quarter of a pound of butter, one glass of wine, one grated nutmeg, and a tablespoonful of warm water; beat together steadily for half an hour. Set a saucepan on the fire, with about a gill of water in it; when it boils put in the sugar, etc., but do not stir it nor let it boil, but simmer gently till all is dissolved; pour into the tureen, and do not cover till cold.

Hard Sauce—No. 1.

Take half as much butter as sugar, and mix, and heat it fifteen minutes in a bowl set in hot water, stirring until it foams. Flavor with wine or grated lemon peel

Hard Sauce—No. 2.

Two tablespoonfuls of butter, ten tablespoonfuls of sugar; work this until white, then add wine or grated lemon peel, and spice to your taste.

Pudding Sauce.

One cup of sugar, a little less than half the quantity of butter, add a wine-glass of sherry wine, flavor with nutmeg, and stir in boiling milk until it is of the consistency of cream. Send to the table, and stir well when served.

Sweet Sauce.

Stir to a cream, one cup of butter with two of sugar; pour into the butter and sugar a teacup of boiling water, beat an egg light, and mix it gradually with the other ingredients before they become hot; mix half a teaspoonful of flour in a little cold water, free from lumps, stir it into the sauce and beat the whole constantly until hot enough to thicken; add nutmeg. This is proper for all boiled puddings, especially berry, and also baked berry puddings.

Cranberry Sauce.

A quart of cranberries, a large pint of sugar, and half a pint of water. Boil slowly, and beat the cranberries to a jelly. When thoroughly bruised put in your moulds.

Creamy Sauce.

One-half cup of butter, one cup of powdered sugar, four tablespoonfuls of cream or milk, four tablespoonfuls of wine, or in place of wine, one teaspoonful of vanilla and three additional teaspoonfuls of milk or cream; beat the butter to a cream, add sugar gradually, then wine gradually and milk gradually. Place the bowl in which the sauce has been made in a basin of boiling water; stir a few minutes until it looks smooth, and it is ready to serve.

Maple Sugar Sauce.

Melt over a slow fire, in a small teacup of water, half a pint of maple sugar; let it simmer, removing all scum; add four tablespoonfuls of butter mixed with a level teaspoonful of flour and one of grated nutmeg; boil for a few moments, and serve with boiled pudding.

Sweet Sauces for Puddings.

For fritters, rub butter and sugar together; serve on little plates. For boiled puddings, English plum puddings and baked puddings, put in a tin sauce pan or tosser, one pint of milk, and let it come to a boil. Take butter the size of an egg, rub into it all the flour it will take, pour on it some cold milk to thin it a little, and put it to the hot milk; sweeten, nutmeg and cinnamon to taste. After you take it from the fire, add brandy or wine. Another way is to take sweet cream sweetened and flavored.

DISHES FOR DESSERT.

Charlotte Russe—No. 1.

Pour one cup of cold water over half a box of gelatine. When it is dissolved add a cup of boiling milk and let it cool. Add to a quart of sweet cream sifted sugar and vanilla to taste. When the gelatine is beginning to harden whip the cream to a froth and add the gelatine gradually, continuing the whipping for some time. Line a glass dish or mould with slices of home-made sponge cake, and pour the mixture into it, and let it stand in a cold place until it is thoroughly congealed. This recipe, it will be observed, does not call for any eggs.

Charlotte Russe—No. 2.

One pint of cream, half a box of gelatine; whip the whites of three eggs with eight teaspoonfuls of white sugar; two teaspoonfuls of vanilla in gelatine.

Charlotte Russe—No. 3.

One quart of cream, four eggs, half a pound of sugar, one ounce of isinglass or gelatine, half a pint of milk. Dissolve one-half box of gelatine in the milk on the back of the stove, beat eggs and sugar together till rising very light; whip the cream and skim off. till all is whipped up, then strain the dissolved gelatine into the eggs, stir this till it begins to thicken, then pour into the whipped cream. Do not beat it but stir it in thoroughly; flavor with vanilla to taste, then pour in the moulds lined with cake.

CHARLOTTE RUSSE—NO. 4.

The sponge cake may be made with four eggs, one cupful of sugar, one and one-half cupfuls of flour, and two even teaspoonfuls of yeast powder. Spread it as evenly as possible on a large sheet of foolscap paper, and bake. When baked cut a piece to fit the bottom of the charlotte pan, then even-sized parallelograms to fit around the sides. Fill with cream made as follows: Whip one pint of cream flavored with vanilla to a stiff froth, and add to it the well-beaten whites of two eggs, and one-half pound of pulverized sugar; mix it all lightly and carefully together. Fill the charlotte pan, or pans, and put them into the ice-chest to set. Cream is much more easily frothed when placed on ice and thoroughly chilled before whipping; when whipping it, place the froth on a sieve, and all that drops through can be returned to the bowl and rewhipped. Many take the trouble to add gelatine, which is unnecessary.

RUSSIAN CHARLOTTE.

Trim about six ounces of lady fingers perfectly straight, so as to make them fit closely to one another, and line the bottom and sides of a plain mould with these; then fill the interior of the charlotte with a Bavarian, coffee, chocolate, pistachio, Italian or any similar cream. The same kinds of fruit as are used for making a Macedoine jelly may be introduced in the cream.

Apple Charlotte.

To prepare this dessert to perfection it is necessary that a crumb-loaf of close-made bread should be made two days previous for the purpose; this, it must be owned, is not positively necessary; therefore, in its stead, a stale quartern loaf may answer the purpose well enough. First of all some apple marmalade must be prepared as follows: Let two or three dozen apples be peeled, cored, sliced up and placed in a stew-pan with one pound of sugar, two ounces of butter, and some lemon peel and cinnamon tied together, moisten with half a pint of water, place the lid on a stew-pan, and then set the apples to boil sharp on a quick stove until they are melted. You then remove the lid, and with a wooden spoon continue stirring the marmalade over a brisk fire until it is reduced to a rather stiff consistency.

A plain round charlotte-mould must now be lined at the bottom with small thin circular pieces of bread, dipped in clarified butter, and placed so as to overlap each other until the bottom of the mould is well covered. Next, cut some oblong-squares of thin bread, also dipped in clarified butter, and set these up the sides of the mould overlapping each other—in order that they may be thus enabled to hold firmly to the sides of the mould. Fill the cavity with the apple marmalade, cover in the top with a thin circular piece of bread dipped in butter, place the charlotte on a baking sheet, and bake it in a rather brisk oven, of a light color; and when done, turn it out on its dish, glaze it on the top with sifted sugar and a red hot salamander; pour some diluted apricot jam around the base, and serve.

Charlotte, a la Parisienne.

First, bake a thin sheet of sponge cake, and when this has become thoroughly cold, proceed to cut it out into twenty-four oblong squares, measuring four inches long, by an inch wide; also about twelve half-moon or crescent shapes, of an equal size, in order that these may closely fit it with each other, so as to effectually cover the bottom of a charlotte mould; a circular piece must also be prepared, with which to finish the centre. All these pieces must be glazed over with icing prepared of two colors in equal numbers; as, for instance, one-half being pink, amber, green or chocolate; while the other half is to be white. With the foregoing, line the mould, and then fill the centre with any kind of Bavarian cream.

Floating Island.

Take one quart of milk and heat it nearly boiling hot; then put the whites of four eggs beaten to a stiff froth on the hot milk for a few moments to cook; then with a skimmer remove the froth from the milk; then beat the yolks of the eggs with one cup of sugar and a pinch of salt, and stir in the milk until boiling, then cool, and flavor with vanilla; lastly, lay the white frosting (at first prepared) on top of the custard.

Tapioca Blanc-mange.

One-half pound of tapioca soaked for an hour in a pint of new milk, then boil until tender; sweeten and flavor to taste; put the mixture in a mould. Serve with cream, custard or preserves.

Blanc-mange—No. 1.

Boil two ounces of isinglass in a pint and a half of water half an hour, strain it to a pint and a half of cream, sweeten it and add some peach-water, or a few bitter almonds. Let it boil up once, and put it into any shaped moulds you desire. If not to be very stiff, a little isinglass will do. Observe to let it settle before you turn it into the forms, or the blacks will remain at the bottom of them, and be on the top when taken out of the moulds.

Blanc-mange—No. 2.

Parboil twelve ounces of Jordan and two ounces of bitter almonds in a quart of water for about two minutes; drain them on a sieve, remove the skins, and wash them in cold water; after they have been soaked in cold water for half an hour, pound them in a mortar with four ounces of sugar, until the whole presents the appearance of a soft paste. This must then be placed in a large basin with twelve ounces of loaf sugar, and mixed with rather more than a pint of pure water; cover the basin with a sheet of paper, twisted around the edges, and allow the preparation to stand in a cool place for about an hour in order to extract the flavor of the almonds more effectually. The milk should then be strained off the almonds through a napkin, with pressure, by wringing it at both ends. Add two ounces of clarified isinglass, or its equal of gelatine, to the milk of almonds; pour the blanc-mange into a mould imbedded in ice, and, when set quite firm, turn it out on its dish with caution, after having first dipped the mould in warm water.

Maraschino Bavarian Cream.

Whip a pint of double cream until it presents somewhat the appearance of snow, taking care not to overdo it, as it would then produce butter When the cream is whipped add one and one-half ounces of clarified isinglass, or its equal of gelatine, a gill and a half of maraschino, the juice of a lemon, and four ounces of granulated sugar; mix these well together and pour the cream into a mould, previously very slightly oiled inside with oil of sweet almonds; set the cream in ice, and when it has become firm, turn it out on its dish. The mould having been oiled, prevents the necessity of dipping this delicate cream in warm water, previously to turning it out.

This kind of cream may also be flavored with all kinds of liquors; also with the essence of orange, lemon, vanilla, roses, bitter almonds, chocolate, coffee, etc.

Strawberry Bavarian Cream.

Take the hulls from two quarts of fine strawberries, and bruise them in a basin with six ounces of pounded sugar; rub this through a sieve, and mix it with a pint of whipped cream, and one ounce and a half of clarified isinglass, or its equal of gelatine. Pour the cream into a mould, previously oiled with oil of sweet almonds, set it on ice, and, when it has become quite firm, turn it out on its dish.

Raspberries, blackberries and currants may be prepared for making Bavarian creams by following the above directions.

Apricot Bavarian Cream.

Split a dozen ripe apricots and remove the stones; place the pieces in a small stew-pan, with twelve ounces of sugar, and a gill of pure water, then stir them over the fire and let them boil until the fruit is entirely dissolved; this *puree* must then be rubbed through a clean fine sieve into a large basin, and mixed with a pint of whipped cream, and one ounce and a half of clarified isinglass, or its equal of gelatine. Pour the cream into an oiled mould, and set it in ice, in the usual way.

This cream may be made of peaches, pears and all kinds of plums, instead of apricots.

Coffee Cream—No. 1.

Roast eight ounces of Mocha coffee-berries, stirring it constantly, until it assumes a light brown color, then blow out the small burnt particles, and throw the roasted coffee into a stew-pan containing a pint of boiling milk or cream; put the lid on the stew-pan and set it aside to allow the infusion to draw out the flavor of the coffee. Next, strain this through a napkin into a stew-pan containing the yolks of eight eggs and twelve ounces of sugar; add a very small pinch of salt, and stir the cream over the fire until it begins to thicken, then quicken the motions of the spoon, and when the yolks of the egg are sufficiently set, strain the cream through a tammy or sieve into a large basin. Mix half a pint of whipped cream and one ounce and a half of clarified isinglass (or gelatine) in, with this, pour the whole into a mould which has been imbedded in ice. When the cream has become firm, dip the mould in warm water and turn out.

Coffee Cream—No. 2.

Boil a calf's foot in water till it wastes to a pint of jelly, clear of sediment and fat. Make a teacup of very strong coffee; clear it with a bit of isinglass to be perfectly bright; pour it to the jelly, and add a pint of very good cream, and as much fine sugar as is pleasant; boil up once and pour into the dish. It should jelly, but not be stiff. Observe that your coffee be fresh.

Chocolate Cream—No. 1.

Grate eight ounces of vanilla chocolate, or use bakers' chocolate and a little essence of vanilla, put this into a stew-pan with eight ounces of sugar, the beaten yolks of eight eggs and a pint of cream; stir the whole over a fire until the it begins to thicken, and the yolks of the eggs are sufficiently set without allowing them to curdle; strain through a tammy or fine sieve, into a basin; add half a pint of whipped cream and one ounce and a half of clarified isinglass. Mix the whole well together, and pour into a mould previously imbedded in rough ice to receive it.

Chocolate Cream—No. 2.

Scrape into one quart of thick cream one ounce of the best chocolate, and a quarter of a pound of sugar; boil and mill it. When quite smooth, take it off, and let it become cold; then add the whites of nine eggs. Whisk, and take up the froth on sieves, as others are done, and serve the froth in glasses, to rise above some of the cream.

Burnt Cream—No. 1.

Boil a pint of cream with a stick of cinnamon, and some lemon peel; take it off the fire, and pour it very slowly into the yolks of four eggs, stirring till half cold; sweeten and take out the spice, etc.; pour it into the dish; when cold, strew white pounded sugar over, and brown it with a salamander.

Burnt Cream—No. 2.

Put two ounces of pounded sugar into a stew-pan, with the grated rind of two lemons; stir these with a spoon over a slow fire, until the sugar begins to assume a light-brown color; then pour in a pint of cream, add to this eight ounces of sugar, the yolks of eight eggs and a little salt, and stir the whole over the fire until the eggs are set; then strain the cream through a tammy into a large basin, and mix in with it half a pint of whipped cream, and one ounce and a half of clarified isinglass. Pour the cream into a mould imbedded in broken ice.

Orange-flower Cream.

Put two ounces of candied orange-flowers into a stew-pan, with two ounces of pounded sugar; stir these over a slow fire until the sugar is nearly melted, and pour in a pint of cream, adding eight ounces of sugar, the yolks of eight eggs, a tablespoonful of orange-flower water, and a very little salt; stir this preparation over the fire to set the yolks of the eggs, and then strain the cream through a tammy into a basin; add half a pint of whipped cream and one ounce and a half of clarified isinglass to it; mix well together, and then pour the cream into a mould imbedded in broken ice.

Note—The flavoring of this kind of cream may be varied according to taste by substituting lemon, orange, vanilla, cinnamon and lemon, or any other kind of essence or liquor, for the foregoing.

Pistachio Cream.

Parboil eight ounces of pistachio kernels for two minutes in boiling water; then remove the skin, wash and wipe the kernels, and pound them in a mortar with six ounces of sugar and a dessert-spoonful of orange-flower water; rub the whole through a fine hair-sieve, and place it in a large basin. Add to the pounded pistachios a spoonful of the green extract of spinach, a pint of whipped cream, and one ounce and a half of clarified isinglass; mix well together; pour the cream into an oiled mould, and then set it in ice in the usual way.

Italian Cream—No. 1.

Put the yolks of eight eggs into a stew-pan with four ounces of ratafias, eight ounces of sugar, the grated rind of an orange, a small stick of cinnamon, a wine-glassful of curacoa, and a pint of cream; stir this over the fire in order to set the yolks of eggs in it, and then strain it through a tammy into a basin. Add thereto half a pint of whipped cream, and one ounce and a half of clarified isinglass, and after having well mixed the whole together, pour it into a mould ready imbedded in broken ice to receive it.

Italian Cream—No. 2.

Whip together a quart of very thick scalded cream, a quart of raw cream, the grated rind of four lemons, and the strained juice, with ten ounces of white-powdered sugar, one hour; then add half a pint of sweet wine, and continue to whip it until it becomes quite solid. Lay a piece of muslin in a sieve, and lade the cream upon it with a spoon. In twenty hours turn it carefully out, but mind that it does not break, and garnish it with a wreath of flowers.

Celestina Strawberry Cream.

Imbed a jelly-mould or plain charlotte-mould in some broken ice contained in an earthen dish; line the bottom and sides of the mould with picked strawberries, which must first be dipped in some perfectly-cold liquid jelly; then fill the interior of this kind of charlotte with some strawberry cream, prepared for the purpose.

Cream, à la Romaine.

Blanch four ounces of Jordan almonds with one ounce of bitter almonds, and when freed from their hulls, washed and wiped dry, let them be chopped rather fine. Next, place them in a sugar boiler and stir them over the fire with a spoon until they have acquired a very light-brown color; the almonds should now be thrown into a pint of milk that has been kept boiling for the purpose; to this add six ounces of sugar and the yolks of eight eggs, and stir the whole quickly over the fire until the yolks are set, when the cream must be immediately removed from the fire, and stirred for a few minutes longer, previously to its being rubbed through a tammy like a *puree*. The produce will present a light fawn-colored thick cream; this must be mixed first, with little better than an ounce of clarified isinglass, and then, three gills of whipped cream are to be lightly yet well incorporated. Pour the cream into a mould, and set it in ice as usual.

Cream, a la Chateaubriand.

Set a jelly-mould in ice, and then proceed to ornament the bottom and sides with blanched almonds that have been split and well soaked to whiten them, each being first dipped in some rather strong and colorless jelly, previously to its being stuck to the sides of the mould. When the mould is thus ornamented, pour some of the same jelly into it, and by gently and gradually moving the mould round (side-ways) in the ice, cause the jelly to form a thin coating over the almonds. When the latter part of the process is satisfactorily effected, proceed to effect another coating about the third of an inch thick, with some pistachio cream; and when this is firmly set, fill up the cavity with some cream *a la Romaine.*

Note—An infinite variety of creams may be thus produced by using two different preparations of different creams, such as currant and orange flower, apricot and vanilla, chocolate and white coffee, etc.

An Excellent Cream.

Whip up three-quarters of a pint of very rich cream to a strong froth, with some finely-scraped lemon peel, a squeeze of the juice, half a glass of sweet wine, and sugar to make it pleasant, but not too sweet. Lay it on a sieve or in a form, and next day put it on a dish, and ornament it with very light puff-paste biscuits, made in tin shapes the length of a finger, and about two thick, over which sugar may be strewed, or a little glaze with isinglass. Or you may use macaroons, to line the edges of the dish.

Rock Cream.

This will be found to be a very ornamental as well as a delicious dish for a supper table. Boil a teacupful of the best rice till quite soft in new milk, sweetened with powdered loaf sugar, and pile it upon a dish; lay on it, in different places, square lumps of either currant jelly or preserved fruit of any kind; beat up the whites of five eggs to a stiff froth, with a little powdered sugar, and flavor with either orange-flower water or vanilla. Add to this, when beaten very stiff, about a tablespoonful of rich cream, and drop it over the rice, giving it the form of a rock of snow.

Snow Cream.

Put to a quart of cream the whites of three eggs well beaten, four spoonfuls of sweet wine, sugar to your taste, and a bit of lemon peel; whip it to a froth, remove the peel, and serve in a dish.

Velvet Cream—No. 1.

Dissolve one paper of gelatine in a pint of cold milk fifteen minutes. Have ready one pint of boiling milk, pour it on the gelatine, strain it through a fine sieve, add one quart of cream well whipped, stir in ten ounces of sugar and flavor to taste with wine or vanilla. Pour into moulds.

Velvet Cream—No. 2.

Half an ounce of isinglass dissolved in one and a half cups of white wine; then add the juice and grated peel of a lemon, three-quarters of a pound of loaf sugar; simmer all together until mixed well; strain and add one and a half pints of rich cream, and stir until cool; pour it into moulds, and let it stand till stiff enough to turn out.

Spanish Cream.

One-half box of gelatine, soaked one hour in one-half pint of milk; beat the whites of six eggs to a stiff froth; put in a deep dish; put one quart of milk on to boil; beat the yolks of the eggs with sugar to taste.

and when the milk is just ready to boil stir in the yolks and gelatine; let it thicken as for soft custard. While boiling hot pour over the whites, stirring some; flavor with vanilla; put in mould and let it cool at least four hours.

Celestine Cream.

Imbed a plain mould in some rough ice. Line the bottom and sides of the mould with fresh-picked strawberries, taking care to put each in dissolved gelatine, in which there has been mixed some maraschino or other wine; when the interior of the mould is completely lined on the bottom and sides, fill the interior with cream.

Rice Cream.

To a pint of new milk add a quarter of a pound of ground rice, a lump of butter the size of a walnut, a little lemon peel and a tablespoonful of powdered sugar. Boil them together for five minutes, then add half an ounce of isinglass which has been dissolved, and let the mixture cool. When cool add half a pint of good cream whisked to a froth, mix all together, and set it for a time in a very cool place or on ice. When used, turn it out of the basin into a dish and pour fruit juice around it; or some stewed apple or pear may be served with it.

Gooseberry Cream.

Take a quart of gooseberries and boil them very quick in enough water to cover them; stir in half an ounce of good butter; when they become soft, press them through a sieve, sweeten the pulp while it is hot, and then beat it up with the yolks of four eggs. Serve in a dish or glass cup.

Everlasting or Solid Syllabubs.

Mix a quart of thick, raw cream, one pound of refined sugar, a pint and a half of fine raisin wine, in a deep pan; put to it the grated peel and the juice of three lemons. Beat or whisk it one way half an hour; then put it on a sieve, with a bit of thin muslin laid smooth in the shallow end till next day. Put it in glasses. It will keep good, in a cool place, ten days.

Croquante of Oranges.

Let the peel and all the white pith be carefully removed with the fingers from about a dozen sound,

and not over-ripe oranges; then divide them by pulling them into small sections with the fingers, taking care not to break the thin skin which envelopes the juicy pulp, then place them on an earthen dish.
Next, put about one pound of granulated sugar into a sugar boiler with sufficient pure water to just cover it, and boil it down until it snaps or becomes brittle, which may be easily ascertained by taking up a little of the sugar, when it begins to boil up in large purling bubbles, on the point of a knife, and instantly dip it into some cold water; if the sugar becomes set, it is sufficiently boiled, and will then easily snap in breaking. (When boiling sugar for this purpose, it is

customary to add a pinch of cream of tartar and powdered alum mixed, or a few drops of acetic acid.) The sugar should now be taken from the fire. The pieces of orange, stuck on the points of small wooden skewers, must be slightly dipped in the sugar, and arranged at the bottom and around the sides of a plain circular mould (previously very lightly rubbed with salad-oil), according to the foregoing design. When the whole is complete and the sugar has become firm by cooling, just before sending to the table, fill the inside of the croquante with whipped cream, seasoned with sugar, a glass of maraschino and some whole strawberries, and then turn it out on a napkin, and serve

Croquante of Fresh Walnuts.

The fittest season for making this, is when the walnuts are just ripe enough to be easily taken out of the shell; about sixty will be required for the purpose. They must be carefully shelled and divided into halves, then freed from the thin whitish skin which covers the kernels, and kept in a clean napkin until used. In all other respects, this kind of croquante must be finished as in the preceding case.

Croquante of Ratafias, a la Chantilly.

Procure one pound of small ratafias; boil down one pound of the finest loaf sugar as directed in the foregoing case. Then slightly rub the inside of a basket-shaped mould with oil, and proceed to line this with ratafias lightly dipped in the sugar—taking care to arrange them in neat and close order; when the croquante is completed and the sugar has become firmly set, turn it out of the mould. With the remainder of the sugar form the handles and a scroll-pattern border, which is to be placed round the join of the basket, and also round the edge; this is effected by dipping the pointed end of the bowl of a spoon into the hot sugar, and then drawing it out and dropping the sugar from the bowl, in the form of the intended design, on a baking sheet slightly oiled; before it becomes set, fix it round the part it is to ornament. Just before sending the croquante to table, fill the inside with whipped cream, arrange some strawberries, preserved cherries, or cut angelica, neatly on the surface and serve.

Orange Dessert.

Peel a dozen oranges and slice them thin, take a preserve dish and first put a layer of oranges then dessicated cocoanut and repeat alternately until the dish is filled. Set in a cool place until ready to serve.

Orange Jelly.

Procure five oranges and one lemon; take the rind off two of the oranges and half of the lemon, and remove the pith, put them in a basin, and squeeze the juice of the fruit into it; then put a quarter of a pound of sugar into a stew-pan, with half a pint of water, and set it to boil until it becomes a syrup, when take it off, and add the juice and rind of the fruits; cover the stew-pan, and place it again on the fire; as soon as boiling commences skim well, and add a gill of water by degrees, which will assist its clarification; let it boil another minute, when add an ounce and a half of isinglass, dissolved, pass it through a jelly-bag or fine sieve; then fill mould and place it on ice; turn out. This jelly does not require to look very clear.

POMEGRANATE JELLY.

Extract the bright pips from six ripe pomegranates, bruise these in a basin, with one pound of pounded sugar, add thereto a gill of pure water, and then filter the preparation through a beaver jelly bag, in order to preserve the delicate flavor of the fruit. The filtered juice of the pomegranates must then be mixed with two ounces of clarified isinglass or gelatine, six drops of cochineal, and, if necessary to make out the quantity of jelly required to fill the mould, some thin clarified syrup may be added. Set a jelly mould in a basin of rough ice, and fill the mould with alternate layers of jelly and the bright pips of this fruit.

PINE-APPLE JELLY.

Peel a pine-apple weighing about one pound, cut it into slices about a quarter of an inch thick, and put these into a basin. Clarify one pound of loaf sugar with a pint of water, the juice of two lemons, and half the white of an egg whipped with a little water; when thoroughly skimmed, strain the syrup on to the pine-apple, allow it to boil for three minutes, then cover it with a sheet of paper twisted round the basin, and allow the infusion to stand for several hours, in order to extract the flavor. When about to mix the jelly, strain the syrup through a napkin into a basin, and put the pieces of pine-apple to drain upon a sieve; add two ounces of clarified isinglass or gelatine to the pine-apple syrup, and then pour the jelly into a mould previously imbedded in ice.

STRAWBERRY JELLY.

Pick the hulls from four quarts of strawberries, put these into a basin, and then pour one pint of clarified boiling syrup and half a pint of red currant juice on them; cover them with a sheet of paper, tightly twisted round the edges of the basin, and allow the infusion to stand in a cool place until it becomes cold; then, filter it through a beaver jelly bag in the usual way, and when the whole has run through perfectly bright, mix it with two ounces of clarified isinglass, and set the jelly in a mould imbedded in ice. This jelly may be garnished with strawberries.

Macedoine of Fruits.

This may be made with any kind of jelly, which should be mixed with a variety of the most delicate fruits in season; these should be arranged with taste, so as to show their forms and colors to the best advantage. The fruits most appropriate for this purpose are peaches, nectarines, apricots, all kinds of plums, strawberries, raspberries, red, white and black currants, cherries, pears, oranges, pomegranates, grapes, etc.

Pistachio Jelly.

Prepare some jelly, with Dantzic brandy (sometimes named "gold and silver water"). Parboil and remove the skin from six ounces of pistachios, and shred each kernel into six strips. Set a jelly mould in some pounded ice contained in a pan, pour a little of the jelly into the bottom of the mould, and then strew some of the prepared pistachios in it; when this has become firm, pour in a little more of the jelly and strew a few of the pistachios in it; as these layers become set, repeat the same until the mould is filled, and allow the jelly to remain imbedded in the ice long enough to congeal it properly.

Variegated Jelly.

This may be prepared with any kind of light colored jelly, which must be divided into two equal parts;

add a few drops of cochineal to one-half, and leave remainder plain. Then imbed the mould in ice, pour the pink jelly into the mould to the depth of about a quarter of an inch, and when this has become set, pour as much of the plain jelly upon it; when this has congealed, repeat another layer of the pink jelly, and go on alternating the different colored layers of jelly until the mould is filled.

The design for this kind of jelly may be varied according to taste, by observing the following directions: Fill two small plain moulds with different colored jelly, such as pink and white noyeau, or amber and very light pink orange jelly, and when these have become firm, turn them out of their respective moulds upon a dish. Next, imbed a plain mould in some broken ice, and then cut the different colored jellies into strips, or fancy-shaped ornaments, which must be so managed as to admit of their being fitted into each other, thus entirely covering the bottom of the mould with the design so formed; a little of the jelly must first be poured at the bottom of the mould, to cause the decoration to adhere together. The sides of the mould should then be ornamented by placing alternate strips of the different jellies in a perpendicular position, and these must first be dipped in a little liquid jelly. The mould being lined according to the foregoing directions, the hollow may be filled up with either a Macedoine jelly of fruits, with any kind of cream, or with the remainder of the same, so arranged in it as to have the appearance of marble when cut.

Russian Jelly.

Put about two-thirds of either of the before-mentioned kinds of jelly into a basin, partially imbedded in ice, then whip the jelly with a whisk, until it assumes the appearance of a substantial froth, and begins to thicken; it must then be immediately poured into a mould, and kept in ice until required to be served.

Punch Jelly.

Put the prepared stock from four calves' feet into a stew-pan, to melt on the stove; then withdraw it, and add thereto the following ingredients: Two pounds of loaf sugar, the juice of six lemons and four oranges, the rind of one orange and of four lemons, half a nutmeg, twelve cloves, two sticks of cinnamon, a small cup of strong green tea, a pint of rum, half a pint of brandy, and a glass of arrack. Stir these well together, then add six whites and two whole eggs whipped up with a little sherry and water, and continue whisking the punch over a brisk fire until it begins to simmer, then set it down by the side of the fire, and cover the stew-pan with its lid containing some live embers of charcoal; about ten minutes after, pour the jelly into a flannel or beaver filtering bag; keep pouring the jelly back into the bag until it becomes quite clear and bright, and when the whole has run through, set it in a mould in ice in the usual way.

Oranges Filled with Transparent Jelly.

Select half a dozen oranges without specks on the rind, make a hole at the stalk end with a circular cutter, about half an inch in diameter, and then use a small teaspoon to remove all the pulp and loose pith from the interior; when this is done, soak the orange skins in cold water for about an hour, then introduce the spoon through the aperture, and scrape the insides smooth, and after rinsing them again in cold water, set them to drain on a cloth. Next, stop up any holes that may have been made in them while scooping out the pulp, and set the oranges in some pounded ice contained in a deep pan; fill three of them with bright pink orange jelly, and the remainder with plain jelly. When the jelly has become firm, wipe the oranges with a cloth, cut each into quarters, dish them up tastefully on a napkin, and send to the table.

Currant and Raspberry Jelly.

Pick the stems from a quart of ripe red currants and two quarts of raspberries; put these into a small preserving pan with one pound of sugar and a gill of water; stir the whole on a stove and keep it boiling for about five minutes; remove the scum as it rises to the surface, and then rub the whole through a hair sieve into a large basin; add two ounces of clarified isinglass or gelatine, and then pour it into a jelly mould, ready imbedded in ice. When this kind of jelly is set firm, dip the mould in warm water, wipe it, and turn the jelly out on its dish; fill the well or cylinder with some stiffly-whipped cream, and serve.

Apricot Jelly.

Remove the stones from eighteen ripe apricots, and put them into a small preserving pan with one pound of loaf sugar and a gill of water; stir this over a brisk fire, until the whole of the fruit is entirely dissolved; and then rub it through a hair sieve into a large basin; add two ounces of clarified isinglass or gelatine, and fill a jelly mould, ready imbedded in ice, with the preparation. When the jelly is set firm, turn it out on its dish, and fill the centre with whipped cream.

Note.—These jellies may be made of any kind of fruit before directed to be used for both jellies and creams; and also with pears, apples and quinces.

Jellied Oranges.

One dozen of oranges, one package of gelatine, dissolved in a cup of cold water, three cups of white sugar, the juice of the oranges and juice of two lemons, two cups of boiling water. Soak the gelatine two hours in cold water, then add the sugar, juices of oranges and lemons and boiling water. Cut the oranges in halves and run out the pulp with a spoon. Take care not to tear the skins; throw the empty skins in cold water; wipe dry before using. Fill with jelly, and put away to cool. The skins can be pointed with scissors for improvement in looks. Do not pour in skins while too hot.

Lemon Jelly—No. 1.

One box of gelatine soaked one hour in a pint of cold water, one quart of boiling water, the juice of five lemons, the grated rind of one lemon, two pounds of white sugar. Strain and let it stand till cold.

Lemon Jelly—No. 2.

One box of gelatine, one quart of cold water, mix and stand one and one-quarter hours; two pounds of white sugar, one pint of wine, juice of three lemons, and grated rind of one lemon; stand one and one-quarter hours; then add one quart of boiling water to the whole and strain through a flannel bag.

Cider Jell

One box of gelatine, soaked one hour in a pint of cold water, two coffee-cups of white sugar, two lemons, grated rind of one, one pint of cider, one quart of boiling water. Let it come to a boil and strain.

Coffee Jelly.

Soak one-half a box of gelatine in a cup of water one hour, and add two cups of boiling water, one cup of sugar, one cup of clear strong coffee.

Gelatine Jelly.

An ounce and a half of gelatine, one quart of water, half a pint of wine, the juice of two lemons, three-quarters of a pound of sugar, two eggs and shells, and boil from fifteen to twenty minutes without touching, then strain through a jelly-bag, and cool for use.

Irish Moss Jelly.

Wash and pick an ounce of this moss; boil it in a pint and a half of water for twenty minutes; strain it and pour it into a dish to jelly.

Wine Jelly

Soak well two ounces of gelatine in a pint of cold water, add the juice of one lemon, one-half pint of wine, one and a half pounds of sugar, a quart of boiling water; boil in a porcelain kettle until dissolved thoroughly, then pour into the moulds, which should first be rinsed with cold water.

Fruit in Jelly.

Put into a basin half a pint of clear calf's foot jelly, and when it has become stiff, lay in three fine peaches, and a bunch of grapes with the stalks upward; over which put a few vine-leaves, and fill up the bowl with jelly. Let it stand till next day, and then set the bowl in hot water up to the brim for a minute; then turn it out carefully on a dish.

Lemon Honeycomb.

Sweeten the juice of a lemon to your taste, and put it in the dish that you serve it in. Mix the white of an egg that is beaten with a pint of rich cream, and a little sugar; whisk it, and as the froth rises, put it on the lemon juice. Do it the day before it is to be used.

Orgeat.

Boil a quart of new milk with a stick of cinnamon, sweeten to your taste, and let it grow cold; then pour into it by degrees three ounces of almonds, and twenty bitter, that have been blanched and beaten to a paste, with a little water to prevent oiling; boil altogether, and stir till cold, then add half a glass of brandy.

Orange Fool.

Mix the juice of three nice oranges, three eggs well beaten, a pint of cream a little nutmeg and cinnamon, and sweeten to your taste. Set the whole over a slow fire, and stir it till it becomes as thick as good melted butter, but it must not be boiled; then pour it into a dish to cool and harden.

Moonshine.

This dessert combines a pretty appearance with palatable flavor, and is a convenient substitute for ice cream. Beat the whites of six eggs in a broad plate to a very stiff froth; then add, gradually, six tablespoonfuls of powdered sugar, beaten for not less than thirty minutes, and then beat in, after being cut in tiny pieces; one-half cup of preserved peaches; or you can use one cup of jelly. In serving, pour into each saucer some rich cream, sweetened and flavored with vanilla, and on the cream, place a liberal portion of the moonshine. This quantity is a sufficient amount for eight or ten persons.

ORNAMENTED CUSTARD.

Put a rich custard into a shallow dish. When it shall have become cold, lay on it, in any shape you please, the beaten whites of two new-laid eggs in a firm froth, and over that sift refined sugar. Put it into an oven to become a fine light brown.

SWEET POTATO CUSTARD.

One pound of potatoes mashed and sifted fine, half pound of sugar, a small cup of cream, one-fourth pound of butter, and four eggs; nutmeg and lemon to suit the taste. If you have no cream put half a pound of butter. This makes two large custards.

RICH CUSTARD.

Boil a pint of milk with lemon peel and cinnamon. Mix a pint of cream and the yolks of five eggs well beaten; when the milk tastes of the seasoning, sweeten it enough for the whole. Pour it into the cream, stirring it well; then give the custard a simmer till of the proper thickness. Do not let it boil. Stir the whole time one way; season as above. If it be extremely rich, put no milk, but a quart of cream to the eggs.

BAKED CUSTARD—No. 1.

Boil one pint of cream, half a pint of milk with mace, cinnamon and lemon peel, a little of each. When cold, mix the yolks of three eggs. Sweeten and make your cups of paste nearly full. Bake them ten minutes.

Baked Custard—No. 2.

Boil a pint of cream with some mace, cinnamon, and a little lemon peel. Strain it, and when cold, add it to the yolks of four eggs, and whites of two eggs, a little orange-flower water, and sugar to your taste. A little nutmeg, and two spoonfuls of sweet wine may be added, if approved. Mix well, and bake in cups.

Snow Custard.

Take one quart of milk and four large eggs; set the milk on the fire in a clean vessel; then separate the eggs, and beat the whites to a stiff froth. When the milk is scalding hot, slip the whites on the top, turning them over gently, so that they will cook; then lift them out and dish; whip up the yolks with two tablespoonfuls of sugar; pour into the milk, stirring rapidly all the time it is scalding. The very moment it comes to the boiling point lift it off; if it boils it will curdle. When it cools sufficiently, pour it into the dish with any kind of flavoring, then put the froth on top.

ADDITIONAL RECIPES.

ADDITIONAL RECIPES.

ICE CREAM AND ICES.

Directions for Freezing.

Break the ice fine enough to go in easily between the pail and can. If the pieces are too large they may dent the can, or the freezer may catch at every turn of the crank. Mix with coarse salt in the proportion of one part of salt to four parts of ice. Put the beater into the can, then pour in the liquid to be frozen. Have the can two-thirds full, put the cover on, then place the point on the bottom of the can into the iron centre at the bottom of the pail. Fill the pail or tub with salt and ice to the top of the can, let it stand fifteen minutes and then begin to turn. In about twenty minutes the cream will be frozen. Keep the ice and salt above the line of the cream in the can. The waste hole in the pail, which should be a little below the top of the can, will not allow the water to get into the cream if kept open. It is important that the bearings of the freezer be kept well oiled.

To Keep Cream after Freezing.

Remove the beater, cover the can, and, should the ice have melted very much, drain off a portion of the water and fill up with ice and salt. Cover and keep in a cool place.

Philadelphia Ice Cream, No. 1.

One quart of cream, one pint of milk, one-half pound of sugar, whites of three eggs beaten to a stiff froth, two teaspoonfuls of vanilla. Stir the egg into the cream, add the sugar and vanilla, and stir until cool; then freeze. This makes two quarts.

Philadelphia Ice Cream, No. 2.

Two pounds of white sugar, one medium sized vanilla bean; cut the bean into small pieces and boil in one pint of the cream; strain, add the sugar, mix well with three quarts and one pint more of cream, and then freeze.

Italian Cream.

One-half box of gelatine, one cup of sweet milk. Put in the stove until the gelatine melts; then cool and strain; flavor with one cup of white sugar, one teaspoonful of vanilla; pour this into one quart of whipped cream; freeze.

Vanilla Ice Cream.

Three pints of cream, one pint of milk, one pound of sugar, one quarter box of gelatine dissolved in a small cup of lukewarm water; add this to the milk and then add the milk to the above, stirring constantly till thoroughly mixed; then add one tablespoonful of vanilla, or soak one vanilla bean in the gelatine. First whipping the cream is a great improvement to the above.

Lemon Ice Cream.

Lemon ice cream is made the same as vanilla if extract of lemon is used. If you choose to use lemons, grate the yellow part of the rind of four lemons off and boil in a little water; then strain and add to the mixture.

STRAWBERRY ICE CREAM.

One quart of strawberries mashed and strained through a jelly-bag, one pint of sugar, one-half pint of milk, three pints of cream. Put in the freezer and let stand fifteen minutes and freeze.

COFFEE ICE CREAM.

One quart of cream, one pint of milk, one-half cup *strong* coffee, one pound of sugar, one-quarter of a box of gelatine dissolved in a little warm water; strain the dissolved gelatine into the above, stirring constantly until thoroughly mixed.

CARAMEL ICE CREAM.

Caramel ice cream is made the same as vanilla, except use burnt sugar for flavoring instead of extract of vanilla, which may be prepared by putting a teacupful of sugar in a small frying-pan, and stir over the fire until the sugar turns to a liquid and begins to smoke.

CHOCOLATE ICE CREAM.

One quart of cream, one pint of milk, one pound of sugar, one-quarter box of gelatine dissolved in half of the milk, and strained; dissolve two ounces of bakers' chocolate in the remainder of the milk; add the dissolved gelatine and chocolate and freeze.

BANANA ICE CREAM.

One quart of cream, one-half pound of sugar, and four bananas rubbed through a fine sieve. Let it stand in the freezer fifteen minutes and freeze.

Pistachio Ice Cream.

One quart of cream, one-half pound of sugar, one ounce of almonds and one-half ounce of pistachio nuts, both blanched and pounded fine. One-half a teaspoonful of spinach green added to this cream gives a delicate color.

Ice Cream without Cream.

One quart of milk, two tablespoonfuls corn starch, three eggs, whites and yolks beaten separately. Scald the milk and corn starch well and then add yolks. Remove from the stove and add the whites and sugar to taste. When cool, flavor.

Orange Ice No. 1.

To each quart of water add the juice of four oranges, the grated rind of one, one pound of white sugar, the grated rind of one-half a lemon, and the juice of one lemon to every four quarts of the mixture. Strain through a fine sieve into the can and freeze.

Orange Ice No. 2.

One quart of water, three-quarters of a pound of sugar, the juice of two lemons, the juice of three oranges and the grated rind of one, the white of an egg, and one-quarter of a box of gelatine dissolved in the water. Strain and freeze.

Lemon Ice.

One quart of water, one pound of sugar, the juice of five lemons, grated rind of one lemon, one-quarter of a box of gelatine dissolved in the water. Strain and freeze.

Pine-apple Ice.

One quart can of pine-apple, or one large fresh pine-apple grated and strained through a fine sieve, one quart of water, one and one-quarter of a pound of sugar, the white of an egg, and one-quarter of a box of gelatine dissolved in the water. Pour in the can and freeze.

Apricot or Peach Ice

May be made the same as pine-apple ice, but use apricots or peaches.

Raspberry Ice.

One quart of water, one pound of sugar, juice of three lemons, white of an egg, the juice of one quart of raspberries, and one tablespoonful of gelatine dissolved in the water. Strain and freeze. Canned raspberries may be used and the quantity of sugar lessened.

Banana Ice.

One quart of water, three quarters of a pound of sugar, juice of two lemons, the whites and yokes of three eggs beaten separately, one teaspoonful of gelatine dissolved in the water, and six bananas grated fine. Strain and freeze.

ADDITIONAL RECIPES

JELLIES AND CANNED FRUITS.

JELLY.

Heat the fruit until soft; then squeeze out the juice and for each pint allow a pint of sugar. Boil the juice for fifteen minutes and add the sugar. Boil two, three or five minutes, till it jellies, testing it by dropping some on a cold saucer. Berries need only to be heated to extract their juice; apples and like fruit need a little water to stew them in. A sure and simple way of covering jelly tumblers is to lay a lump of paraffine on the hot jelly, letting it melt and spread over the top. It is more successful as an air-tight covering than the white of an egg and similar appliances, and is easily removed by slipping a knife around the edges. The paraffine can be used another year.

PLUM JELLY.

Take sound plums, put them in a stone jar, cover the jar with a bladder, put it in a deep pan of water over the fire, and let the water boil gently till all the juice has come from the fruit, strain through a jelly bag, and boil with an equal weight of loaf sugar, stirring all the time. Damsons should have a slight incision.

Apple Jelly.

Cut and core apples without paring, cover with water, and let them cook slowly until the apples look red; then pour into a bag and gently squeeze out all the liquid that will flow freely; boil the liquor again half an hour. Then add one-half pound of sugar to a pint of juice, and boil quickly fifteen minutes.

Peach Jelly.

Pare well ripened peaches, and remove the pits; boil until soft in water to cover them; strain through a cloth. To a quart of liquor add a pound of white sugar; then boil till thick.

Currant Jelly.

Strip the fruit from the stems, and in a stone jar stew them in a sauce pan of water; strain off the liquor, and to every pint weigh a pound of loaf sugar; put the latter in large lumps into it, in a stone or china vessel, till nearly dissolved; then put it in a preserving pan; simmer and skim as necessary. When it will jelly on a plate, put it in small jars or glasses.

Cranberry Jelly.

Wash and pick over the fruit, and boil till soft in water enough to cover it. Strain through a sieve, and weigh equal quantities of the pulp and sugar. Boil gently fifteen or twenty minutes, taking care it does not burn.

Currant Jelly without Cooking.

Press the juice from the currants, and strain it; to every pint put a pound of fine white sugar; mix them together until the sugar is dissolved; then put in jars, seal them, and expose them to a hot sun for two or three days.

Preserved Peaches.

Take ripe free-stone peaches; pare, stone and quarter them. To six pounds of cut peaches allow three pounds of the best brown sugar. Stew the sugar among the peaches, and set them away in a covered vessel Next morning, put the whole into a preserving kettle, and boil it slowly about an hour and three-quarters, or two hours, skimming it well.

Preserved Pears.

Take six pounds of pears to four pounds of sugar; boil the parings in as much water as will cover them; strain it through a colander; lay some pears in the bottom of your kettle, put in some sugar, and so on alternately; then pour over the pears the liquor from off the pear skins; boil them until they begin to look transparent, then take them out and let the juice cool, and clarify it; put the pears in again, and add some ginger; boil till done; let the liquor boil after taking them out, until it is reduced to a syrup.

Yellow Tomato Preserves.

One peck of yellow tomatoes, one dozen lemons, one-half ounce of sliced ginger root, six pounds of sugar; add one pint of vinegar to the preserves when cold.

Preserved Cherries.

Stem and stone them carefully, preserving the juice. To one quart of cherries allow one pound of sugar. Make a syrup, allowing half a pint of water to a pound of sugar. Boil and skim it, and when the scum has ceased to rise, put in the cherries and their juice, and boil them up slowly.

Grape Preserves.

Squeeze with your fingers the pulp from each grape. Put the pulps over the fire, and boil them till they are tender; then press them through a colander, so that the seeds may be taken out; now add the skins to the pulps and juice. Put a cupful of sugar to each cupful of fruit, and boil all together until of a thick consistency. Green grape preserves are also nice. In managing the green grapes, halve them and extract the seeds with a small knife. Put also a cupful of sugar to a cupful of fruit. Many prefer the green to the ripe grape preserves.

Marblehead Preserved Peaches.

Take a peck of ripe peaches, stone and pare them; allow a bowl of white sugar to a bowl of peaches; put a layer of peaches into the stone jar, then a layer of sugar, and so on until they are used up. Let them stand for two days; drain off the syrup, boil and skim and turn over the peaches; stand two days; drain off the syrup, scald and skim, and again return to the peaches, and it is fit for use.

Preserved Quinces.

Into two quarts of boiling water put a quantity of the fairest golden pippins, in slices not very thin, and not pared, but wiped clear. Boil them very quick, covered closely, till the water becomes a thick jelly;

then scald the quinces. To every pint of pippin jelly put a pound of the finest sugar; boil it, and skim it clear. Put those quinces that are to be done whole into the syrup at once, and let it boil very fast; and those that are to be in halves by themselves. Skim it, and when the fruit is clear, put some of the syrup into a glass to try whether it jellies before taking off the fire. The quantity of quinces is to be a pound to a pound of sugar, and a pound of jelly already boiled with the sugar.

Preserved Strawberries.

Take equal weights of the fruit and sugar; lay the former in a large dish, and sprinkle half the sugar, in fine powder, over; give a gentle shake to the dish, that the sugar may touch the under side of the fruit. Next day make a thin syrup with the remainder of the sugar, and, instead of water, allow one pint of red currant juice to every pound of strawberries; in this simmer them until sufficiently jellied. Choose the largest when not dead ripe. In the above way they are nice served in thin cream, in glasses.

Preserved Pears.

Pare them very thin, and simmer in a thin syrup; let them lie a day or two. Make the syrup richer, and simmer again; and repeat this till they are clear; then drain and dry them in the sun or a cool oven a very little time. They may be kept in syrup, and dried as wanted, which makes them more moist and rich.

Preserved Pine-apples.

Twist out the crown of the pine-apple, and pare off the hard, yellow rind; next slice the fruit about half an inch thick, and trim it quite clean round the edges, taking care of the trimmings. Put them into the preserving pan with one quart of cold water, and boil till reduced to half a pint; strain it, then put in the slices on the fire with the juice and equal weight of fine white sugar. Boil gently half an hour.

Preserved Siberian Crab-apples.

Boil a pint of water and a pound and a half of refined sugar to a fine clear syrup; skim it, and let it become cold; and to this quantity of syrup put a pound of fruit, and simmer slowly till tender. Carefully remove each apple separately, and pour the syrup over when a little cooled, and add orange and lemon peel boiled tender.

Canned Fruit.

Allow three pints of fruit, one cup of water and one cup of sugar to every one-quart can of strawberries, raspberries, cherries, currants and grapes. Put in the water, then the sugar, and when it is boiled, put in your fruit. Let it boil slowly for ten minutes, skim well and then can. Be sure to fill your can so that when you put on your cover they will run over. Press the glass cover firmly with your hand before putting on the ring. If this is done right, and the rubber rings are new, which they should be every year, they will seal without any difficulty.

CANNED PINE-APPLE.

For six pounds of fruit when cut and ready to can, make syrup with two and a half pounds of sugar and nearly three pints of water; boil syrup five minutes and skim or strain if necessary; then add the fruit and let it boil up; have your cans hot; fill and shut up as soon as possible. Use the best white sugar. As the cans cool keep tightening them up.

ORANGE MARMALADE.

Rasp the oranges, cut out the pulp, boil the rinds very tender, and beat fine in a mortar. Boil three pounds of loaf sugar in a pint of water, skim it and add a pound of the rind. Boil fast until the syrup is very thick, but stir it carefully. Then put in a pint of the juice (the seeds and pulp having been removed) and a pint of apple liquor. Boil all gently until well jellied, which will take about half an hour.

LEMON MARMALADE.

It is made the same as the orange. It is an elegant sweetmeat.

APPLE MARMALADE.

Scald apples till they will pulp from the core; then take an equal weight of sugar in large lumps, just dip them in water, and boil it till it can be well skimmed, and is a thick syrup; put to it the pulp, and simmer it on a quick fire a quarter of an hour. Grate in a little lemon peel before boiling; too much will make it bitter.

CRAB-APPLE MARMALADE.

Boil the apples in a kettle until soft, with just water enough to cover them. Mash and strain through a coarse sieve. Take a pound of apples to a pound of sugar. Boil half an hour and put in jars.

QUINCE MARMALADE.

Pare and quarter quinces; weigh an equal quantity of sugar; to four pounds of the latter put a quart of water, boil and skim, and have ready against four pounds of quinces. They are made tolerably tender by the following mode: Lay them into a stone jar, with a teacup of water at the bottom, and pack them with a little sugar strewed between, cover the jar close, and set it on a stove or cool oven, and let them soften till the color becomes red; then pour the fruit-syrup and a quart of quince-juice into a preserving pan, and boil all together till the marmalade be completed, breaking the lumps of fruit with the preserving ladle. This fruit is so hard, that if it be not done as above, it requires a great deal of time. Stewing quinces in a jar, and then squeezing them through a cloth, is the best method of obtaining the juice to add as above, and dip the cloth in boiling water first, and wring it.

TOMATO MARMALADE.

To two pounds of tomatoes allow two pounds of sugar, and the juice and grated rind of one lemon. Scald the tomatoes, take off the skins, mix the sugar with them, and boil them slowly for an hour, skimming and stirring; add the juice and grated rind of the lemon, and boil another half hour, or until it is a thick smooth mass.

TRANSPARENT MARMALADE.

Cut the oranges to be used in quarters; take the

pulp out and put in a basin, pick out the seeds and skins. Let the outsides soak in water with a little salt all night, then boil them in a good quantity of pure water till tender; drain and cut them in very thin slices, and put them to the pulp; and to every pound, a pound and a half refined sugar beaten fine; boil them together twenty minutes, but be careful not to break the slices. If not quite clear, simmer five or six minutes longer. It must be stirred all the time very gently. When cold, put it into glasses.

CHERRY MARMALADE

Stem and stone your cherries, saving as much of the juice as possible; allow one pound of sugar to one pint of cherries. Boil the fruit and sugar together uncovered for an hour, skimming and stirring well. When cool, put in pots and cover tight.

MARMALADE.

Select very ripe fruits—grapes, crab-apples or quinces. Cut the fruit having a core in halves and stew until tender in water enough to cover the bottom of the kettle; strain through a fine colander or sieve to remove the skin and seeds. For each pint of pulp allow a pound of sugar, and boil half an hour, stirring constantly. Spice may be added if desired. The marmalade should be firm and hard when cold.

SPICED CURRANTS.

Five pounds of whole currants, three and one-half pounds of white sugar, one pint of vinegar, two teaspoonfuls of ground cloves, two teaspoonfuls of ground cinnamon, two teaspoonfuls of ground allspice, one nutmeg. Boil one hour, and be careful about burning.

To Can Currants without Cooking.

To every pound of stemmed currants pour on one pound of white sugar, not cooked. They want to stand on ice from twelve to sixteen hours. The sugar wants to be thoroughly mixed in among the currants. After you take them off the ice, put them in cans.

Apple Jam.

Weigh equal quantities of brown sugar and good sour apples; pare, core and chop them fine; make a good, clear syrup of the sugar. Add the apples, the juice and grated rind of three lemons, and a few pieces of white ginger. Boil it till the apples look clear and yellow; this resembles foreign sweetmeats. On no account omit the ginger.

Quince Jam.

Twelve ounces of brown sugar to one pound of quince. Boil the fruit in as little water as possible, until the fruit will mash easily. Pour off the water, mash the fruit with a spoon, put in the sugar, and boil twenty minutes, stirring often.

Gooseberry Jam for Tarts.

Put twelve pounds of gooseberries, when ripe, into a preserving pan, with a pint of currant juice, drawn as for jelly. Let them boil pretty quick, and beat them with a spoon. When they begin to break, put to them six pounds of pure white sugar, and simmer slowly to a jam. It requires long boiling, or it will not keep. It is an excellent and not expensive thing for tarts or puffs. Look at it in two or three days, and if the syrup and fruit separate, the whole must be boiled longer. Be careful it does not burn to the bottom.

Raspberry Jam.

Weigh equal quantities of fruit and sugar. Put the former in a preserving pan, boil and break it, stir constantly, and let it boil very quickly. When most of the juice is wasted, add the sugar, and simmer half an hour. This way the jam is greatly superior in color and flavor to that which is made by putting the sugar in at first.

Currant Jam.

Let the fruit be very ripe, pick it clean from the stalks, bruise it, and to every pound put three-quarters of a pound of loaf sugar; stir it well, and boil half an hour.

Grape Jam.

Boil grapes soft and strain through a sieve. Weigh the pulp thus obtained, and put a pound of sugar to one pint of pulp. Boil twenty minutes, stirring frequently.

Green Gage Jam.

Rub ripe green gages through a sieve, put all the pulp into a pan with an equal weight of loaf sugar pounded and sifted. Boil the whole till sufficiently thick, and put into pots.

Quince Sauce.

Cut, pare and core a quart of quinces, cover in water and boil till perfectly tender, then add three-quarters of a pound of sugar, and continue boiling for ten or fifteen minutes, that the sugar may penetrate the quince.

Brandy Peaches.

Drop the peaches in hot water, let them remain till the skins can be taken off; make a thin syrup, and let it cover the fruit; boil the fruit till they can be pierced with a straw; take it out, make a very rich syrup, and add, after it is taken from the fire, and while it is still hot, an equal quantity of brandy. Pour this, while it is still warm, over the peaches in the jar. They must be covered with it.

Brandy Apricots or Peaches.

Wipe, weigh and pick the fruit, and have ready a quarter of the weight of fine powdered sugar. Put the fruit into an ice pot that shuts very close; throw the sugar over it, and then cover the fruit with brandy. Between the top and cover of the pot, put a piece of double cap paper. Set the pot into a sauce pan of water till the brandy be as hot as you can possibly bear to put your finger in, but it must not boil. Put the fruit into a jar, and pour the brandy on it.

Brandy Grapes.

Take some close bunches, black or white, not over-ripe, and lay them in a jar. Put a good quantity of pounded white sugar-candy upon them, and fill up the jar with brandy. Tie them down with a bladder, and keep in a dry place. Each grape should be pricked thrice.

Raspberry Brandy.

Pick fine dry fruit, put it into a stone jar, and the jar into a kettle of water or on a hot hearth, till the juice will run; strain, and to every pint add half a pound of sugar, give one boil, and skim it; when cold put equal quantities of juice and brandy; shake well, and bottle. Some people prefer it stronger of the brandy.

Stewed Pears.

Pare and halve, or quarter, large pears, according to their size; throw them into water, as the skin is taken of, before they are divided, to prevent their turning black. Pack them round a block tin stew pan, and sprinkle as much sugar over as will make them pretty sweet, and add lemon peel, a clove or two, and some allspice cracked; just cover them with water. Cover them close, and stew three or four hours.

DRINKS.

COFFEE.

The variety of coffees is much larger than most people imagine, as that grown in Brazil and also in other places is sold as Java and Mocha. More than one-half of the coffee produced by the world is of Brazilian growth, and yet the coffee of Brazil has very little reputation, simply because the best produced there is sold under other names, as before stated. Coffee should be carefully roasted, as the flavor largely depends upon it. The natural color of the coffee bean is pale green, and should be evenly roasted till it acquires a chestnut-brown color. If roasted to a black color it gives a burnt and disagreeable flavor to the beverage. Slightly heating the dry coffee before making improves it. There are numberless modes of preparing coffee, each, of course, having its advantages and disadvantages, but all should combine the two important principles, viz: to extract the largest amount of aroma and body, and to render the fluid clear and free from grounds. Good cream adds much to the flavor of coffee, but when cream cannot be procured, boil the milk, as it makes the coffee richer and more palatable. The milk should merely come to a boil, and then be taken off the fire, as too much boiling makes it oily and strong.

Coffee to many people is injurious, but taken without cream is said by physicians to be harmless. Do not buy ground coffee, as it is very extensively adulterated, and also harmful in its effects upon the system. One-third Mocha and two-thirds Java is the correct proportion for good coffee. A small egg, shell and all, broken into the pot with the dry coffee improves it greatly, as it makes it richer. It should boil from five to ten minutes, counting from the time it begins to boil. Take the coffee from the stove and let it stand a little while to settle. Probably the most economical way to prepare the beverage is to filter it. A filtering coffee pot can be obtained at any hardware store, and consists of two cylindrical tin vessels, one fitting into another, and the bottom of the upper being a fine strainer. The strength of the coffee can be more effectually obtained by this method.

Chocolate.

Those who use much of this article will find the following mode of preparing it both useful and economical: Cut a cake of chocolate in very small bits; put a pint of water into the pot, and, when it boils, put in the chocolate; mill it off the fire until quite melted, then on a gentle fire till it boils; pour it into a basin, and it will keep in a cool place eight or ten days, or more. When wanted, put a spoonful or two into milk, boil it with sugar, and mix it well.

Cocoa or Broma.

To one pint of milk put four heaping teaspoonfuls of cocoa or broma, dissolved smoothly in one-half cup of milk. Stir in the milk when at boiling point. Remove from the fire, after allowing it to boil briskly three minutes, and stir in sugar to taste.

Verder.

Pare six oranges and six lemons as thin as you can, grate them after with sugar to get the flavor. Steep the peels in a bottle of rum or brandy tightly corked twenty-four hours. Squeeze the fruit on two pounds of sugar, add to it four quarts of water, and one of new milk, boiling hot; stir the rum into the above, and run it through a jelly bag till perfectly clear. Bottle, and cork close immediately.

Ice Punch.

Make a rich sherbet, and grate a piece of sugar on a lemon or citron for flavor; then beat the whites of five or six eggs to a froth, and by degrees stir it into the sherbet; add rum and ice, and serve in glasses.

Milk Punch.

Take two tablespoonfuls of brandy, a little sugar and a gill of hot water; add a gill of milk and a little nutmeg.

Roman Punch.

Three coffee cups of lemonade, strong and sweet, one glass of champagne, one glass of rum, the pieces of two oranges, two eggs, whites well whipped, one-half pound of powdered sugar, beaten into the stiffened whites. Ice.

Currant Shrub.

Boil currant juice and sugar, in proportion of one pound of sugar to one pint of juice, five minutes. Stir it constantly while cooling; when cold, bottle it. Use like raspberry shrub, one spoonful or two to a tumbler of water.

Pine-apple Sherbet.

One can of pine-apple, a small pint of sugar, one pint of water, one tablespoonful of gelatine. Cut the hearts and eyes from the fruit, and chop it very fine, add the juice from the can, the water and boil them in thin clarified sugar, let them imbibe the sugar, and be careful to preserve their form; make a marmalade with some other apples, adding to it four ounces of rice, previously boiled in milk, with sugar and butter and the yolks of two or three eggs; put them into a dish for the table; surround it with a border of rice and marmalade, and bake it.

Lemon Sherbet.

The juice of five lemons, one pint of sugar, one quart of water, one tablespoonful of gelatine. Put together like the pine-apple.

Sassafras Mead.

Three pounds of brown sugar, one pint of molasses, one-quarter pound of tartaric acid. Mix together; pour over them two quarts of water and stir until dissolved. When cold, add half an ounce of essence of sassafras, and bottle. When you wish to drink it, put three tablespoonfuls of it in a tumbler, filled half full with ice water, add a little more than one-quarter of a teaspoonful of soda. An excellent summer beverage.

Sarsaparilla Mead.

Three pounds of sugar, three ounces of tartaric acid, one ounce of cream tartar, one ounce of flour, one ounce of essence of sarsaparilla, three quarts of water. Strain and bottle it, then let it stand ten days before using.

Raspberry Shrub.

Take three quarts of red raspberries, and one quart of cider vinegar, and put together in a vessel, adding one pound of sugar to the pint, and let it stand twenty-four hours; then strain, scald and skim it. Bottle when cold.

Ginger Beer.

Pour four quarts of boiling water on one ounce and a half of ginger, one ounce of cream of tartar, one pound of brown sugar, and two lemons sliced thin. Put in two gills of yeast, let it ferment twenty-four hours, and bottle it. It improves by keeping a few weeks, unless it is very hot weather, and it is a very nice beverage.

Maple Beer.

To four gallons of boiling water, put one quart of maple syrup, and one tablespoonful of essence of spruce; when about milk-warm, add one pint of yeast, and when fermented, bottle it. In three days it is fit for use.

Blackberry Cordial.

To each quart of blackberry juice add one pound of white sugar, one tablespoonful of cloves, one of allspice, one of cinnamon and one of nutmeg. Boil all together for fifteen minutes, and add a wine-glass of pure brandy. Put while hot into bottles, cork and seal. This will keep several years.

Egg Nogg.

The yolks of six eggs, with four tablespoonfuls of sugar, a little nutmeg, a glass of wine, and two glasses of brandy; then add, when well mixed, a quart of milk. It is refreshing in summer to add ice, pounded very fine.

Lemonade.

Take one dozen lemons and squeeze the juice into a bowl or glass (not into a tin); strain out all the seeds; remove the pulps from the peels, and boil in one pint of water a few minutes; then strain the water into the juice of the lemons; put in a pound of sugar to each pint of juice Bottle it. Use one or two tablespoonfuls of this syrup into each glass of ice water.

Cream Nectar.

Three pounds of sugar, three pints of water, white of one egg, and three ounces of tartaric acid. Dissolve the sugar in the water, add the beaten white of the egg, and let it come to a boil. When cold, add tartaric acid, and flavor to taste.

Sauterne Cup.

One bottle of Sauterne, one pint of Vichy water, two oranges sliced, a bunch of balm, the same of burrage, one ounce of pulverized sugar candy. Place these ingredients in a covered jug imbedded in ice for an hour and a quarter previous to the cup being required for use, and then strain through a jelly bag.

Claret Cup.

One bottle of claret, one pint bottle of German seltzer water, a small bunch of balm, the same of burrage, one orange cut in slices, half a cucumber sliced thick, a liquor glass of cognac, and one ounce of pulverized sugar candy. Put the ingredients in a covered jug well imbedded in ice, stir all together with a spoon, and when the cup has been iced for about an hour, strain it off free from the herbs, etc.

Pine-apple Cup.

Eight ounces of pine-apple sliced very thin, one bottle of Ai wine, a sprig of verbina, a wine-glassful of Maraschino, one quart bottle of double soda water, and one ounce of pulverized sugar candy. Thoroughly imbed the wine and the soda water in ice for an hour previous to its being required for use; and then, first place the slices of pine-apple, the verbina, the Maraschino, and the sugar candy in a glass jug, and afterwards add thereto the iced wine and soda water.

Champagne Cup.

One bottle of champagne, one quart bottle of German seltzer water, two oranges sliced, a bunch of balm, the same of burrage, and one ounce of pounded sugar candy. Place the ingredients in a covered jug imbedded in ice for an hour and a quarter previous to its being required for use, and then strain it free from the herbs, etc.

Chablis Cup.

One bottle of Chablis, one pint of German seltzer water, one bunch of balm, the same of burrage, one orange sliced, and one ounce of pulverized sugar candy. Put the ingredients in a covered jug imbedded in ice for an hour and a quarter previous to its being required for use, and then strain the cup free from the herbs, etc.

Badminton Cup.

One bottle of red Burgundy, one quart of German seltzer water, the rind of one orange, the juice of two, a wine-glass of curacoa, a bunch of balm, the same of burrage, a sprig of verbina, one ounce of pulverized sugar candy, and a few slices of cucumber. Place the ingredients in a covered jug imbedded in ice for about an hour previous to its being required for use, and afterward strain the cup free from the herbs, etc.

Cider Cup.

One quart of cider, one pint of German seltzer water, a small glass of cognac, a bunch of balm, the same of burrage, a sliced orange, one ounce of pulverized sugar candy. Place the ingredients in a covered jug imbedded in ice for an hour and a quarter, and then strain the cup free from herbs, etc.

Note.—Any other aerated water may be substituted for seltzer, or the cup may be prepared without the addition of any water.

Unfermented Wine.

Weigh the grapes, pick from the stems, put in a porcelain kettle, add very little water, and cook until stones and pulp separate; press and strain through a thick cloth, return the juice to the kettle, and for every ten pounds of grapes add three pounds of sugar; heat to simmering, and seal up hot. This quantity makes about a gallon of wine.

Grape Wine.

Three quarts of juice, two pounds of sugar; let it stand six weeks, or until it has stopped working; then skim and bottle.

Wine Whey.

Boil half a pint of new milk; while it is boiling, put in a cup of white wine; stir it up, turn it into a bowl, and let it stand about ten minutes; then turn it off from the curd, and flavor it as you like with sugar.

Currant Wine—No. 1.

Four pounds of currants, three pounds of sugar, and one gallon of water. Place the currants, stems and all, in a tub, and mash them well; add the water, set in a cool place, and stir occasionally; continue the stirring for three days; then drain the liquor through a sieve, squeeze the pulp in a cloth, add the sugar, stirring until it is all dissolved, and put into a barrel or cask, which should stand in a dry, cool cellar. When fermentation is over, bung up tight and leave all winter. Rack off in the spring before the second fermentation, and bottle after the second fermentation.

Currant Wine—No. 2.

To one gallon of currant juice put nine pounds of the best sugar, and two gallons of water. Set it where it will not be disturbed, and bottle at the end of one year.

Currant Wine—No. 3.

Eleven quarts of currant juice, and thirty-four pounds of the best brown sugar. Put it in a ten gallon keg, and fill the keg with water; after a few days cork, and let it remain until winter.

A Rich and Pleasant Wine.

Take new cider from the press, mix it with as much honey as will support an egg, and boil gently fifteen minutes, but not in an iron, brass or copper pot. Skim it well. In March following, bottle it, and it will be fit to drink in six weeks; it will be less sweet if kept longer in the cask. You will have a rich and strong wine, and it will keep well. This will serve for any culinary purposes which sweet wine is directed for.

RASPBERRY WINE.

To every quart of well-picked raspberries, put a quart of water; bruise, and let them stand two days; strain off the liquor, and to every gallon put three pounds of lump sugar; when dissolved, put the liquor in a barrel, and when fine, which will be in about two months, bottle it, and to each bottle put a spoonful of brandy, or a glass of wine.

BLACK CURRANT WINE.

To every three quarts of juice, put the same of water unboiled; and to every three quarts of the liquor, add three pounds of very pure moist sugar. Put it into a cask, reserving a little for filling up. Put the cask in a warm dry room, and the liquor will ferment of itself. Skim off the refuse, when the fermentation shall be over, and fill up with the reserved liquor. When it has ceased working, pour three quarts of brandy to forty quarts of wine. Bung it close for nine months, then bottle it, and drain the thick part through a jelly bag until it is clear, and bottle that. Keep it ten or twelve months.

ELDER WINE.

To every quart of berries put two quarts of water, boil half an hour, run the liquor and break the fruit through a hair sieve; then to every quart of juice put three-quarters of a pound of sugar. Boil the whole a quarter of an hour, with some Jamaica peppers, ginger, and a few cloves. Pour it into a tub, and when of a proper warmth, into a barrel, with toast and yeast to work, which there is more difficulty to make it do than most other liquors. When it ceases to hiss, put a quart of brandy to eight gallons, and stop up. The liquor must be in a warm place to make it work.

White Elder Wine.

Boil eighteen pounds of white powdered sugar, with six gallons of water, and the whites of two eggs well beaten; then skim it, and put in a quarter of a peck of elder flowers from the tree that bears white berries; do not keep them on the fire. When near cold, stir it, and put in six spoonfuls of lemon juice, four or five of yeast, and beat well into the liquor; stir it every day; put six pound of the best raisins, stoned, into the cask, and tun the wine. Stop it close, and bottle in six months. When well kept, this wine will pass for Frontiniac.

Cherry Rum.

A peck of black wild cherries, soaked in cold water for twenty-four hours. Put them in a demijohn, add two pounds of brown sugar, two quarts of blackberries, and a gallon of the best New England rum. The older it is the better, if kept well corked. It is excellent for summer complaints.

ADDITIONAL RECIPES.

CONFECTIONERY.

COCOANUT CANDY QUICKLY MADE.

Grate the meat of a cocoanut, and having ready two pounds of finely sifted white sugar, the beaten whites of two eggs, and the milk of the nut, simply mix all together, and make into little cakes. In a short while the candy will be dry enough to use, and found to be as good as if boiled.

CHOCOLATE CARAMELS—No. 1.

Three pounds of sugar (brown will do), half a pound of butter, one teacupful of milk or cream—the latter, of course, preferable, and two cupfuls of chocolate. Boil rapidly until candied, when it may be either cut into squares or moulded into small thin cakes.

CHOCOLATE CARAMELS—No. 2.

One cupful of chocolate cut up fine, two cupfuls of brown sugar, one cupful of warm water, and three-quarters of a cupful of butter. Boil until it will harden when dropped in cold water; then pour into shallow buttered pans, and when almost cold, cut into small squares.

Cocoanut Taffy.

One cup of cocoanut grated, one cup of sugar, one cup of molasses, butter the size of an egg.

Cocoanut Drops.

Beat the whites of four eggs with one-half pound of powdered sugar until very light; flavor with lemon. Add grated cocoanut until it is thick enough to stir easily with a spoon. Lay in little heaps on sheets of paper. Bake in a quick oven.

Molasses Candy—No. 1.

Two cupfuls of molasses, one tablespoonful of sugar; stir occasionally while boiling; before taking from the fire add butter half the size of an egg, and one-third teaspoonful of soda. Pour into buttered tins, and when cool enough pull it.

Molasses Candy—No. 2.

Two cupfuls of sugar, one cupful of molasses, one-half cupful of water; after it begins to boil add one-quarter teaspoonful of cream of tartar; cook in the usual way, but do not stir; before taking from the fire, add butter half the size of an egg. Do not butter your hands while pulling.

Chocolate Cream Drops.

White of one egg beaten thoroughly, one pound of lozenge sugar, and one teaspoonful of water; make into a stiff dough, and mould in drops on marble; take two squares of bakers' chocolate, melt it, and roll the cream drops into it until covered well; then set away to cool.

CONFECTIONERY.

CARAMELS.

Take one cupful of molasses, two cupfuls of sugar, and boil ten minutes; then add one large tablespoonful of flour, butter the size of an egg, and one-half pound of chocolate. Boil twenty minutes.

CREAM CANDY.

One pound of loaf sugar, two-thirds of a coffee cup of water, one-half teaspoonful of cream of tartar, two teaspoonfuls of vinegar, butter the size of a walnut; flavor with vanilla; boil and stir twenty minutes.

ICE CREAM CANDY.

Two cupfuls of granulated sugar, one-half cupful of water, add one-fourth teaspoonful of cream of tartar dissolved in water, as soon as it boils. Boil about ten minutes; do not stir it. When done, it will be brittle if dropped in cold water; add butter half the size of an egg just before taking off the stove. Pour into a buttered tin to cool, and pull it as hot as possible; flavor while pulling, with vanilla, checkerberry or any extract to suit taste.

LEMON DROPS.

Grate three large lemons, with a large piece of double-refined sugar; then scrape the sugar into a plate, add half a teaspoonful of flour; mix well, and beat it into a light paste with the white of an egg. Drop it upon white paper, and put them into a moderate oven on a tin plate.

MARSHMALLOW DROPS.

Dissolve one-half pound of gum arabic in one pint of water; strain and add one-half pound of white sugar, and place over the fire, stirring constantly until the syrup is dissolved and of the consistency of honey; then add gradually the whites of four eggs well beaten. Stir the mixture until it becomes somewhat thin and does not adhere to the fingers. Flavor to taste, and pour all into a pan slightly dusted with powdered starch, and when cool, divide into small squares.

Fig Candy.

One cupful of sugar, one-third of a cupful of water, one-fourth of a teaspoonful of cream of tartar; do not stir while boiling; boil to an amber color, and stir in the cream of tartar just before taking from the fire. Wash the figs, open and lay in a tin pan and pour the candy over them.

Vinegar Candy.

Two cupfuls of sugar, one-half cupful of water, four tablespoonfuls of vinegar; stir before putting on the stove, and not after.

Taffy.

Two cupfuls of brown sugar, one-half cupful of butter, four tablespoonfuls of molasses, two tablespoonfuls of water, two tablespoonfuls of vinegar. Boil fifteen minutes.

Everton Taffy.

One pound of powdered loaf sugar, one teacupful of water, one-quarter of a pound of butter, six drops of essence of lemon. Put the water and sugar in a brass pan on the stove. Beat the butter to a cream; when the sugar is dissolved, add the butter, and keep stirring the mixture over the fire until it sets. Just before the taffy is done add the lemon.

NUT CANDY.

Three cupfuls of sugar, one-half cupful of vinegar, one-half cupful of water. Prepare two cupfuls of any kind of nutmeats, spread them on well-buttered plates, and pour the candy over; when done, test it by dropping a little in cold water; when it hardens into a little lump it is done.

CORN BALLS.

Boil one cupful of molasses and two tablespoonfuls of sugar twenty minutes. When done, rub one-half of a teaspoonful of soda smooth; then stir in pop corn. Butter the hands, and ball.

ADDITIONAL RECIPES.

FOR THE SICK ROOM.

INDIAN MEAL GRUEL.

To make a cupful of gruel, take a tablespoonful of Indian meal, wet it with a little water; pour on to it half a pint of boiling water, and let it boil half an hour. Nutmeg, sugar and cream may be added if approved.

CAUDLE FOR INVALIDS.

A highly nourishing caudle for invalids is made with two moderate spoonfuls of manioca stirred into a quart of cold water, with a little butter, a blade or two of mace, and some grated lemon peel. Boil a quarter of an hour or twenty minutes, stirring constantly that it may be quite smooth. Sweeten with refined honey, or sugar if preferred. Add spice to taste, and one glass of brandy or white wine. Should the mixture become too thick, stir in a little boiling water while the mixture is yet warm.

COUGH SYRUP.

Five cents' worth of licorice, five cents' worth of horehound candy, five cents' worth of gum arabic, all steeped together in one pint of water; then pour in one ounce of paregoric.

Oatmeal Gruel.

Put on a cupful of raisins in a quart of water to boil; boil them hard for half a hour. Take two tablespoonfuls of oatmeal and make smooth with cold water; add a little salt; when the raisins are boiled enough, stir in the thickening; let it boil up and skim it well; then add a bit of butter, a little white sugar, and grate a little nutmeg on the top when it is served.

Scotch Broth.

Two pounds of the scraggy part of a neck of mutton; cut the meat from the bones, and cut off the fat; then cut the meat into small pieces and put into the soup pot with one large slice of turnip, two of carrot, one onion and a stalk of celery, all cut fine, half a cupful of barley and three pints of cold water. Simmer gently two hours. On to the bones put one pint of water; simmer two hours, and strain upon the soup. Cook a tablespoonful of flour and one of butter together until perfectly smooth; stir into the soup, and add a teaspoonful of chopped parsley. Season with salt and pepper.

Beef Tea—No. 1.

One pound of lean beef, cut into small pieces; put into a jar without a drop of water; cover tightly and set in a pot of cold water. Heat gradually to a boil, and continue this steadily for three or four hours, until the meat is like white rags, and the juice all drawn out. Season with salt to taste, and when cold, skim. The patient will often prefer this ice cold to hot.

Beef Tea—No. 2.

Cut a pound of fleshy beef in thin slices; simmer with a quart of water twenty minutes, after it has once boiled and been skimmed. Season, if approved, but it has generally only salt.

MUTTON OR CHICKEN BROTH.

One pound of lean mutton or chicken cut small, one quart of cold water, one tablespoonful of rice or barley, soaked in a very little warm water, four tablespoonfuls of milk, salt and pepper, with a little chopped parsley. Boil the meat, unsalted, in the water, keeping it closely covered, until it falls to pieces. Strain it out, add the soaked barley or rice; simmer half an hour, stirring often; stir in the seasoning and milk, and simmer five minutes after it heats up well, taking care it does not burn. Serve hot, with cream crackers.

CHICKEN PANADA.

Boil a chicken until about three parts ready in a quart of water; take off the skin, cut the white meat off when cold, and put into a marble mortar. Pound it to a paste with a little of the water it was boiled in; season with a little salt, a grate of nutmeg, and the least bit of lemon peel. Boil gently for a few minutes to the consistency you like; it should be such as you can drink, though tolerably thick. This conveys great nourishment in small compass.

SIPPETS.

On an extremely hot plate put two or three sippets of bread, and pour over them some gravy from beef, mutton, or veal, with which no butter has been mixed. Sprinkle a little salt over. This is an excellent dish when the stomach will not receive meat.

FLOUR CAUDLE.

Into five large spoonfuls of the purest water rub smooth one dessert-spoonful of fine flour. Set over the fire five spoonfuls of new milk, and put two teaspoonfuls of sugar into it; the moment it boils, pour into it the flour and water, and stir it over a slow fire twenty minutes. It is a nourishing and gently astringent food. This is an excellent food for babies who have weak bowels.

SALEP.

Boil a little water, wine, lemon peel, and sugar together; then mix with a small quantity of the powder, previously rubbed smooth, with a little cold water; stir it all together, and boil it a few minutes.

MILK PORRIDGE.

Make a fine gruel of half grits, long boiled; strain off; either add cold milk, or warm with milk, as may be approved. Serve with toast.

FRENCH MILK PORRIDGE.

Stir some oatmeal and water together, let it stand to become clear, and pour off the latter; pour fresh water upon it, stir it well, let it stand till next day; strain through a fine sieve, and boil the water, adding milk while doing. The proportion of water must be small. This is often ordered with toast, for the breakfast of weak persons.

GROUND RICE MILK.

Boil one spoonful of ground rice, rubbed down smooth, with a pint and a half of milk, a bit of cinnamon, lemon peel, and nutmeg. Sweeten when nearly done.

Sago Milk.

Cleanse the sago, and boil it slowly, and wholly with new milk. It swells so much that a small quantity will be sufficient for a quart, and when done it will be diminished to about a pint. It requires no sugar or flavoring.

Toast and Water.

Toast slowly a thin piece of bread till extremely brown and hard, but not the least black; then plunge it into a jug of cold water, and cover it over an hour before used. This is of particular use in weak bowels. It should be of a fine brown color before drinking it.

Wine Whey.

Boil a quart of milk, add to it half a pint of wine, put on the fire till it boils again, then set aside till the curd settles, pour off the whey, and sweeten to taste. It is said good country cider is as nice as the wine.

Veal Broth.

Stew a small knuckle in about three quarts of water, two ounces of rice, a little salt, and a blade of mace, till the liquor is half wasted away.

Boiled Rice.

Wash a cupful of rice, and add four cupfuls of water, and a teaspoonful of salt; let it simmer on the back of the range for two hours, and do not stir it.

Toast Water.

Two slices of stale bread, toasted brown, cut in pieces, and a pint of boiling water poured over. Invalids relish it with a glass of white wine added, and a little nutmeg grated over.

Fresh Eggs for Invalids.

Break an egg into a tumbler, add two teaspoonfuls of white sugar, and whip briskly; then add a glass of wine, and fill up the tumbler with milk.

Hop Tea.

Take a large spoonful of hops, and simmer in a pint of water; when strong enough of hops, strain off and add white sugar and a tablespoonful of gin. It is a quieting drink, most excellent for nervous headache.

ADDITIONAL RECIPES

PERTAINING TO PLANTS.

CONCERNING HOUSE PLANTS.

The best temperature for house plants is from forty-eight degrees at night to seventy degrees during the day.

Water thoroughly, but not too often.

Give air on every warm, sunny day.

Shower all smooth-leaved plants frequently.

Wash the leaves of English ivy with clean, cold water and a sponge—nothing else.

In giving liquid manure—a heaping tablespoonful stirred into a water-pailful of water is enough.

Fix up all plants neatly.

Clip off all dead or dying leaves.

The oleander, calla lily, and hydranges may have water standing in the saucers under the pots.

Vines should be watered more frequently than other plants.

To kill the green fly or plant louse smoke the plants with tobacco.

Very weak lime water will kill worms in the pots.

Red spiders may be gotten rid of by frequently wetting the foliage and keeping the atmosphere moist.

A pinch of flour of sulphur, sprinkled now and then on the leaves, will keep off mildew.

Do not forget to send your flowers to your sick neighbors. They do a world of good, and your plants thrive all the better for having the blossoms picked.

If your plants should at any time get nipped with frost shower them with very cold water, and keep them in the shade for a day or two.

If you want your plants to bloom well in winter, do not let them bloom in summer.

Use water of the same temperature as the room.

Keep the air moist; a pan of water kept on the stove, or a damp towel hung on the register, will do this.

All plants need rest after blooming; set them away in the shade.

A few drops of ammonia added to a pail of water, and applied once a week, will prevent the earth in the pots from getting sour.

The mealy bug, which looks like a little more than a bit of dirt, must, like the scaly bug, be removed by hand picking.

Do not be discouraged at one failure, but keep trying, until your windows are a living protest against frost and snow, and your room a bower of living green, that will never let the memory of summer days go out of your heart.

One of the prettiest arrangements for plants is a window with two narrow shelves, placed one above the other, on which were three home-made flower pots containing a heliotrope, geraniums, pinks, begonias and other plants, all as thrifty as if grown in a green house.

Plants may be protected from the frost by placing newspapers between the window and the plants.

OLEANDER SLIPS.

Oleander slips may be rooted as follows: Cut a little slit in the end of the slip large enough to put an oat kernal in; put the slip with the kernal in it in a bottle of water and hang it up on the wall. In a short time little rootlets will appear, and it may then be put in a pot, but without removing the oat.

CALLA LILIES.

Calla lilies should be placed in a shady corner of the garden during the months of June and July and be given no water except that which falls from the clouds early in August; they should be put in a size larger pot with very rich earth, that is, loam-peat mixed; you cannot give too much water when growing and they are wanted to bloom.

WATER LILIES.

Water lilies may be successfully grown by sinking half a hogshead even with the ground, placing in soil taken from the bottom of a pond and planting a few roots therein. The hogshead is to be kept full of water, and the year following a crop of lilies surpassing those usually found in ponds in a wild state will be produced.

FLOWERS IN SAND.

Many pretty little blossoms of bulbs of violets, primroses and other spring flowers having short stalks, will keep fresh for a long time if each flower be pricked into a saucer or plate of wet sand. The great advantage of the sand over water used in the usual way, is that each bloom remains in its place just where fixed. It is a good idea to keep a flat glass dish filled as stated above, on the sideboard, and as these flowers decay, remove them, and stick in a few more in their places.

ASHES AND IRON FOR FLOWERS.

The observation of practical and experimental gardners seems to confirm the fact that to procure brilliant colors in flowers, it is necessary to cover the soil with an abundance of ferruginous constituents and silica. The latter supplies a material (says S. E. Todd in one of his foreign exchanges) which is one of vast importance in the production of that brilliancy of the petals and the dark green clusters of the leaves. Then, if potash be added, or the ground be dressed round about the growing flowers with unleached wood ashes, an increased brilliancy will appear in every petal and leaf. Any person who cultivates only a few flowers in pots, or on grassy lawns, or on spacious piazzas, may readily satisfy himself of the exceedingly useful part the foregoing materials play in the production of beautiful flowers. Even white flowers, or roses that have petals nearly white, will be greatly improved in brilliancy by providing iron sand and unleached ashes for the roots of growing plants. Ferruginous material may be applied to the soil where flowers are growing, or where they are to grow, by procuring a supply of oxide of iron, in the form of the dark colored scales that fall from the heated bars of iron when the metal is hammered by the blacksmiths. Iron turnings and iron filings, which may be obtained for a trifle at most machine shops, should be worked into the soil near the flowers, and in a few years it will be perceived that all the minute fragments will have been dissolved, thus furnishing the choicest material for painting the gayest colors of the flower garden. When there is an excess of vegetable mold in a flower bed, and a deficiency of silica or sand, the flowers will never be so rich in color, nor so brilliant as they would be were a liberal dressing of sand, or sandy loam, worked down into the bed, where the growing roots could reach it. If wood ashes can be obtained readily, let a dressing be spread over the surface of the ground, about half an inch deep, and raked in. A dressing of quicklime will be found excellent for flowers of every description. It is also of eminent importance to improve the fertility of the soil where flowers are growing, in order to have mature, plump, ripe seeds. Let the foregoing materials be spread around the flowers, and raked in at any convenient period of the year. When soil is prepared for flowers in pots, let some sand, some oxide of iron and ashes be mingled thoroughly with the leaf mold.

Religious Value of Flowers.

The Bible, the most valuable of all books, speaks of the "Rose of Sharon" and the "Lily of the Valley." Christ pointed to the latter for the purpose of illustrating and enforcing the truth. The poet feels the inspiration of flowers, and employs them as rich materials. One speaks of never-fading flowers that smile upon the everlasting fields of Paradise, and another of the shady rills of Sharon, where the lily and the rose contribute with their beauty and fragrance to the happiness of the devout. Their influence on the health and happiness of families, where cultivated, is proverbial. Absolutely we must surround ourselves with things beautiful and agreeable, or sink to a kind of heathenism.

Lilies for Pot Culture.

If anyone wishes a showy plant for winter blooming, let a bulb of Japan lily be set in a deep flower pot, with a compost surface soil from the woods, well rotted leaves, and enough rich, black loam to give it weight, all thoroughly mixed up together. Water slightly at first, but abundantly supply with moisture as growth progresses. Place in a sunny window, and the gorgeous flowers that are produced will sufficiently reward any one for the slight trouble required in taking care of them. After putting the bulb in the earth, the pot should be set in some cool, dark place until the roots get a good start. All bulbs for pot culture should be so treated. The calla lily is also very fine for window culture, and even if it produced no flowers at all, its large, bright, green leaves should make it a general favorite. It is a plant not affected much by insects, except the green fly, which can be easily removed by sponging.

To Raise Hyacinths in Winter.

Put the bulbs in glasses on earth, and set them in a dark closet to sprout. If in glasses the water should not be higher than one inch below the bulb, until the roots have reached the water, when the glasses may be filled up, a piece of charcoal put in the water, and the plants set in the sun to grow.

To Preserve Flowers.

Flowers may be preserved for many months by dipping them carefully as soon as gathered in perfectly limpid gum water; after allowing them to drain for two or three minutes, arrange them in a vase. The gum forms a complete coating on the stems and petals, and preserves their shape and color long after they have become dry.

Hanging Garden.

A hanging garden of sponge is a very pretty window ornament. Take a good-sized sponge and sow it full of rice, oats or wheat, placing it for a week or ten days in a shallow dish containing water. The sponge will absorb the moisture and the seeds will begin to sprout before many days. When this has fairly taken place, the sponge may be suspended by a cord from a hook at the top of the window, so as to swing free, where it will get a little sun. It will thus become a living mass of green, and require but little moisture.

A Parlor Vine.

To grow a pretty vine from the sweet potato, put a tuber in pure sand, or sandy loam, in a hanging basket and water occasionally. It will throw out tendrils and beautiful leaves, and climb freely over the arms of the basket and upwards toward the top of the window. There will not be one visitor in a hundred but that will suppose it to be some foreign plant. The dark green leaves might easily be taken for some new variety of ivy. As much pleasure can as often be got out of a common plant like the above as from one costly and rare.

How to Slip Geraniums.

Slipping geraniums or other plants for winter flowering may be successfully done by cutting the slips diagonally partly off. Let them remain on the parent stock long enough to harden, after which, if put in wet sand, they will certainly take root and thrive.

Autumn Work Among Flowers.

Many persons who have taken great delight and pleasure in their brilliant flowers all through the summer are often at a loss to know what to do with their favorites so that they may be ready to grow and blossom another season. Perhaps a little light may be thrown upon this subject which will relieve perplexity. When the blackening touch of the frost has withered the stalks of tender bulbs and roots, such as dahlias, tuberoses, gladiolus, and Madeira vines, they should be taken up on the first bright, sunny day. Take the forenoon for the work, and dig up the bulbs carefully, letting them lie in the sun for three or four hours, so that the earth attached to them will easily shake off. Then cut off the stalks a few inches from the bulbs, and put each variety in a paper bag, fastening it so as to hang it up in a cool, but frost-proof cellar; heat and dampness will cause them to decay. Tuberoses, however, will not blossom another season, but the numerous little bulbs which adhere to the parent bulb will, if kept in a dry, warm closet, and planted out in May or June, grow well another summer.

Ferns.

Nothing is more beautiful for interior decoration than the ferns which grow so luxuriantly in almost every pasture and woodland. The ferns are pressed and used in their natural state in decorating walls, fire screens, vases, etc., and produce a very pleasing effect. This style of decoration is growing in popularity, and promises to open a way to a productive industry. Let anybody who wishes to earn an honest penny, gather a supply of ferns, and in the holiday season they will sell readily.

Mounting Ferns.

By taking a little trouble, pretty pictures may often be made out of fern fonds, considered useless in the greenhouse, or, at all events, by the use of a few which may be cut off and never missed. After the ferns have been removed, they should be dried between sheets of botanical drying paper; even old newspaper or blotting paper will answer the purpose. Presuming that a collection of dried ferns is at hand, a sheet of nice cardboard should be procured; some like white cardboard, other, nicely tinted—which is the best. The ferns should then be laid lightly on it, and arranged according to taste; they should be lifted up again, and their backs glued with a fine brush, so as to make them stick to the paper. Should any gold or silver varieties be among those selected, they should be placed so as to show the colors of the under sides of the fonds. The light colored moss, which is to be found growing on old trunks of trees, if interspersed through the ferns, tends to give the arrangement a light and elegant appearance, if placed round or under a handsomely illuminated text.

Effective Arrangement for Cut Flowers.

The first thing to be considered in arranging cut flowers is the vase. If it is scarlet, blue, or many-colored, it must necessarily conflict with some hue in your bouquet. Choose, rather, pure white, green, or transparent glass, which allows the delicate stems to be seen. Brown Swiss wood, silver, bronze, or yellow straw conflict with nothing. The vase must be subordinate to what it holds. A bowl for roses; tall spreading vases for gladiolus, fern, white lilies and the like; cups for violets and tiny wood flowers; baskets for vines and gay garden blossoms. A flower will in time collect shapes and sizes to suit each group. Colors should be blended together with neutral tints, of which there are an abundance—whites, grays, purples, tender greens—and which harmonize the pink, crimsons, and brilliant red into soft unison. The water should be warm for a winter vase; cool, but not iced, for a summer one. A little salt or a bit of charcoal should be added in hot weather, to obviate vegetable decay, and the vase filled anew each morning. With these precautions your flowers, if set beside an open window at night, will keep their freshness for many hours even in July, and reward by their beautiful presence the kind hand which arranged and tended them.

A Good Way to Plant Spring Bulbs.

The only objection made to beds of spring bulbs is that though beautiful beyond description while the bulbs are in flower, the time of blooming is short; and thereafter the beds look bare and are not available for other purposes. This fault can be overcome by a little management and the use of such bulbs as bloom successively. The following arrangement has proved successful for several years. Make a round bed of any size and plant an inner circular row of crocus, and next outside a row of crocus, and next outside a row of hyacinths; then a second row of crocus, and next one of tulips between them. The row on the extreme edge must be crocus, and the space inside of the first row should be filled with tulips or hyacinths. The effect of a bed thus prepared is extremely pretty for a long time, and, thus arranged, it may remain undisturbed two or three years. Snow has no sooner gone than the bed is bright with the cheery little crocus, which apparently covers the whole surface. These will hardly have passed away when you will have a bed of hyacinths, in their delicate, lovely tints. The tulips then form a climax of gorgeousness that will last till the middle of June. The foliage of the crocus, which is extremely delicate and pretty, is in perfection during the flowering of the hyacinths and tulips, and covers the bed as with a lovely green carpet, taking away the usual bare look of bulb beds, when out of their time of bloom.

How to Make Moss Baskets.

Very beautiful baskets for holding flowers can be made of the longer and more feathery kinds of mosses. A light frame of any shape you like should be made with wire and covered with common pasteboard or calico, and the moss, which should first be well picked and cleansed from any bits of dirt or dead leaves, which may be hanging about it, gathered into little tufts, and sewed with a coarse needle and thread to the covering, so as to clothe it thickly with a close and compact coating, taking care that the points of the moss are all outward. A long handle made in the same manner should be attached to the basket, and a tin or other vessel filled with either wet sand or water, placed within to hold the flowers. By dipping the whole fabric into water three or four days, its verdure and elasticity will be fully preserved, and a block of wood about an inch thick, and stained black or green, if placed under the basket, will prevent all risk of damage to the table from moisture.

Care of Indoor Plants.

Everyone knows that a plant grown in the dark is weak and colorless; and if it has plenty of light and little air, it will be slender and sickly. The gardner, therefore, is careful to give his green houses and hot beds not only light, but air at every convenient opportunity. In winter he hails a bright, sunny day with delight. Plants will suffer from a currant of cold air just as their owner would, but will be benefited by an invigorating breath of fresh air. Provide, therefore, for air in some way, especially on pleasant days. Cleanliness is as necessary to the health of plants as to animals, and it is therefore necessary to secure them from dust as much as possible; and also to cleanse the plants frequently by syringing or washing. Even here a little caution is necessary, for while the smooth-leaved plants are benefited, not only by showering, but even by washing the leaves with a cloth or sponge, the rough-leaved plants, like the begonia rex, do not like to have the surface of their leaves frequently moistened. It would, therefore, be well to remove such plants before syringing. Take every precaution, however, to prevent the accumulation of dust upon the plants. The essentials of success in plant culture are suitable soil, air, light, moderate and regular heat, a moist atmosphere, regular and moderate watering and freedom from dust and foul gas.

Pretty Hanging Pots.

Very pretty hanging baskets, or pots, can be made of the tops of goblets or the half of a cocoanut shell, by crocheting a net of some bright worsteds to hang them in. A petunia placed in one of these and suspended in the window is what people who are extremely fond of flowers would call "lovely," when the long stems fall over the sides and are all covered with blossoms. The purple and white variety are the most beautiful. Very handsome hanging pots can be made in this manner at a cost of comparatively nothing. Try it.

Pot Flowers.

Many of those who attempt the raising of flowers in pots, make a fatal mistake at the very foundation, in the selection of the soil. Many use a soil which is too compact to allow water to pass freely through it, and the plants soon become "water logged." The soil should be porous enough to admit of the free passage of water, and yet not so open as to dry up. A pile composed of equal parts of partially decayed sods, manure and wood loam, will, when thoroughly decayed, make the best possible soil for pots. If sods and manure are used, garden soil may do, but most of it contains too much clay; this may be counteracted by using sand. The soil must allow the water to pass freely through it, and too much should not be applied at one time; little and often is the safest rule.

MISCELLANEOUS.

Pot-Pourri.

Put into a large china jar the following ingredients in layers, with bay salt strewed between the layers: Two pecks of damask roses, part in buds and part blown; violets, orange flowers and jasmine, a handful of each; orris root sliced, benjamin, and storax, two ounces of each; a quarter of an ounce of musk; a quarter of a pound of angelica root sliced; a quart of the red parts of clove gillyflowers; two handfuls of lavender flowers; half a handful of rosemary flowers; bay and laurel leaves, half a handful of each, three oranges, stuck as full of cloves as possible, dried in a cool oven, and pounded; half a handful of knotted marjoram; and two handfuls of balm of Gilead. Cover all quite close. When the pot is uncovered, the perfume is very fine.

How to Make Bandoline.

Simmer one ounce of quince seed and one-quarter of an ounce of Iceland moss in one quart of water. Add a little rectified spirits to make it keep well. Perfume. Cork tight. It is an excellent recipe to hold the hair in place.

To Remove the Unpleasant Odor of Perspiration.

The unpleasant odor produced by perspiration is often the cause of much vexation to persons who are subject to it. Instead of using perfumery, wash the whole body with warm water, to which has been added two tablespoonfuls of the compound spirits of ammonia. It will leave the skin as sweet, clean and fresh as one can wish. It is recommended on the authority of an experienced physician.

To Remove Corns.

Take a piece of lemon, cut it so as to let the toe through, and put the pulp next to the corn. Two or three applications will cure.

Soft Corns.

Soft corns between the toes may be cured by a weak solution of carbolic acid.

Ingrowing Nails.

Cut a notch in the centre of the nail, or scrape it thin in the middle. Put a small piece of tallow in a spoon and heat it over a lamp until it becomes very hot. Drop two or three drops between the nail and granulation. The pain and tenderness will soon be relieved, and in a few days the granulation will be gone. One or two applications will cure the most obstinate case.

To Remove Warts.

Dissolve three cents' worth of sal ammoniac in a gill of soft water. Wet the warts frequently. They will soon disappear.

How to Make Rose Water.

Take two drachms of magnesia and one-half ounce of powdered sugar; mix with these twelve drops of otto of roses; add two ounces of alcohol, and one quart of water filtered through blotting paper.

Tincture of Roses.

Take the leaves of the common rose (centifolious) and place, without pressing them, in a bottle. Pour some good spirits of wine upon them, close the bottle and let it stand until required for use. This tincture will keep for years, and yields a perfume little inferior to otto of roses. A few drops of it will impregnate the atmosphere of a room with a delicious odor.

Ratafia.

Blanch two ounces of peach and apricot kernels, bruise and put them into a bottle, and fill nearly up with brandy. Dissolve half a pound of white sugar-candy in a cup of cold water, and add to the brandy after it has stood a month on the kernels, and they are strained off; then filter through paper, and bottle for use.

Protection Against Moths.

Closets that have been infested with moths should be well rubbed with a decoction of tobacco and repeatedly sprinkled with spirits of camphor. Pieces of paper soaked with the same are good.

To Clean the Hair.

Take one ounce of borax and half an ounce of camphor. Powder these ingredients fine, and dissolve in one quart of boiling water. When cold, the solution will be ready for use. Dampen the hair with this frequently. It is claimed that this not only effectually cleanses and beautifies, but strengthens and preserves the hair. It also preserves the color and prevents baldness.

To Prevent Hair from Turning Gray.

The hair should be well brushed every day, and be wet at the roots with strong sage tea. One ounce of borax to every quart of the tea. Wet the scalp, and then brush for fully ten minutes. This will make harsh, rough hair, smooth and glossy.

To Restore Gray Hair.

Hair may be restored (when any remedy in the world will do it) to its natural color and beauty by the daily use of the following: Five grains of sulphurate of potassium, half an ounce of glycerine, one ounce of tincture of acetate of iron, and one pint of soft water. Mix and let the bottle stand open until the smell of the potassium has disappeared; then add a few drops of otto of roses. The hair should be rubbed with a little of this daily.

Tonic for the Hair.

Two ounces of French brandy, two ounces of bay rum, and one ounce of the best castor oil, well mixed. It is an excellent tonic for the hair.

To Beautify the Hair.

The hair may be made more beautiful and darkened by taking four ounces of bay rum, two ounces of olive oil and one drachm of the oil of almonds. Mix, shake well and apply.

For the Care of the Teeth.

Never allow a partical of food to remain between the teeth. Use the brush before breakfast and after each meal. Brush the back of the teeth as well as the front. Pure castile soap is better than powder. Use a tooth-pick freely after each meal.

To Clean Black Teeth.

Pulverize equal parts of salt and cream of tartar, and mix them thoroughly. After washing the teeth in the morning, rub them with this powder. After a few applications the blackness will disappear.

To Beautify the Teeth.

Dissolve in three pints of boiling water two ounces of borax. Add one teaspoonful of spirits of camphor. When you take a glass of water to brush your teeth, pour in a little. It is very pleasant and will strengthen the gums

For the Complexion.

One-half pint of new milk, one-half ounce of white brandy, one-quarter ounce of lemon juice, boiled together. Skim clean from scum, and use night and morning. It will remove tan and freckles caused by the sun and wind.

Complexion Wash.

A good and perfectly harmless wash for the face can be made by adding one ounce of powdered gum of benzoin to a pint of white whisky; add water until it becomes milky. Pour a little into the palm of the hand, rub it all over the face and neck, and wipe downwards with the palm of the hand until dry. It should not be used until after the face has been washed an hour.

To Make Cold Cream.

Twenty grains of white wax, two ounces of pure oil of sweet almonds, one-half ounce of pure glycerine, and six drops of oil of roses. Melt the first three ingredients together in a shallow dish over hot water. As it begins to cool, add the glycerine and oil of roses. Strain through muslin. Beat with a silver spoon until snowy white. It is excellent for chapped face and hands, and makes the skin fine and soft.

To Make Lip Salve.

Place a jar in a basin of boiling water. Melt one ounce each of white wax and spermaceti, fifteen grains of flour of benzoin, and half an ounce of oil of almonds. Stir until the mixture is cold. Color with a little alkanet root.

To Clean Hair Brushes.

Put a tablespoonful of ammonia into tepid water, dip the brushes up and down in it until clean; then dry with the brushes downward and they will look like new.

Measures for Housekeepers.

Wheat flour, one pound is one quart; Indian meal, one pound and two ounces is a quart; butter (when soft), one pound is one quart; loaf sugar (broken), one pound is one quart; white sugar (powdered), one pound and one ounce is one quart; best brown sugar, one pound two ounces is one quart; eggs, ten are one pound; flour, eight quarts are one peck.

To Clean Zinc.

Wash it in a solution of oxalic acid and water, and rub off with finely powdered slacked lime.

To Wash Woolen.

To every pail of water add one tablespoonful of ammonia, and the same of beef gall; wash out quickly, and rinse in warm water, adding a very little beef gall to the water. This will remove spots from carpets, making them look fresh.

To Clean Carpets.

Mix ox gall and water; rub the carpet with a flannel dipped in the mixture; then rub dry with a linen cloth.

How to Use Beef's Gall in Setting Colors.

Pour the gall from the bladder into a bottle, let it stand corked two or three days to settle. Pour about half of it into a pailful of warm bran water, stir it well together; then wash whatever you want to set the color quickly; rinse in two waters, and dry in a shady place. Most dark colors are "set" or fixed by using the gall, but some light, delicate colors, pink, blue, violet and lavender require the following treatment: Dissolve one tablespoonful of sugar of lead in half a pail of cold water. Put the article to be soaked into the water, and let it soak two or three hours; then wash quickly in bran water, no soap; rinse and dry as usual. In using sugar of lead, be careful not to put the hands into the water if there is a scratch or cut on them, as the lead is poisonous if it gets beneath the skin. It is better to take the article out with a stick, drain, and then put it into the bran water and wash.

Camphor Ice.

One-half ounce each of camphor gum, white wax, spermaceti, and sweet oil or lard; melt slowly the hard ingredients, and then add the oil.

Lime Water.

Put four ounces of quick lime into six pints of water; mix well, and let it stand in a covered vessel an hour; then pour off the liquid.

Cure for Sore Throat.

One ounce of tincture muriate of iron, and one ounce of chlorate of potash. Place one teaspoonful of the potash with the same quantity of the iron in a bottle holding one-half pint; shake well, and add enough syrup to fill the bottle. The syrup is prepared by placing in a vessel one cupful of white sugar, with just sufficient water to dissolve it; heat, and when the sugar is dissolved, fill the bottle. Dose for an adult, one teaspoonful three or four times a day; dose for children, one-half teaspoonful three or four times a day.

Grafting Wax.

One and one-quarter pounds of beeswax, two pounds of resin and three-quarters of a pound of tallow

To Remove Ink Stains.

Ink can be removed from furniture, carpets, floors, etc., as follows: Wipe the spot with oxalice, let it remain a few minutes, then rub it with a cloth wet with warm water. Colored paint, mahogany and carpets will require washing with ammonia water to restore the original color.

Cure for a Bone Felon.

Take soft soap and air-slacked lime and mix to a putty. Apply in a leather cot.

Soft Soap.

Twelve pounds of potash, eighteen pounds of grease and boiling water enough to fill the barrel. Then put in potash and grease. Stir often for a few days.

Mrs. Woods's Salve.

Three pounds of lard, one pound of bayberry-tallow, three ounces of oil of rosemary, a piece of beeswax the size of a butternut. Stir in the rosemary when cooled a little.

A Strong Paste for Paper.

To two large spoonfuls of fine flour put as much pounded resin as will lie on a shilling; mix with as much strong beer as will make it of a due consistence, and boil half an hour. Let it become cold before it is used.

A Cure for Rheumatism.

Lemon juice is recommended as a certain cure for acute rheumatism. It is given in quantities of a tablespoonful to twice the quantity of cold water, with sugar, every hour. The effect of the lemon juice is almost instantaneous.

To Extract Grease from Cloth.

For removing grease from cloth the following is infallible: To half a pint of pure alcohol add ten grains of carbonate of potash, half an ounce of oil of bergamot, and one ounce of sulphuric ether; mix, and keep in a glass-stopped bottle. Apply with a piece of sponge, soaking the cloth thoroughly when the grease is not recent. The mixture emits a peculiarly fragrant odor, and being a fluid soap, chemically composed, will be found a perfect solvent of oily matter.

To Restore Crape.

When a drop of water falls on a black crape veil or collar it leaves a conspicuous white mark. To obliterate this, spread the crape on a table (laying on it a large book or a paper weight, to keep it steady), and place underneath the stain a piece of old black silk. With a large camel-hair brush dipped in common ink go over the stain, and then wipe off the ink with a bit of old soft silk. It will dry immediately, and the white mark will be seen no more.

An Ant Trap.

Procure a large sponge, wash it well, and press it dry, which will leave the cells quite open; then sprinkle over it some fine white sugar, and place it near where the ants are most troublesome. They will soon collect upon the sponge, and take up their abode in the cells. It is then only necessary to dip the sponge in scalding water, which will wash them out "clean dead" by ten thousands. Put on more sugar, and set the trap for a new haul. This process will soon clear the house of every ant, uncle and progeny.

Ink Stain.

Housewives who are horrified at the sight of ugly ink stains will like to get a recipe for removing them:

The moment the ink is spilled, take a little milk and saturate the stain; soak it up with a rag, and apply a little more milk, rubbing it well in. In a few minutes the ink will be completely removed.

To Clean Decanters.

Cut some raw potatoes in pieces, put them in the bottle with a little cold water; rinse them, and they will look very clean.

To Clean Cut Glass.

Cut glass should be rubbed with a damp sponge dipped in whiting; then brush this off with a clean brush, and wash the vessel in cold water.

To Remove Rust.

To remove rust from steel, cover with sweet oil, well rubbed on it; in forty-eight hours use unslacked lime powdered very fine. Rub it until the rust disappears. To prevent the rust, mix with fat oil varnish four-fifths of well rectified spirits of turpentine. The varnish is to be applied by means of a sponge; and articles varnished in this manner will retain their brilliancy, and never contract any spots of rust. It may be applied to copper philosophical instruments, etc.

To Take Stains of Any Kind Out of Linen.

Stains caused by acids.—Wet the part, and lay on it some salt of wormwood. Then rub it without diluting it with more water.

Another.—Let the cloth imbibe a little water without dipping, and hold the part over a lighted match at a due distance. The spots will be removed by the sulphureous gas.

Another way.—Tie up in the stained part some pearl ash; then scrape some soap into cold water to make a lather, and boil the linen until the stain disappears.

Stains of wine, fruit, etc., after they have been long in the linen.—Rub the part on each side with yellow soap. Then lay on a mixture of starch in cold water very thick; rub it well in, and expose the linen to the sun and air until the stain comes out. If not removed in three or four days, rub that off, and renew the process. When dry, it may be sprinkled with a little water.

To Prevent a Felon.

When a soreness is felt, immerse the finger in a basin of ashes and cold water, set it on the stove while cold, and stir it continually, without taking it out, until the lye is so hot it cannot be borne any longer. If the soreness is not gone in half an hour, repeat it.

To Prevent Flies Injuring Picture Frames.

Boil three or four onions in one pint of water. Brush your frames over with the liquid. No fly will touch them, and it will not injure the frames.

How to Tell Good Eggs.

If you desire to be certain that your eggs are good and fresh, put them in water; if the buts turn up, they are not fresh. This is an infallible rule to distinguish a good egg from a bad one.

Linen Whitened.

Cut a pound of fine white soap into a gallon of milk and hang it over the fire in the wash kettle.

When the soap is entirely melted, put in the linen, and boil half an hour; then take it out; have ready a lather of soap and warm water; wash the linen in it, and then rinse through two cold waters, with a very little blue at the last.

To Cure Diphtheria.

Take a common tobacco pipe, place a live coal in the bowl, drop a little tar upon the coal, draw the smoke into the mouth, and discharge it through the nostrils.

Cure for a Cough.

A patient, who, for nearly two months, could not pass a night in quiet without large doses of laudanum, has been cured of a most harassing cough by suet boiled in milk.

To Keep and Prepare Lard.

To a gallon of lard, before it is washed, put one ounce of sal soda. The soda makes it foam and boil over. No other water is required than that the soda is dissolved in. Lard put up in this way keeps for two years hard through the whole summer. When your lard is done, it will be as clear as spring water. Strain through a coarse cloth into your jars, and set to cool.

Butterflies and Moths.

All that is required for collecting these insects is the following: A net, killing bottle, some setting boards, a collecting box, a store box, and some pins. The best time for catching butterflies is on a hot sunny day during the middle of the day—from eleven, to three or four o'clock in the afternoon. The moths are out in force in the evening, and may be captured by "sugaring" for them. Boil together half a pint of beer, a quarter of a pound of sugar and the same of molasses, add half a gill of rum, and apply this mixture with a brush to the trunks of trees, making a streak two inches wide. This will attract the moths, and those desired may be captured and put in the killing bottle. Having killed the moth, fasten it in the collecting box with a pin stuck through its side, thus avoiding any injury to the back.

Wasp Stings.

The following will cure almost instantaneously a wasp or bee sting: Press a common hollow trunk key over the puncture until the pain ceases. In the case of a bee sting on the cheek, apply a hollow trunk key over the sting, and in less than one minute the sting will be forced upon the surface. The same principle applied to the bite of any poisonous animal, even that of a rabid dog, snakes or mosquito bites, would effect a cure by preventing the poison from entering the circulation.

Home-made Water Filter.

Place a wine cask on end, fit a faucet at the bottom and remove the head. In this bore holes all over it with a small bit; place four clean bricks on the bottom of the cask and on these rest the perforated top. On this perforated top put about four inches of charcoal broken into bits the size of peas, and over this a layer of clean sand six inches deep. Water passing through this layer of sand and that of charcoal under it will leave its impurities behind it, and run from the faucet clear and sparkling. Once in two or three months the filter should be renewed.

Cleansing Carpets.

Where carpets cannot readily be taken up and thoroughly shaken, they may be very much brightened and freshened by being wiped with a mop wrung from warm water. The water should be frequently changed. If the mopping precedes and follows through sweeping, but little dust will be raised in the room. With the aid of a mop-wringer this may be easily done, without wetting even the finger tips, and the mopping will be less tiresome than the sweeping. A little ox gall or ammonia in the water will brighten the color. If a carpet sweeper is used the carpet may be entirely cleansed without raising a particle of dust, though it is well to cover bric-a-brac while the work is going on.

Night Sweats.

A gentleman went to a celebrated physician and told him that his child was suffering from night sweats consequent on nervous exhaustion. "Rub him," was all the response he could get. So he rubbed the child persistently every morning and night with his hands, and in a short time the trouble ceased. The same father sent his little daughter to the country for the summer. While there she ran incessantly. Her friends perceived that she began to draw long breaths, and longer breaths, until she sighed almost continually. A physician being interrogated as to the cause of this sighing, simply replied: "Runs too much." So the girl was kept more quiet, and soon the sighing ceased. These hints may be beneficial

Milk Diet.

Milk is called by some constipating food, and food likely to produce biliousness. But without just reason. Every constituent of milk can be assimilated and there is no waste in it, so there is nothing left to cause any action on the bowels. If milk were taken into the stomach as slowly and were as perfectly mingled with saliva as is an equivalent amount of solid food, when slowly eaten and thoroughly masticated, the probabilities are that the liver would not be stimulated to send bile into the stomach, where it does not belong, to aid in digesting the milk. Milk should be sipped slowly and with pauses between, not gulped at a draught. Those who are troubled with headache after eating should drink milk very slowly or not at all. The acids of the stomach convert it promptly into curd, and everybody knows that curd, like cheese, is a very hearty food.

Cement.

For a stove that has a crack in it buy silicate of potash or soluble glass, mix it with ashes, and apply to the crack. This cement will stick to red-hot iron and bricks without crumbling off, but will not bear moisture. If holes are to be stopped in hard-finished walls mix the silicate and whiting; if in holes in grates, mix with fire clay.

Ink from Mahogany.

Touch the stain with a feather dipped in a spoonful of water with six or eight drops of nitre mixed with it. As soon as the ink disappears wash the place with a cloth wrung from cold water, or a white spot will be left. Repeat if necessary. Ink stains may be removed from other dark woods in this way.

Chilblains.

1.—One ounce of sulphureous acid, one ounce of

glycerine, and two ounces of distilled water; mix, and apply night and morning. 2.—Rub the feet with snow. 3.—Bathe in strong oak-leaf tea, or in liquor from the tan vats heated hot. 4.—Apply strong copperas water. 5.—Hold the foot, with the sock on, as near the fire as can be borne, withdrawing it when too hot, and returning it again to the fire for five or ten minutes. One or two successive applications will effect a cure. 6.—One part of muriatic acid to eight parts of water. Just wet the chilblains before the fire, if not broken; if they are, apply poultices and healing ointment.

Disinfection.

One of the most important methods of disinfection is the following: Into an iron kettle put some live coals, set the kettle in the room to be disinfected and lay stick sulphur on the coals. The doors and windows should be closed before the sulphur is lighted, and whatever will be likely to be bleached by the sulphureous acid fumes should be removed.

To Cure a Wen.

Wash it with common salt dissolved in water every day, and it will be removed in a short time. Or make a strong brine of alum salt; simmer it over the fire. When thus prepared, wet a piece of cloth in it every day, and apply it constantly for one month, and the protuberance will disappear.

Cure for Chills.

One ounce each of cream of tartar, pulverized Peruvian bark and ground cloves. Mix well together, and take a tablespoonful three times a day, half an hour before eating, in a wine-glass of sweet cider. It has never been known to fail.

For Sick Headache.

Put the feet into hot mustard water, lay a cold wet cloth on the stomach with dry flannel over it, and swallow a few spoonfuls of lemon juice.

Cure for Headache.

Put a handful of salt into a quart of water, add one ounce of spirits of hartshorn and half an ounce of camphorated spirits of wine. Put them quickly into a bottle, and cork tightly to prevent the escape of the spirits. Soak a piece of rag with the mixture, and apply it to the head; wet the rag afresh as soon as it gets heated.

To Clean Brass.

Rub the tarnished or rusted brass, by means of a cloth or sponge, with diluted acid, such as sulphuric, or even with strong vinegar. Afterward wash it with hot water, to remove the acid, and finish with dry whiting.

Soap for Whitening the Hands.

Take a wine-glassful of *eau de cologne*, and another of lemon juice; then scrape two cakes of brown Windsor soap to a powder, and mix well in a mould.

To Wash White Lace.

The following recipe for washing white lace is generally found more successful than any other: Cover a glass bottle with white flannel, then wind the lace round it, tack it to the flannel on both sides, and cover the whole with a piece of flannel or linen, which sew firmly round it. Then steep the bottle over night in an ewer, with soap and cold water. Next morning wash it with hot water and soap, the soap being rubbed on the outer covering. Then steep it again for some hours in cold water, and afterwards dry it in the air or near the fire. Remove the outer covering, and the lace is ready, no ironing being required. If the lace is very dirty, of course it must be washed a great deal.

To Remove Mortar or Paint from Window Glass.

Rub mortar spots with a stiff brush dipped in sharp, hot vinegar, and paint spots with camphene and sand.

To Take off Starch or Rust from Sad Irons.

Tie a piece of yellow beeswax in a rag, and when the iron is almost hot enough for use, rub it with the beeswax quickly, and then with a clean coarse cloth.

To Purify a Sink or Drain.

Dissolve half a pound of copperas in two gallons of water. Pour in half this liquor one day and the other half the next day.

To Take Out Mildew.

Get the dryest chloride of lime you can buy, and for strong fabrics, dissolve four tablespoonfuls of the lime in half a pint of water. Let the mildewed article lie in this solution fifteen minutes. Take it out, wring it gently, and put immediately into weak muriatic acid, one part acid and four parts soft water. For delicate fabrics, the solution of lime should be made much weaker, three or four times the quantity of water should be put on the lime. Let the article lie in it only fifteen minutes, and then put into the muriatic acid.

Tooth Powder.

Two ounces of Peruvian bark, two ounces of myrrh, one ounce of chalk, one ounce of Armenian bole, and one ounce of orris root.

To Clean Silk and Make it Like New.

Put an old kid glove in a pint of cold water. Let it boil until the water is reduced to one-half the quantity. Sponge the silk with this water on the right side, and iron it on the wrong side. This will make old silks or ribbons look like new.

To Drive Away Ants.

The little red ants will leave a place where sea sand is sprinkled, or where oyster shells are laid. Scatter sprigs of wormwood where black ants are troublesome.

To Extract Oil or Grease Spots from Carpets.

If oil is spilled on a carpet, put on plenty of white flour, and do it as soon as possible, to prevent the oil spreading. If the oil is near a seam, but does not reach it, rip the seam, in order to stop it. Put flour on the floor under the oil spot. The next day brush up all the flour from the carpet and floor with a stiff brush, and repeat the putting on of fresh flour. It will not need it the third time. To take out grease spots rub them with a bit of white flannel dipped in spirits of turpentine. If they show again, repeat the process. It is well to put paper under the carpet, when grease spots are on the floor, as no scouring will remove them entirely.

To Renovate Velvet.

Wet a clean sponge in warm soap suds, squeeze it very dry in a cloth, and wipe the velvet with it. Then pass the velvet over the edge of a hot sad iron, turned down sideways—the wrong side of the velvet next to the iron.

To Keep Steel Knives from Rusting.

Have them rubbed bright, and perfectly dry; have a soft rag, and rub each blade with dry wood ashes. Wrap them in thick brown paper, and lay them in a dry closet. If taken care of in this way, they may be kept years free from rust.

To Keep Ivory Knife Handles from Cracking.

Never let the knife blades stand in hot water. The heat expands the steel that runs up into the handle, and cracks it. Of course the handles must never lie in water.

To Take Out Fruit Stains.

Tie up cream of tartar in the spotted places, and put the garment into cold water and boil it. If the stains are much spread, stir cream of tartar in the water. If still visible, boil the garment in a mixture of super carbonate of soda, a tablespponful to a pail of water.

To Purify a Well.

When the well is cleaned out, if any offensive substance is found in it, have the bottom sprinkled with two or three quarts of quicklime.

To Destroy Grass in Gravel Walks.

Scatter the cheapest coarse salt along the edges, and wherever the grass is springing up. Even the Canada thistle can be destroyed by cutting the stalks close to the ground and putting salt on them.

To Make Grass Thrifty.

Spread wood ashes on it just before a rain. If you cultivate raspberries and blackberries, have a lot of sawdust and put round them once a year. It wil improve them a great deal.

Black Paper for Drawing Patterns.

Mix and smooth lampblack and sweet oil; with a bit of flannel cover a sheet or two of large writing paper with this mixture; then dab the paper dry with a bit of fine linen, and keep it by for using in the following manner: Put the black side on another sheet of paper, and fasten the corners together with small pins. Lay on the back of the black paper the pattern to be drawn, and go over it with the point of a steel pencil; the black paper will then leave the impression of the pattern on the under sheet, on which you must draw it with ink. If you draw patterns on cloth or muslin, do it with a pen dipped in a bit of stone blue, a bit of sugar, and a little water, mixed smooth in a teacup, in which it will be always ready for use, if fresh wet to a due consistence as wanted.

To Extract Oil from Boards or Stone.

Make a strong ley of pearl ashes and soft water, and add as much unslacked lime as it will take up; stir it together, and then let it settle a few minutes; bottle it, and stop close; have ready some water to lower it as used, and scour the part with it. If the liquor should lay long on the boards, it will draw out the color of them; therefore, do it with care and expedition.

To Take Stains from Marble.

Mix unslacked lime in finest powder, with the strongest soap ley, pretty thick, and instantly, with a painters' brush, lay it on the whole of the marble. In two months' time wash it off perfectly clean; then have ready a fine thick lather of soft soap, boiled in soft water; dip a brush in it, and scour the marble with powder, not as common cleaning. This will, by very hard rubbing, give a beautiful polish. Clear off the soap, and finish with a smooth hard brush until the end be effected.

Hard Soap.

Four pounds of grease, three pounds of quicklime, and six pounds of sal soda. Put the lime and soda together in four gallons of hot water; let it stand over night, and then add the grease and boil four hours.

To Color Seal Brown.

One pound of cutch, half a pound of bichromate potash to four pounds of goods. Put potash in brass kettle and cutch in iron kettle.

To Take Iron Stains from Marble.

Mix an equal quantity of fresh spirits of vitriol and lemon juice in a bottle, shake well. Wet the spots, and in a few minutes rub with soft linen until they disappear.

Hair Tonic.

Two ounces of tincture of cantharades, half a pint of Jamaica rum and one pint of rain water.

Paste for Chapped Hands.

Mix a quarter of a pound of unsalted hog's lard, which has been washed in water, and then in rose water, with the yolks of two new-laid eggs, and a large spoonful of honey. Add as much fine oatmeal or almond paste as will work into a paste. This will keep the hands smooth by its constant use.

Fine Blacking for Shoes.

' Take four ounces of ivory black, three ounces of the coarsest sugar, a tablespoonful of sweet oil, and a pint of small beer; mix them gradually cold.

To Cement Broken China.

Beat lime into the most impalpable powder, sift it through fine muslin; then tie some into a thin muslin; put on the edge of the broken china some white of an egg, then dust some lime quickly on the same and unite then exactly.

Kitchen Pepper.

Mix together one ounce of the finest powdered ginger, half an ounce each of cinnamon, black pepper, nutmeg and Jamaica pepper, ten cloves and six ounces of salt. Keep it in a bottle. It is an agreeable addition to any brown sauces or soups.

To Make Essence of Anchovies.

Take two dozen anchovies, chop them, without the bone, but with some of their own liquor strained; add them to sixteen large spoonfuls of water; boil gently until dissolved, which will be in a few minutes; when cold, strain and bottle. The quicker the process, the finer will be the color.

To Clarify Sugar for Sweetmeats.

Break as much as required in large lumps, and put a pound to half a pint of water, in a bowl, and it will dissolve better than when broken small. Set it over the fire, with the well-whipped white of an egg; let it boil up, and, when ready to run over, pour a little cold water in to give it a check; but when it rises a second time, take it off the fire, and set it by in a pan for a quarter of an hour, during which the foulness will sink to the bottom, and leave a black scum on the top, which take off gently with a skimmer, and pour the syrup into a vessel very quickly from the sediment.

To Keep Lemon Juice.

Buy the fruit when cheap and keep it in a cool place two or three days; if too unripe to squeeze readily, cut the peel off from some and roll them under your hand to make them chop with the juice more readily; others you may have unpared for grating, when the pulp shall be taken out and dried. Squeeze the juice into a china basin; then strain it through some muslin which will not permit the least pulp to pass. Fill half and quarter-ounce phials—which should be perfectly dry—with the juice so near the top as only to admit half a spoonful of sweet oil into each, or a little more if for larger bottles. Cork tight, and set them upright in a cool place. When you wish to use the juice, wind some clean cotton around a skewer, and you can easily dip the oil from the juice, which will be as fine as when first bottled.

To Pot Mushrooms.

Choose large buttons, or such whose inside is not yet the least brown; peel and wipe out the fur of the larger ones; and to every two quarts put half a drachm of pounded mace, two drachms of white pepper, and six or eight cloves in powder; set them over the fire; shake and let the liquor dry up into them. Then put to them two ounces of butter, and stew them in it until they are fit for eating; pour the butter from them, and let them become cold. Pack them close into a pot, making the surface as even as possible; add some lukewarm butter, and lay a bit of white paper over them, and pour clarified suet upon it to exclude the air.

Colorings for Jellies, Ices or Cakes.

For a beautiful red, boil fifteen grains of cochineal in fine powder, with a drachm and a half of cream of tartar, in half a pint of water, very slowly, half an hour. Add in boiling a bit of alum the size of a pea. Or use beet root sliced and some liquor poured over. For white, use almonds finely powdered, with a little water; or use cream. For yellow, the yolks of eggs, or a bit of saffron, steeped in liquor and squeezed. For green, pound spinach leaves or beet leaves, express the juice, and boil in a saucepan in a teacupful of water to take off the rawness.

Extract of Spinach.

Wash and pound in a mortar a sufficient quantity of spinach for a small dish, until it assumes a pulpy appearance; turn it out upon a strong kitchen rubber, the opposite ends of which are to be gathered up and held in the left hand by two persons, who must take care to fold the extremity of the cloth firmly round the handle of a wooden spoon, which will give them a strong purchase, acting as a windlass, and will enable them to wring the cloth so tightly as to express all the moisture of the spinach. To receive this extract, a stew pan should be placed ready; it should be held over the fire until it becomes coagulated, and must be put upon a hair sieve to drain off any remaining watery particles. Work the spinach green through the sieve with a spoon, and this will form the extract.

For Filtering Orange or Lemon Juice for Jellies.

Wash several sheets of white blotting paper (of the best quality) in cold water; then boil them in two quarts of water for about twenty minutes, strain the water from the paper, and pound it in a mortar until reduced to a fine pulp; mix this with a spoonful of washed white sand; then add both to the juice intended to be filtered, and throw the whole into a clean beaver jelly bag. Pass the juice through the filtering bag until it drops as bright as spring water.

BILLS OF FARE.

BREAKFAST, NO. 1.

Oatmeal and Cream.

Lamb Chops. Broiled Steak.

Stewed Potatoes. Fried Potatoes.

Rolls. Corn Cakes.

Tea. Coffee.

BREAKFAST, NO. 2.

Fruit.

Hominy and Milk.

Porterhouse Steak. Broiled Ham.

Omelets, with Mushrooms.

Stewed Potatoes.

Rolls. Graham Gems.

Tea. Coffee. Chocolate.

BREAKFAST, NO. 3.

Fruit.

Oatmeal and Cream.

Mutton Chops.   Cold Tongue.

Spanish Mackerel.

Lyonnaise Potatoes.   Sliced Tomatoes.

Griddle Cakes.

Graham Gems.   Toast.

Tea.   Coffee.

BREAKFAST, NO. 4.

Canteloupe Mellons.

Broiled Spanish Mackerel.   Broiled Chicken.

New Stewed Potatoes.

Fancy Baked Potatoes.

Rice Griddle Cakes.   Waffles.

Tea.   Coffee.   Chocolate.

DINNER, NO. 1.

Tomato Soup.

Baked Blue Fish, Oyster Sauce.

Roast Beef.   Roast Lamb.   Boiled Ham.

Mashed Potatoes.   Green Peas.

Stewed or Sliced Tomatoes.   String Beans.

Rice Pudding.

Lemon Meringe Pie.   Berry Pie.

Chocolate Cream.

Fruits.   Nuts.

Coffee.   Tea.

DINNER, NO. 2.

English White Soup.

Chow Chow.   Tomato Catsup.   Lettuce.

Soles, a la Portugese.   Riced Potatoes.

Beef, a la Mode.

Spare Rib of Pork.

Roast Chicken.

Mashed Potatoes.   Squash.   Asparagus.

Fig Pudding, Wine Sauce.

Cream Pie.   Orange Tartlets.   Assorted Cake.

Cream, a la Romaine.

Oranges.   Nuts.   Raisins.

Tea.   Coffee.   Chocolate.

DINNER, NO. 3.

Ox Tail Soup.

Mushroom Catsup.   Sweet Pickles.
Spiced Tomatoes.

Baked Turbot.   Fancy Baked Potatoes.

Veal, a la Daube.
Sweet Breads.   Pigeon Pie.

Stewed Asparagus.   Stewed Green Peas.
Riced Potatoes.   Onion Ormoloo.

Apple Pudding, a la Cremone, Sweet Sauce.
Apple Pie.   Apricot Jelly.   Orange Pie.
Pistachio Cream.
Sponge Cake.

Tea.   Coffee.

SUPPER, NO. 1.

Deviled Turkey.   Pickled Oysters.
Preserved Pine Apples.
Rusks.   Hot Biscuit and Butter.
Cheese Cakes.
Watermelon Cake.   White Fruit Cake.
Tea.   Coffee.

SUPPER, NO. 2.

Potted Lobster. Cold Lamb.
Sardines.

Strawberries and Cream. Brandied Peaches.

Bread and Butter. Cottage Cheese.

Angels' Food.
Pound Cake. Banana Cake.

Tea. Coffee.

SUPPER, NO. 3.

Oyster Salad. Chicken Croquettes.

Preserved Pears. Brandied Apricots.

Cream Biscuits. Crackers.

Pickled Crab Apples. Pickled French Beans.
Sage Cheese.

Geneva Cake. Black Fruit Cake. Lady Fingers.

Tea. Coffee.

INDEX.

Soups.

	PAGE.
American Lobster	24
Bean	23
Beef	22
Brown Stock	16
Chicken Broth	23
Clam	25
Coloring for Soups and Gravies	15
Common	22
Dried Pea	20
Eel	24
English Gravy	19
English Lobster	24
English Mock Turtle	17
English White	17
French Stewed Oysters	25
French Vegetable	20
Green Pea	21
Grouse	18
Ham or Pea	21
Macaroni	18
Mock Stewed Oysters	23
Noodles	17
Ox Tail	20
Oyster Stew, No. 1	25
Oyster Stew, No. 2	25
Partridge	18
Plain White	18
Portable	16
Scotch Barley Broth	19
Scotch Mutton Broth	20
Soup, a la Sap	23
Soup Powder	26
Split Pea	22
Tomato	16
Tomato	19

Fish.

	PAGE.
Brook Trout, Fried	39
Codfish Cakes	37
Codfish, Scrambled	37
Eels, collared	37
Eels, fried	37
Fish Cake	38
Fish Chowder	38
Flounders	35
Fresh Fish, broiled	39
Herrings, broiled	36
Herrings, fried	36
Observations on Dressing	29
Pike, to dress	36
Plaice, to dress	36
Red Mullet	35
Salmon, collared	33
Salmon, dried	33
Salmon, pickled	33
Salmon, to boil	32
Salmon, to broil	32
Salmon, to pot	33
Salt Cod or Ling, to dress	34
Salt Fish, to dress	34
Smelts, to Fry	37
Soles	34
Soles, a la Portuguese	34
Soles, stuffing for	35
Sturgeon, to dress	32
To Fry	30
To Select	29
Trout, cream baked	39
Turbot	31
Turbot, baked	31
Turbot, boiled	31

Shell-Fish.

	PAGE.
Clam Chowder, No. 1	41
Clam Chowder, No. 2	42
Lobster, buttered	46
Lobster Patties	46
Lobster Pudding	45
Lobsters, Rissoles of	46
Lobsters, to pot	46
Oysters, baked in shell	45
Oysters, fancy roast	45
Oysters, fried, No. 1	42
Oysters, fried, No. 2	42
Oyster Fritters	45
Oyster Loaf	44
Oyster Macaroni	45
Oyster Patties	43
Oyster Pie	43
Oysters, roasted	44
Oysters, scalloped	44
Oysters, steamed	43
Oyster Toast	44
Oysters, to pickle	42

Meats.

	PAGE.
Beefsteak	51
Beefsteaks, Italian	51
Beefsteaks and Oyster Sauce	51
Beefsteaks, Staffordshire	52
Beef, a la mode	52
Beef Heart	52
Beef Palates	52
Beef Palates, to pickle	52
Beef, to pot	53
Beef, minced	54
Beef, to dress the inside of a sirloin of	54
Beef, to select	49
Beef, to salt	74
Beef Savory	55
Beef, spiced	50
Calf's Head, to dress like Turtle	57
Calf's Head, to collar	61
Calf's Liver	62
China Chilo	66
Collops, to dress quick	60
Cutlets	60
Cutlets Maintenon	59
Forcemeat, ingredients of	75
Ham Croquets	72
Ham and Eggs, fried	71

Meats—Continued.

	PAGE.
Ham, how to choose a	70
Ham, roast	72
Ham, toast	72
Hams, to cure	69
Harrico	64
Head Cheese	70
Lamb Cutlets, with spinach	66
Lamb, fore quarter of	66
Lamb's head and hinge	67
Lamb, leg of	66
Lamb's sweet-breads	67
Meat, to curry	55
Mutton, a la venison	63
Mutton, breast of	64
Mutton Chops	65
Mutton Cutlets	65
Mutton, fillet of glazed	64
Mutton, hashed without herbs	62
Mutton or Lamb Steaks and Cucumbers	65
Mutton Kidneys	62
Mutton Kidneys	63
Mutton, roast saddle of	64
Mutton Steaks, with beans	63
Mutton, to collar a breast of	65
Ox Cheek, to dress	54
Pettitoes	68
Pig's Feet and Ears Soused	69
Pig, to roast a suckling	68
Pork, boiled leg of	68
Pork, roast leg of	67
Pork Steaks	68
Pork, to select	67
Pork and Beans	70
Practical Hints	49
Rice Hash	73
Sausage	74
Sausage, mutton	73
Sausage, pork	73
Sausage, veal	73
Sausage, to eat cold	74
Spare-ribs	68
Sweet-breads, a la Daube	62
Tongues, cold	55
Tripe	54
Tripe, soused	55
Veal, breast of	57
Veal, chump of, a la Daube	58
Veal Collops	60
Veal, dish made from roasted	61
Veal, fricandeau of	59

VEGETABLES—*Continued.*

	PAGE.
Potatoes, Lyonaise, No. 3.	128
Potatoes, mashed	127
Potatoes, riced	128
Potatoes, Saratoga	127
Potatoes, stewed	126
Potatoes, to boil	125
Salsify, or Oyster Plant	140
Sea Kale	141
Shallots	130
Spinach	136
Squash, Summer	131
Squash, Winter	132
Succotash	134
Tomatoes, baked	140
Tomatoes, fried	140
Tomatoes, scalloped	140
Tomatoes, stewed	140
To Can Corn	142
Turnips, with sauce	129
Vegetables, to boil	125

Pickles.

Apples	149
Blackberries	157
Butternuts	150
Cauliflower	148
Celery Chowder	149
Cherries	157
Chili Sauce	152
Chow Chow	145
Crab Apples	147
Cucumbers	145
Cucumbers, to Salt	146
Cucumbers, Sliced Onions	146
French	150
French Beans	151
Gooseberry	158
Grape Catsup	153
India	155
Lemon	151
Mixed	145
Mushroom Catsup, No. 1	154
Mushroom Catsup, No. 2	154
Nasturtiums	152
Nasturtiums, for capers	158
Onions	146
Orka and Tomato	151
Oyster	150
Peaches, No. 1	156
Peaches, No. 2	156

PICKLES—*Continued.*

	PAGE.
Pears	156
Peppers	150
Piccollily	149
Plums	156
Raspberry Vinegar	157
Red Cabbage	147
Ripe Cucumber	146
Shallot Vinegar	157
Sugar Vinegar	157
Sweet	153
Tomato	148
Tomatoes, spiced	148
Tomato Catsup, No. 1	153
Tomato Catsup, No. 2	153
Tomato Sauce for Meats	147
Virginia Damson	147
Walnuts	152
Walnut Catsup	154
Wine Vinegar	158

Yeast.

Augusta's	162
Hop	161
Potato, No. 1	161
Potato, No. 2	161
Yeast Cakes	162

Bread and Biscuits.

BREAD.

Boston Brown	167
Corn	166
German	166
Good Brown	167
Graham	166
Hoyleton	165
Margaret's Wheat	163
Mississippi Corn	166
Quick	165
Unfermented	165
Wheat, No. 1	164
Wheat, No. 2	164
Wheat and Indian	164
Yeast	163

BISCUITS.

Biscuits	166
Corn	166
Crackers	168
Cream	166
German	166
Graham	168

Breakfast and Tea Cakes.

	PAGE.
Buns	181
Cakes, Boston Corn	178
Cakes, Buckwheat	175
Cakes, Connecticut Corn	177
Cakes, Corn	178
Cakes, Dixie Corn	178
Cakes, Georgia Indian	179
Cakes, Johnny	177
Cakes, Little Milk	177
Cakes, Round Lake Corn	178
Cakes, Rice	175
Cakes, Rye	176
Cakes, Rye and Indian Johnny	179
Cakes, Rye Drop	176
Cakes, Susan's Rye Drop	175
Cheese, stewed	186
Cheese, roasted	186
Cheese Cakes	186
Cheese Omelette	187
Corn Omelette	183
Dumplings, Light Dough	182
Flap Jacks	174
Fritters	183
Fritters, Apple	183
Fritters, Corn	184
Fritters, Potato	183
Fritters, Spanish	183
Gems, Breakfast	176
Gems, Graham	176
Gems, Kentucky corn meal	178
Muffins, No. 1	171
Muffins, No. 2	171
Muffins, Breakfast	172
Muffins, French	172
Muffins, Graham	172
Muffins, Hominy	173
Muffins, Mrs. D's	173
Muffins, Mrs. H's	172
Muffins, Rice	173
Muffins, Rye and Indian	171
Muffins, Saratoga Graham	172
Muffins, Water	172
Mush, Fried	177
Oatmeal	187
Pancakes, bread, with water	174
Pancakes, Corn, to eat with meat	174
Pancakes, Ground Rice	174
Pancakes, New England	173

Breakfast and Tea Cakes—

	PAGE.
Pancakes, Rice	175
Pancakes, Soda	174
Pan Doddlings	176
Pop Overs	187
Puffs, Indian Meal	179
Rolls, Brentford	180
Rolls, Cincinnati	180
Rolls, Delmonico	179
Rolls, Dutch	181
Rolls, Flannel	180
Rolls, French	180
Rolls, Parker House	179
Rolls, Superb	180
Rolls, Unique	181
Rusks	181
Rusks, Barrington	181
Sally Lunn, No. 1	175
Sally Lunn, No. 2	175
Toast	184
Toast, Anchovy	186
Toast, broiled and deviled	185
Toast, Cheese	185
Toast, French	185
Toast, Milk	184
Toast, Soft	185
Toast, Welsh Rare-bit on	175
Waffles, Breakfast	182
Waffles, Mrs. Bleeker's	182
Waffles, Rice	182

Cake.

Cake, Angel's Food	211
Cake, Banana	206
Cake, Bernard	209
Cake, Bread	192
Cake, Burwick	193
Cake, Butternut	203
Cake, Chocolate, No. 1	208
Cake, Chocolate, No. 2	208
Cake, Chocolate, No. 3	208
Cake, Christmas	203
Cake, Cocoanut, No. 1	198
Cake, Cocoanut, No. 2	199
Cake, Cocoanut, No. 3	199
Cake, Coffee, No. 1	201
Cake, Coffee, No. 2	202
Cake, Cream, No. 1	193
Cake, Cream, No. 2	194
Cake, Cream, No. 3	194
Cake, Cream, No. 4	194
Cake, Cup	197

Meats—*Continued.*

	PAGE.
Veal, hashed	59
Veal Olives	60
Veal, ragout of cold	58
Veal, roast fillet of	56
Veal, shoulder of	56
Veal Sweet-breads	56
Veal, to select	56
Veal, to collar a breast of	57
Venison, breast of	51
Venison, stewed shoulder of	50
Venison, roast	50

Poultry and Game.

Blanching	79
Braising	79
Chicken, a la Mode	84
Chicken and Cream	83
Chicken Croquettes	84
Chicken, fricassee of	87
Chicken Pot Pie	85
Chicken Short Cake	86
Chicken, to braise	87
Chicken, to pull	88
Ducks, boiled	90
Ducks, Goose or Sucking Pig, dressing for	81
Ducks, roasted	90
Fowls, to force	80
Fowls, to boil	82
Fowls, to stew	82
Fowls, to roast	84
Glazing, without braising	80
Grouse	91
Meat, Fowls, &c., to card	80
Pigeon, broiled	90
Pigeon Pie	89
Pigeon, roasted	89
Pigeon, stewed	89
Poultry, roast	85
Quail, broiled	88
Quail Pie	88
Rabbit, baked	91
Rabbit, fricasseed	91
Rabbit, to pot	92
Spring Chicken, baked	83
Spring Chicken, broiled	83
Snipe, roasted	90
Turkey, Baltimore	82
Turkey, boiled, No. 1	81
Turkey, boiled, No. 2	81

Poultry and Game—*Continued*

	PAGE.
Turkey, deviled	82
Turkey or Chicken, dressing for	80
Wild Fowls, to roast	87
Wild Duck, Teal, &c	88

Sauces and Dressings for Meats and Fish.

Anchovy Sauce, No. 1	96
Anchovy Sauce, No. 2	96
Apple Sauce for Pork	103
Bechamel or White Gravy	193
Benton Sauce, for hot or cold roast beef	104
Boiled Chicken Sauce	98
Bread Sauce for Fowl or Fish	98
Caper Sauce for Mutton	99
Celery Sauce	97
Cheap Gravy	103
Chutney	97
Curry Balls	104
Curry Powder	97
Cullis, or Brown Gravy	102
Drawn Butter Sauce	96
Dressing for Sandwiches	104
Gibert Gravy	101
Gravy	95
Gravy, that will keep a week, to dress	95
Gravy, clear	95
Horseradish Sauce	99
Lemon White Sauce for Boiled Fowls	101
Lobster Sauce	98
Mayonnaise Dressing	103
Mint Sauce for Lamb	99
Mushroom Sauce	101
Onion Sauce	97
Oyster Sauce	100
Oyster Sauce for turkeys, &c	100
Shallot	97
Tomato Sauce	99
Trout in White Sauce	100
Trout in Green Sauce	100
Veal Gravy	102
Vinaigrette, for cold fowl or meat	104
Wild Fowl Sauce	101
Wild Fowl Sauce	102
Worcestershire Sauce	96

Salads.

	PAGE.
Beef	111
Cabbage, No. 1	108
Cabbage, No. 2	109
Cabbage or Celery	108
Chicken, No. 1	107
Chicken, No. 2	108
Cream Cabbage	109
Cold Slaw	109
Dressing for Cabbage	109
French	111
Ham	110
Lobster, No. 1	110
Lobster, No. 2	110
Oyster	112
Potato	109
Tomato and Onion	111
Watercress	112

Eggs.

Boiled	115
Dumplings	118
Eggs, a la mode	120
Egg Sauce	117
Eggs and Sausages	117
French Omelet	119
Ham Omelet	120
Omelet, No. 1	118
Omelet, No. 2	118
Omelet, No. 3	118
Omelet, au Naturel	119
Pickled	117
Poached	116
Puff Omelet	118
Rolled	117
Scrambled	116
Smoked Beef and Eggs	120
Stuffed	117
To Keep Eggs	120

Rare-bits, Cheese, Cakes, Etc.

Cheese Cakes	124
Cheese Cakes, lemon	124
Roasted Cheese	123
Veal Cheese	124
Welsh Rare-bit, No. 1	123
Welsh Rare-bit, No. 2	123

Vegetables.

	PAGE.
Artichoke Bottoms	139
Artichokes, how to dress	139
Asparagus, stewed	136
Asparagus on Toast	136
Asparagus Omelet	136
Beans, French	141
Beans, Lima	141
Cabbage, stewed, No. 1	130
Cabbage, stewed, No. 2	130
Cabbage, ladies	131
Cabbage, stuffed	131
Cale Cannon	129
Carrots, boiled	138
Carrots, stewed	138
Cauliflower, No. 1	137
Cauliflower, No. 2	137
Cauliflower, fried	137
Cauliflower in white sauce	137
Celery, stewed	138
Cucumbers, to stew	139
Egg Broccoli	135
Egg Plant	134
Egg Plant, fricasseed	135
Egg Plant, fried	135
Green Peas	133
Green Peas, to boil	133
Green Peas, to stew	133
Green Corn	142
Green Corn Stewed	142
Green Corn Fritters	142
Hot Slaw	131
Macaroni, how to dress and boil	139
Old Peas, to stew	134
Onions, boiled	129
Onion Ormoloo	130
Onions, stewed	129
Oysters, artificial	141
Parsley, to crisp	133
Parsnips, boiled	132
Parsnips, fried	132
Parsnips, fricassee of	132
Parsnips, mashed	132
Potatoes, broiled	127
Potato Cakes	128
Potato Croquette, baked	128
Potatoes, fancy	126
Potatoes, fried	126
Potatoes, hashed	126
Potatoes, Lyonaise, No. 1	127
Potatoes, Lyonaise, No. 2	128

Cake—*Continued.*

	PAGE.
Cake, Delicate, No. 1	200
Cake, Delicate, No. 2	200
Cake, Delicate, No. 3	200
Cake, Fancy	195
Cake, Feather	203
Cake, Fool	193
Cake, French	193
Cake, Fruit, No. 1	205
Cake, Fruit, No. 2	205
Cake, Geneva	207
Cake, Gold, No. 1	202
Cake, Gold, No. 2	202
Cake, Graham	192
Cake, Hickory Nut	202
Cake, Jelly	209
Cake, Jelly Cocoanut	199
Cake, Ladies'	196
Cake, Layer	210
Cake, Lemon, No. 1	203
Cake, Lemon, No. 2	203
Cake, Lemon Layer	204
Cake, Marble, No. 1	211
Cake, Marble, No. 2	211
Cake, Midnight	213
Cake, Minnehaha	198
Cake, Mountain	198
Cake, Mrs. Burnham's Fig.	210
Cake, Nut	202
Cake, Preserved Ginger	191
Cake, Pine-apple	196
Cake, Pink Marble	212
Cake, Pound	207
Cake, Pork	209
Cake, Puff	213
Cake, Queen	212
Cake, Roll Jelly	219
Cake, Roll Sponge	210
Cake, Romeo and Juliet	208
Cake, Round	196
Cake, Seed	194
Cake, Shrewsbury	209
Cake, Silver, No. 1	210
Cake, Silver, No. 2	210
Cake, Spice	214
Cake, Sponge, No. 1	200
Cake, Sponge, No. 2	200
Cake, Sponge, No. 3	200
Cake, Soda, No. 1	193
Cake, Soda, No. 2	193
Cake, Tea	199
Cake, Watermelon	205

Cake—*Continued.*

	PAGE.
Cake, Washington	210
Cake, Washington and Domestic	194
Cake, Wedding, No. 1	206
Cake, Wedding, No. 2	206
Cake, White	213
Cake, White Citron	204
Cake, White Fruit, No. 1	204
Cake, White Fruit, No. 2	204
Cake, White Mountain	198
Cake, White Sponge	201
Cake, Wilson's Ginger	192
Cookies, Ginger	191
Cookies, Graham Ginger	191
Cookies, Molasses	190
Cookies, Sugar, No. 1	191
Cookies, Sugar, No. 2	191
Cream Puffs	212
Crullers	213
Doughnuts, No. 1	214
Doughnuts, No. 2	214
Dominoes	206
Drops, Cocoanut	199
Drops, Sponge	201
Fried Cakes, No. 1	214
Fried Cakes, No. 2	214
Frosting, No. 1	214
Frosting, No. 2	214
Frosting, No. 3	215
Frosting, No. 4	215
Gateaux Madeleines	207
Ginger Bread, No. 1	192
Ginger Bread, No. 2	192
Ginger Snaps	190
Icing for Cake	215
Jumbles	202
Jumbles, No. 1	195
Jumbles, No. 2	195
Kisses, No. 1	196
Kisses, No. 2	197
Kisses, No. 3	197
Kisses, No. 4	197
Lady Fingers	206
Macaroons, Almond, No. 1	195
Macaroons, Almond, No. 2	196
Macaroons, Walnut	195
Noodles	195
Puff Overs	213
Weights and Measures	190
Whip Churn for Creams	215

Pastry and Meat Pies.

	PAGE.
Apple Custard	229
Banana	228
Beefsteak	236
Beefsteak and Oyster	236
Bread	230
Cold Veal or Chicken	237
Cocoanut, No. 1	227
Cocoanut, No. 2	228
Cream, Dedham	221
Cream, Lemon	222
Cream, No. 1	222
Cream, No. 2	222
Cream, No. 3	223
Custard	228
Crust for Venison Pastry	236
Delicate	229
Giblet	235
Lemon, No. 1	224
Lemon, No. 2	224
Lemon, No. 3	225
Lemon, No. 4	225
Lemon Custard	225
Lemon Fruit	225
Lemon Tart	230
Marlboro	224
Meat	233
Mock Mince, No. 1	226
Mock Mince, No. 2	227
Mock Mince, No. 3	227
Mince Meat, No. 1	226
Mince Meat, No. 2	226
Orange	230
Orange, No. 1	227
Orange, No. 2	227
Orange Tartlets or Puffs	229
Pastry, Custard or Cream	233
Patties, Good Mince for	235
Patties, Resembling Mince Pies	234
Patties, Sweet	235
Patties, Turkey	234
Patties, Veal	234
Pie Crust, New England	220
Pie Crust, No. 1	221
Pie Crust, No. 2	221
Pie Paste, Common	221
Pie Paste, French	221
Pine-apple	228
Puff Paste	220
Puff Paste (less rich)	220
Puff Paste, Francatelli	231

Pastry and Meat Pies—

	PAGE.
Pumpkin	223
Rabbit	235
Raspberry Tarts with cream	230
Rhubarb	223
Squash	224
Squash (Eggless)	224
Tomato	229
Veal	236

Puddings.

Almond	257
Apple	251
Apple, a la Cremone	250
Apple, Baked	251
Apple, Snow	243
Arrow Root	244
Baked Dumplings	248
Baked Sponge	241
Baked Indian	243
Baked Vermicelli	251
Batter	251
Batter	243
Beefsteak	258
Beefsteak, baked	258
Bird's Nest	248
Blue Berry	242
Boiled Custard	255
Brown Bread	252
Cabinet	255
Cocoanut	241
Cocoanut Bread	241
Cottage	245
Corn Meal	244
Crumb	248
Delicate	252
Delmonico	246
Dorchester Corn	255
Fig, No. 1	244
Fig, No. 2	245
Flour Suet	241
Green Corn	240
Green Bean	257
Light or German	257
Little Bread	250
Macaroni	252
Maizena	255
Marblehead Apple	256
Mutton	258
Norfolk Dumplings	256
Old-fashioned Indian	241
Orange	243

INDEX.

PUDDINGS—*Continued.*

	PAGE.
Orange	258
Pea, for Beef or Pork	256
Plain Fruit	249
Plum	246
Plum, English	246
Plum, English Christmas	246
Plum, Saratoga	247
Porcupine	253
Poverty	243
Poverty	252
President's	247
Pretty Supper Dish	259
Quaker	253
Rice, with fruit	253
Rice, frosted	253
Rice, meringne	254
Rice, without eggs	254
Royal	254
Snow	245
Stale Bread, what to do with	259
Steak or Kidney	258
Strawberry	245
Suet, No. 1	242
Suet, No. 2	242
Suet, No. 3	242
Swiss	244
Tapioca, No. 1	249
Tapioca, No. 2	249
Tapioca, No. 3	250
Troy	248
Yorkshire	257

Sauces for Puddings.

Cranberry	264
Cream	265
Hard, No. 1	264
Hard, No. 2	264
Maple Sugar	265
Pudding	264
Sweet	264
Sweet	265
Wine, No. 1	263
Wine, No. 2	263
Wine, No. 3	263

Dishes for Dessert.

Blanc-Mange, No. 1	270
Blanc-Mange, No. 2	271
Blanc-Mange, Tapioca	270
Charlotte, a la Parisienne	270
Charlotte, Apple	269

DISHES FOR DESSERT—

	PAGE.
Charlotte, No. 1	267
Charlotte, No. 2	267
Charlotte, No. 3	267
Charlotte, No. 4	268
Charlotte, Russian	268
Cream, a la Chateaubriand	277
Cream, a la Romaine	277
Cream, an excellent	278
Cream, Bavarian, Apricot	272
Cream, Bavarian, Maraschino	271
Cream, Bavarian, Strawberry	272
Cream, Burnt, No. 1	274
Cream, Burnt, No. 2	274
Cream, Celestine	280
Cream, Chocolate, No. 1	274
Cream, Chocolate, No. 2	274
Cream, Coffee, No. 1	273
Cream, Coffee, No. 2	273
Cream, Gooseberry	280
Cream, Italian, No. 1	276
Cream, Italian, No. 2	276
Cream, Orange-flower	275
Cream, Pistachio	275
Cream, Rice	280
Cream, Rock	278
Cream, Snow	279
Cream, Spanish	279
Cream, Strawberry Celestina	276
Cream, Velvet, No. 1	279
Cream, Velvet, No. 2	279
Croquante of French Walnuts	282
Croquante of Orange	281
Croquante of Ratifias, a la Chantilly	282
Custard, Baked, No. 1	292
Custard, Baked, No. 2	293
Custard, Ornamented	292
Custard, Rice	292
Custard, Snow	293
Custard, Sweet Potato	292
Everlasting or Solid Syllabubs	281
Floating Island	270
Jelly, Apricot	288
Jelly, Cider	289
Jelly, Coffee	299
Jelly, Currant & Raspberry	288

Dishes for Dessert—

	PAGE.
Jelly, Fruit in	290
Jelly, Gelatine	290
Jelly, Irish Moss	290
Jelly, Lemon, No. 1	289
Jelly, Lemon, No. 2	289
Jelly, Orange	283
Jelly, Pine-apple	284
Jelly, Pistachio	285
Jelly, Pomegranite	284
Jelly, Punch	287
Jelly, Russian	286
Jelly, Strawberry	284
Jelly, Transparent, Oranges filled with	287
Jelly, Variegated	285
Jelly, Wine	290
Lemon Honeycomb	291
Macedoine of Fruits	285
Moonshine	291
Orange Dessert	283
Orange Fool	291
Oranges, Jellied	289
Orgeat	291

Jellies and Canned Fruits.

Apricots, Brandied	309
Brandy, Raspberry	310
Cherries, Preserved	300
Crab-apples, Siberian, Preserved	303
Currants, Spiced	306
Currants, to Can, without cooking	307
Fruit, Canned	303
Grapes, Brandied	309
Grapes, Preserved	301
Jam, Apple	307
Jam, Currant	308
Jam, Grape	308
Jam, Green Gage	308
Jam, Gooseberry, for Tarts	307
Jam, Quince	307
Jam, Raspberry	308
Jelly	298
Jelly, Apple	299
Jelly, Cranberry	299
Jelly, Currant	299
Jelly, Currant, without cooking	299

Jellies and Canned Fruits—

	PAGE.
Jelly, Peach	299
Jelly, Plum	298
Marmalade	306
Marmalade, Apple	304
Marmalade, Cherry	306
Marmalade, Crab-apple	304
Marmalade, Lemon	304
Marmalade, Orange	304
Marmalade, Quince	305
Marmalade, Tomato	305
Marmalade, Transparent	305
Peaches, Brandied	309
Peaches, Preserved	300
Peaches, Preserved, Marblehead	301
Pears, Preserved	300
Pears, Preserved	302
Pears, Stewed	310
Pine-apples, Canned	304
Pine-apples, Preserved	303
Quinces, Preserved	301
Quince Sauce	308
Strawberries, Preserved	302
Tomatoes, Yellow, Preserved	300

Drinks.

Beer, Ginger	317
Beer, Maple	317
Chocolate	314
Cocoa, or Broma	314
Coffee	313
Cordial, Blackberry	317
Cup, Badminton	320
Cup, Chablis	319
Cup, Champagne	319
Cup, Cider	320
Cup, Claret	318
Cup, Pine-apple	319
Cup, Sauterne	318
Egg Nogg	317
Lemonade	318
Mead, Sarsaparilla	316
Mead, Sassafras	316
Nectar, Cream	318
Punch, Ice	315
Punch, Milk	315
Punch, Roman	315
Rum, Cherry	323
Sherbet, Lemon	316
Sherbet, Pine-apple	316

INDEX.

DRINKS—*Continued.*

	PAGE.
Shrub, Currant	315
Shrub, Raspberry	317
Verder	315
Wine, a rich and pleasant	321
Wine, Black Currant	322
Wine, Currant, No. 1	321
Wine, Currant, No. 2	321
Wine, Currant, No. 3	321
Wine, Elder	322
Wine, Grape	320
Wine, Raspberry	322
Wine, Unfermented	320
Wine, White Elder	323
Wine Whey	321

Confectionery.

Candy, Cocoanut, quickly made	326
Candy, Cream	328
Candy, Fig	329
Candy, Ice Cream	328
Candy, Molasses, No. 1	327
Candy, Molasses, No. 2	327
Candy, Nut	330
Candy, Vinegar	329
Caramels	328
Caramels, Chocolate, No. 1	326
Caramels, Chocolate, No. 2	326
Corn Balls	320
Drops, Chocolate Cream	327
Drops, Cocoanut	327
Drops, Lemon	328
Drops, Marshmallow	328
Taffy	329
Taffy, Cocoanut	327
Taffy, Everton	329

For the Sick Room.

Beef Tea, No. 1	334
Beef Tea, No. 2	334
Broth, Mutton or Chicken	335
Broth, Scotch	334
Broth, Veal	337
Caudle for Invalids	333
Caudle, Flour	336
Cough Syrup	333
Eggs, Fresh, for Invalids	338
Gruel, Indian Meal	333
Gruel, Oatmeal	334
Hop Tea	338
Milk, Ground Rice	336
Milk, Sago	337

FOR THE SICK ROOM—

	PAGE.
Panada, Chicken	335
Porridge, French Milk	336
Porridge, Milk	336
Rice, Boiled	337
Salep	336
Sippets	335
Toast, Water	337
Toast and Water	337
Wine Whey	337

Pertaining to Plants.

A Good Way to Plant Spring Bulbs	349
Ashes and Iron for Flowers	343
Autumn Work among Flowers	347
Care of Indoor Plants	350
Concerning House Plants	340
Effective Arrangement for Cut Flowers	348
Ferns	347
Ferns, Mounting	348
Flowers, to Preserve	345
Flowers, Religious value of	344
Flowers in Sand	342
Geraniums, How to Slip	346
Hanging Garden	346
Hanging Pots, Pretty	351
Hyacinths, to raise in winter	345
Lilies, Calla	342
Lilies, Water	342
Lilies for Pot Culture	345
Moss Baskets, how to make	350
Oleander Slips	342
Parlor Vine, a	346
Pot Flowers	352

Miscellaneous.

Anchovies, Essence of	376
Ants, to Drive Away	372
Ant Trap	362
Bandoline, How to Make	353
Black Paper for Patterns	374
Blacking for Shoes	376
Bone Felon, Cure for	361
Brass, to Clean	370
Butterflies and Moths	365
Camphor Ice	360
Carpets, to Clean	359
Carpets, to Clean	367
Cement	368

MISCELLANEOUS—*Continued.*

	PAGE.
Cement for Broken China.	376
Chapped Hands, Paste for.	376
Chilblains	368
Chills, Cure for	369
Clarified Sugar and Sweetmeats	377
Cold Cream, to Make	358
Complexion, for the	357
Complexion, Wash for the.	357
Corns, to Cure	354
Corns, Soft, to Remove	354
Cough, to Cure	365
Crape, to Restore	362
Cut Glass	363
Decanters, to Clean	363
Diphtheria, to Cure	365
Disinfection	369
Felon, to Prevent	364
Filtering Orange or Lemon Juice	379
Fruit Stains, to Remove	373
Good Eggs, How to Tell	364
Grafting Wax	360
Grass, to Make Thrifty	374
Gravel Walks, to Destroy Grass in	374
Grease, to Remove	361
Grey Hair, to Prevent	356
Grey Hair, to Restore	356
Hair Brushes, to Clean	358
Hair, to Clean	355
Hair, to Beautify	356
Hair Tonic	356
Hair Tonic	376
Hard Soap	375
Headache, Sick	370
Headache, Cure for	370
Ink Stains	362
Ink Stains, to Remove	360
Ink from Mahogany	368
Ivory Handle Knives, to Keep from Cracking	373
Jellies, Ices, &c., Colorings for	378
Kitchen Pepper	376
Lard, to Keep and Prepare	360
Lemon Juice, to Keep	377
Lip Salve, to Make	358
Lime Water	360
Linen Whitened	364
Measures for Housekeepers	358
Mildew, to Remove	371

MISCELLANEOUS—*Continued.*

	PAGE.
Milk Diet	367
Mortar or Paint, to Remove	371
Moth, Protection against	355
Mushrooms, to Pot	378
Nails, Ingrowing	354
Night Sweats	367
Oil or Grease Spots from Carpets, to Remove	372
Oil from Boards or Stone, to Extract	374
Paste for Paper	361
Perspiration, to Remove Odor of	354
Picture Frames, to Prevent Flies Injuring	364
Pot-pourri	353
Ratafia	355
Rheumatism, Cure for	361
Rose Water, How to Make	355
Roses, Tincture of	355
Rust, to Remove	363
Sad Irons, Starch or Rust from	371
Salve, Mrs. Wood's	361
Seal Brown, to Color	375
Setting Colors with Beef's Gall	359
Sink or Drain, to Purify	371
Soft Soap	361
Sore Throat, Cure for	360
Soap for Whitening the Hands	370
Spinach, Extract of	378
Silk, to Clean	372
Stains from Marble	375
Stains, Iron, from Marble	375
Stains from Linen, to Remove	363
Steel Knives from Rusting.	373
Teeth, to Beautify	357
Teeth, Care of	357
Teeth, to Clean Black	357
Velvet, to Renovate	373
Wasp Stings	366
Warts, to Remove	354
Water Filter, Home-made.	366
Wen, to Cure	369
Well, to Purify	373
White Lace, to Wash	370
Woolen, to Wash	359
Zinc, to Clean	359

www.ingramcontent.com/pod-product-compliance
Lightning Source LLC
Chambersburg PA
CBHW022111290426
44112CB00008B/637